The Wines of the World

The Wines of the World

**Edited by
Jeremy Roberts and José Northey**

ORBIS PUBLISHING - LONDON

Contents

Title page: Wine harvest in Ingleheim am Rhine, Germany (Picturepoint)

Endpapers: Fields in Champagne (A. Howarth/Daily Telegraph)

© Istituto Geografico de Agostini, Novara 1971
© Grange Batelière SA, Paris 1972
English edition © Orbis Publishing Limited, London 1974
Reprinted 1976
Adapted from the Italian *Vini Bianchi e Rosati* and *Vini Rossi,*
and the French *Vins Français* and *Vins Etrangers*
ISBN 0 85613 237 3

Introduction

All over the world the wine industry is expanding to meet the demands of an increasingly discerning wine-drinking public. New vineyards are being planted, new machinery introduced and new wines created; however, modern methods cannot alter the fact that wine, which has been known and loved for centuries throughout the western world, still benefits from the scrupulous care and attention of the dedicated individual. And an understanding of wine rewards the enthusiastic wine-drinker.

The Wines of the World is an up-to-date, practical guide to the wines of the major wine-producing countries. While the classic wine regions of Europe, which produce the very best estate-bottled wines, are described in detail, the newer wine-producing countries (which now account for a sizeable proportion of the world market, especially in the cheaper ranges) are also included. You will be able to find out about wines you encounter on holiday abroad or in your local stores.

This book provides a thorough introduction to every aspect of wine from grape-growing to serving wine at table. Country by country, it gives a brief survey of the local wine history, followed by a description of the geographical conditions which influence every vineyard area and have an enormous effect on the qualities of the wines produced. The numerous maps of all the countries featured make it easy to locate the major wine regions.

Each wine area has its own distinctive wine-making processes which give its wines their identifying characteristics. In some countries these methods have hardly changed for centuries – such as the French *méthode champenoise* by which the only wine that may legally be called Champagne is produced. In the USA, for example, research into the science of wine-making is being undertaken and experimentation with new methods aiming to improve on existing wines is unceasing. All the different methods, which may take from only a few months for *vins ordinaires* to up to 20 years for a really fine port, are described here.

Without a knowledge of the laws that govern vinification in different countries and the terms that may be used to categorize their various wines, it is hard to know the value of the wine you are buying. Here you will find the meanings of the most common terms, including the descriptive ones, that you may encounter on bottles of wine from any of the countries described.

Advice on buying and storing wine is included for those who wish to start a home cellar on however small a scale. The table of comparative vintages will help you to know which wines and which years are likely to be especially good. Some guidelines on tasting and serving wine, and on partnering wine and food are also given.

Although the choice and appreciation of wine must ultimately be a matter of personal preference, the wealth of information contained in this guide should certainly enhance your enjoyment of one of the most pleasurable of interests and activities.

The nature of wine

Wine is a 'living thing'; it is in a continual state of development and reacts to changing circumstances in different ways. There are a number of elements that directly affect the development of wine from the moment the vine is planted in the ground to the time the wine is bottled or stored in cask. Even within regions there are important differences that have to be taken into account – and it is these contrasting characteristics that identify the origin and year of a wine.

Location and climate

The vine flourishes best in a temperate climate – dry and sunny, with a moderate amount of rain and mild winters. Yet, as will be seen, the vine can also produce good wine in areas where there are extremes – desert heat by day and cold by night, high altitude or excessive rainfall over a very short period of time. It is the way these factors are balanced that is important.

The nature of the soil – both its chemical and physical qualities – can determine the type and taste of wine. Although the vine will grow virtually anywhere, it favours a light, pebbly soil that enables water to penetrate the topsoil, causes reflection of the sun's rays onto the grapes and helps to protect the root. So the wine-grower must understand the composition of his soil to get the best results from the vine and grapes he has chosen to grow.

Most wine-growing countries now have wine institutes whose researches and experimental plantings have led to improved methods of growing and harvesting grapes.

The vine and the grape

The most important vine is the *Vitis vinifera*, used throughout Europe for both wine-making and table grapes. There are 18 kinds of native American vine that are used to create hybrids and root stocks. The American vines have been found to produce better wines with European vine stocks grafted onto them. It is the American vine that saved the European vineyards at the end of the last century, when they had been decimated by a terrible epidemic of the root louse phylloxera. American root stocks were found to be resistant to the phylloxera bug, and the European vines were grafted onto them; in this way the European vineyards were slowly able to flourish once more.

There are 19 Asiatic species of vine as well but these are purely ornamental.

No single grape gives exactly the type of wine wanted; this is why so many different kinds are grown, either together or separately, and the resulting wines blended. Every wine zone varies in its choice of grapes, and there are about 50 grape varieties used throughout the world purely for wine-making.

The principal red grapes used are cabernet sauvignon, gamay, pinot noir, cabernet franc, merlot and grenache;

the principal white ones are chardonnay, sauvignon blanc, riesling and sémillon.

To learn what grapes are used to make every type of wine and why they are used would be a formidable task, but here we give a brief outline. Taking the most common red grapes, their uses may be listed as follows:

Cabernet sauvignon used for red wines principally in Bordeaux, Chile, South Africa and Australia.

Gamay used mainly for Beaujolais and rosé wine in California.

Pinot noir one of the best red wine grapes, used especially in Champagne and Burgundy, as well as in Germany and Eastern Europe.

Cabernet franc one of the important red wine grapes of Bordeaux, the Loire Valley and south-west France; it is also used in Argentina, Chile, Australia and Algeria.

Merlot blanc and **merlot noir** used for red wines in Bordeaux and south-west France as well as in Chile, Romania and Yugoslavia.

Grenache used for rosé wines and found in the Rhône Valley, Spain, Australia and California.

The principal white grapes and their uses are:

Chardonnay finest grape of white Burgundy and Champagne; also used in California and Bulgaria.

Sauvignon blanc principal grape of white Bordeaux and wines from Pouilly-sur-Loire/Sancerre in the Loire Valley; also used in California and Chile.

Riesling noblest grape of Germany and Alsace; also used in Austria, Australia, South Africa, California and Chile.

Sémillon used for making the great golden wines of Sauternes and Barsac in Bordeaux; also in California and Australia.

Muscat this grape, which may also be black, is renowned for its intensely sweet wines, usually known as Muscat or Muscatel, found particularly throughout the Mediterranean wine-growing countries. There are exceptions to this rule with Muscat grown in Provence and Alsace in France, and in Italy, Portugal and Bulgaria. In the French areas, a very dry, heavily perfumed white wine is made.

Other lesser known, though equally important grapes include the malbec, carignan, barbera, chasselas, muscadet or melon, ugni blanc, savagnin, chenin blanc, tintas, nebbiolo, folle blanche, syrah, pedro ximenez, palomino, verdelho and sylvaner. These and many more grape varieties are used throughout the world.

The bottle label

In Europe it is not customary to mention the individual grape type used for the wine on the bottle label, although there are a few exceptions where the grape name has evolved into the name of the wine, for example, Barbera from Italy and Gewürztraminer from Alsace.

In America, however, the reverse is true for here it is usual to name the wine after the grape, and Chenin Blanc or Pinot Noir is likely to be a far more familiar term to an American than to a Frenchman.

The great Château Lafite of Bordeaux

Protecting the vine

From spring until the vintage, the grower must care for his plants unceasingly. Not only must he contend with vagaries of weather, for frost and hail can ruin his vineyard, but he must also fight a host of insects, bugs and moulds that attack the flower, fruit, roots and leaves. These range from the red spider and caterpillars to mildew.

The most persistent of the insects are several species of moth – *eudemis*, *pyralis* and *cochylis* – that attack the grape and its leaf. The most deadly fungi are the oidium and mildew which attack both the leaves and the grapes.

Fortunately, there is a veritable army of modern sprays which the wine-grower may apply by hand, with machinery or, in the case of very large vineyards, from the air. Sulphur and multi-purpose fungicides are used to combat oidium and mildew and systemic insecticides are used for pests.

Work in the vineyard

The vineyard is the object of constant attention. Practically all the work demands a skilled and delicate touch, especially pruning, and methods vary from area to area according to the size and way of growing the vines.

There are two basic methods of pruning. Dry pruning takes place during the vine's dormant season to encourage the growth of the plant and the bearing of fruit; green pruning involves pinching out unwanted shoots and buds, thinning out leaves and clipping branches. Ploughing and hoeing must also be done winter and summer.

The vintage or harvest

The vintage is the climax of the wine-grower's year, when he reaps the rewards for his labours. The ripening period is about 50 days and during this time the grape swells and changes colour. The black grape turns from green to red, the white grape from green to yellow. When the grapes have reached maturity they must be gathered, without undue damage, in two to four weeks, and taken to the presses.

Prior to the vintage, the wine-grower has, at regular intervals, had grape samples analysed and has followed the grapes' progress at all times so that he can judge the moment when the natural acidity in the grapes has been converted to enough sugar to ensure a good fermentation and the correct percentage of alcohol in the finished wine. He fixes the date for picking and the vintage is under way.

The differences in climate and growth of the vine mean that the harvest does not take place at the same time everywhere. In Germany, for example, it is very late so the grapes can benefit from all the available sunshine; in Champagne it takes place earlier because it is essential to pick the grapes before the onset of frosts. But the procedure is virtually the same everywhere.

Before the vintage, though, there are routine but important tasks to carry out in preparation for the grapes. All equipment is thoroughly checked and cleaned. Wooden

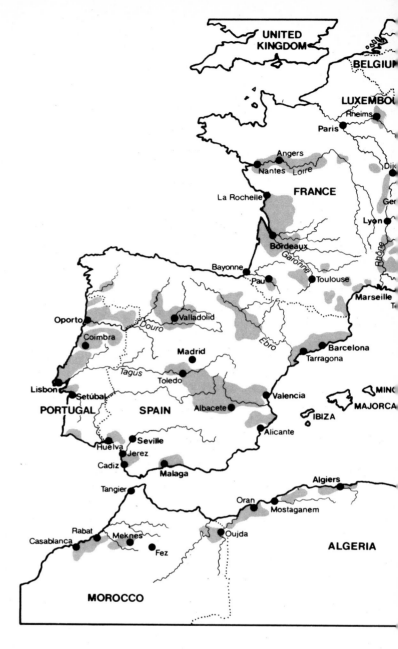

casks and hods are washed and soaked so the swelling wood seals any cracks, they are then fumigated with sulphur to ensure that they are free of infection. Baskets are checked over, and secateurs and knives sharpened.

How wine is made

The process that turns grape juice into wine is the natural one of fermentation. This is the chemical change of sugar into alcohol and carbon dioxide caused by the action of yeasts – minute organisms which are found on the skins of the grapes. The yeasts start their work as soon as the skins are broken.

To promote fermentation, the temperature must be very steady between 18°C–30°C. Fermentation is controlled by adding selected yeasts to the natural yeasts in order to avoid a slow or incomplete fermentation.

The duration of fermentation varies: it is between 10–15 days in the Médoc, four to eight days in Burgundy, and still less in North Africa. A wine that has fermented out is

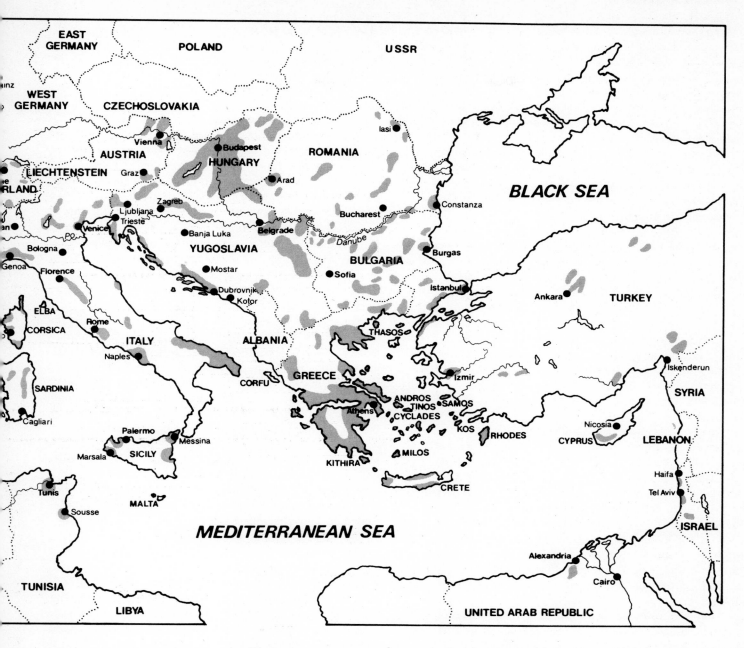

completely dry, for no sugar remains. This natural process can be stopped or speeded up at the wine-grower's discretion, to determine the type of wine produced – dry, medium dry or sweet. Rapid but controlled fermentation, aided by modern techniques, is increasingly employed today to obtain soft wines that mature quickly and can be sold earlier without loss of quality.

Red wines are made by crushing the grapes with the skins, pips, and sometimes the stalks; the resulting mixture is put into huge vats for fermentation. All the parts of a grape colour wine red, and black or white grapes with red juice can be used.

White wines are treated differently. The juice must be separated as quickly as possible from the skins, pips and stalks for they add tannin, give a bitter taste and can lend a brownish tinge to the wine. So the grapes are gently crushed rather than pressed and the juice is strained off. Only grapes with white juice may be used.

Rosé wines follow the same pattern as red wines, but the skins, pips and stalks are removed a short while after

fermentation starts, depending on the depth of colour and taste required.

Once the grape juice, or must, has been put into the vats (wood is the traditional material for vats for fine wines, although stone, brick, cement, stainless steel and vats that are lined with glass or treated with glass-paint are used today) the fermentation begins. It is now that the art of the wine-grower comes into its own.

Once the yeasts have done their job, they fall to the bottom of the vats and constitute what is known as the lees, most of which will be removed when the wine is drawn off in casks; this job is known as racking.

The first racking takes place two to four weeks after fermentation, the second between January and April, according to the climate and the wine. When the lees have been removed by filtering, the wine starts to clear. The cellarman assists this process by fining. This consists of adding to the wine different substances which, by coagulating with the tannin (a natural substance in grape skins which helps a wine's keeping properties) already present, form a kind of net that catches and sinks floating particles. Dried blood is sometimes used for very fine wines but gelatine and dry albumen are more common.

The young wine must be filtered several times, preferably into airtight containers, as contact with air must be avoided at this stage. To fill the empty space left after filtering, the barrel is topped up with wine from a similar source.

As economic pressures on wine-makers increase the lengthy and gentle technique of allowing wines to rest after fermentation so that unwanted organic particles can settle out is being replaced by a mechanical system called centrifuging.

Centrifuging is used in everyday wine-production, especially in bulk wine-making; the particles in the wine are centrifuged out after the fermentation, usually in the spring following the vintage. Great care must be taken to centrifuge the wine without aeration because oxidation will spoil the wine slightly and affect its freshness on the palate.

The advantage of the centrifuging system is that it saves time, money and labour, making new wines faster to process for mass markets.

Even after all these precautions, the young wine is still not ready for drinking and must be protected from harm as it develops.

There are a number of factors that have a detrimental effect on the flavour and health of young wine, particularly wines with a low alcohol content. Bad wine-making and the use of dirty equipment cause unpleasant flavours as may any temporary or permanent changes in the wine.

Wine soon suffers if it is left exposed to the air for it can be attacked by yeasts and bacteria which cause an 'off' flavour and eventually make the wine undrinkable.

Other bacteria turn wine sour or cause unpleasant musty, damp or rotten smells. If wine turns sour, there is nothing left to do but throw it away or make vinegar from it.

Temperature is another vital factor; too low or too high a temperature can kill the natural yeasts and stop fermentation prematurely. So great care is required.

The wine-making cycle has sometimes to be helped along, and there are a number of alternatives open to the wine-maker. One method known as *chaptalisation* consists of adding sugar to must that is poor in natural sugar (because the grapes have not ripened enough) to raise its alcohol level. Wine laws of most countries control the process very carefully for it can have a detrimental effect when used to raise the alcohol content of a wine that was perfectly well-balanced in the first place. The addition of salt is tolerated and is often necessary to hide such dubious practices as the addition of alcohol and water. The addition of glycerine to soften a wine and strengthen its qualities is illegal; so is the use of saccharine and other artificial sweeteners, antiseptics, and colouring matter.

Chemical manipulations are spurned by reputable wine-growers. Such actions debase wine (the legal definition of wine requires that it should be held to be a natural substance when it is chemically analysed; chemicals added should not exceed official limits).

Ageing wine

Certain wines, such as true Beaujolais and some of the Loire Valley wines, are best drunk young or before their freshness is lost. Ageing improves great red wines and some white ones.

Red wines are aged both in wooden barrels and in bottles. In contact with a well-chosen wood, usually oak, the wine acquires a very pleasant taste and aroma from the resins in the wood.

Oxygen plays an important part in ageing. It seeps through the wood and causes oxidation, the initial phase of the process. At first there is an intense precipitation of various substances, while the colour, bouquet and taste are gradually modified and lose all the characteristics, notably the acidity, of a young wine. Except for high-quality red wines the wine is bottled within six months of fermentation.

The most important changes, however, take place in bottle and bring about a notable improvement in the wine's characteristics. The roughness of the tannin is mellowed but the wine retains its astringency; the colour loses some of its intensity but becomes enriched with shades of brown; finally, oxidation allows the bouquet or aroma to grow while the taste is refined. The alcohol content diminishes due to continuous oxidation through the cork, while acidity decreases proportionately.

White wines are aged in a similar manner except that a long stay in barrel is not essential as all the necessary changes take place in the bottle. This is why most white wines are bottled shortly after fermentation. Contact with oxygen must be avoided to prevent over-oxidation which darkens the colour and gives the wine a dull taste.

The length of time a wine is aged is not subject to precise rules and varies noticeably according to the wine. The keeping properties of wine vary according to its acidity and alcohol content. The richer a wine is in body and in alcohol, the more it will benefit from ageing, though this does not normally hold good for more than 10–12 years. This is a very general rule, for the ageing capacity of a wine depends on many factors which may vary even among wines of a similar quality, from the same source and made in the same year.

Many wines are capable of reaching extreme old age. Such wines include the great clarets from the Médoc, Graves, St Emilion and Pomerol, some of the best Burgundies, Italian wines and port. White wines include top quality Sauternes and Barsacs, some Burgundies, and a number of fine German wines from the best vineyards in the Rheingau, Rheinpfalz, Rheinhessen and Mosel districts.

Conditions for ageing wine in barrel and bottle are stringent. Wines must be kept in deep, cool cellars (*chais*) at a constant temperature, for any change in temperature may be extremely damaging. Strong light must be avoided as it can cause photo-chemical changes; so should excessive vibration (notably that of traffic). Humidity must be regulated as dampness encourages the formation of fungi, and an over-dry atmosphere causes the cork to dry out. It is preferable to lay the bottles horizontally so that the wine covers the cork and keeps it moist.

Major wine laws

The modern system of controls over production and sales of French wines dates back to the phylloxera disaster that struck France's vineyards in the late 19th century. Wine-growers, concerned at the decline of standards and the effect on the reputation of famous vineyards, formulated standards for each area of production, and subsequently pressed for laws to enforce them.

Successive laws were passed in 1905, 1908 and 1919 all aimed at creating an *appellation d'origine* (literally 'name of origin', although it actually meant that the wine was entitled to bear the name of the area) to protect the reputation and quality of good wines. It was not until 1935 that the Appellation d'Origine Contrôlée (AOC) laws were passed and rules finally laid down applicable to all French vineyards.

The laws determine the grape varieties to be grown, the methods of cultivation, control of volume, production, fermentation, cellaring and finishing of wines; they limit the use of established vineyard names to wines that are produced only in those areas and ensure that they meet the traditional standards for that type of wine.

In 1947 the laws were laid down in greater detail and L'Office International du Vin was formed to act as a supervisory body.

There are basically three classes of French wines. The most common and least expensive wines are called Appellation Simple; they are really *vins ordinaires* or *vins du pays.* There is little control over grape types, growing conditions or wine-making processes, and many of these wines may be blended with imported wines.

The second class of wines is called Vins Délimités de Qualité Supérieure (VDQS – wines of superior quality with limited production). These wines are usually made from specified grapes in particular wine-growing areas, and can be very good value and moderately priced.

The third and finest class of wines is called Appellation d'Origine Contrôlée (AOC). These wines are made from the best vineyards and every stage of their making is carefully supervised. Wines accorded AOC status are sold under the name of the region, district, village or commune, or individual vineyard from which they originate. So, in order to understand wine labels, one needs to know a little about the structure of the French wine-making regions.

Other European countries have not been so forward-looking in creating control laws for their wines. Germany recently took steps to simplify the names of her vineyards; this and other changes had a considerable effect on her wine industry. Place names are in future to be more clearly defined, the type of grapes and the sugar content are to be more strictly controlled, and the wording on the labels is generally being simplified. The laws also split German wines into three main types: Tafelwein (table wine), Qualitätswein (quality wine) and Qualitätswein mit Prädikat (quality wine with certification). However, it will be a few years before these changes take full effect.

Médoc wine label for a 'great year', with AOC information

Italy passed a set of laws in 1963 that started a form of control over her wine industry. Although not nearly so detailed, it followed the French pattern. The code of laws is called Denominazione di Origine Controllata (DOC – controlled denomination of origin). It defines the wine regions of Italy, the grape types most suitable for specific areas, districts, towns and vineyards, the permitted methods of cultivation and wine-making, and the terminology for use on wine labels that carry the DOC stamp.

Italy is an extremely prolific wine-making country where standards of quality vary enormously. Accordingly, the wines, like those of France and Germany, have been divided into three main classes. The most common and least expensive wines are called Denominazione Semplice (DS); only the region of the wine's origin is specified. The second class embraces higher quality wines that come from specified grapes and areas with established production standards. These are called Denominazione di Origine Controllata (DOC).

The third class – the best Italian wines – is small; it is called Denominazione di Origine Controllata e Garantita (DOCG). Such wines must originate from one of the famous, traditional districts or sub-districts, and be made from the highest quality grapes by the most closely controlled wine-making processes.

As a result of Britain's entry into the European Economic Community, the AOC rules apply to Britain as from 1974. Stricter labelling, even at the lower end of the price range, will have a number of effects – some good, some bad. Although the consumer will now know he is buying exactly what is described on the label, he will however have to exchange familiar names for new ones which comply with Common Market rules. And in the light of rising world prices for wine, the wine-drinker will have to pay more for his wine.

Glossary

A

Abboccato *(Italian)* Sweet, semi-sweet

Acetic Describes vinegary taste of undrinkable wine; *aigre* is the French term which describes the sourness in wine caused by acetic acid

Acid, -ity Natural quality of wine due to the presence and proportion of various acids, some present in the grape, others caused during fermentation. Not only an essential keeping quality, it also gives a wine its bite and bouquet. Degrees of acidity vary: it is high in Mosel and Saar wines and is responsible for their refreshing qualities; it is low in wines from hot, southerly regions like North Africa and southern Italy. Lack of acidity makes a wine dull with a watery finish; excess acidity makes a wine tart and possibly undrinkable; acidity in a young wine will decrease with ageing

Adamado *(Portuguese)* Sweet

Adega *(Portuguese)* Producer's cellar

Aerate, to To draw the cork from a bottle of wine, allowing air to mingle with the wine in order to diminish its potency

Age, to To keep wine in wooden casks or barrels, or in bottle for specific periods of time so that it will develop flavour, aroma and colour

Alba *(Romanian)* White

All'annata *(Italian)* Literally 'of the year'; young wine drunk in the year after the vintage

Amabile *(Italian)* Sweet, medium sweet

Amaro *(Italian)* Bitter; may also describe a dry red wine

Amontillado *(Spanish)* Light-amber dry sherry with a mellow flavour

Aperitif Appetizer, drunk before meals

AOC Appellation d'Origine Contrôlée; the term which indicates that a wine conforms to certain geographical and qualitative standards laid down by the French government

Apre Harsh, raw-tasting, especially in a young wine; it does not necessarily indicate a poor or bad wine

Aroma Smell of a wine

Asztali bor *(Hungarian)* Table wine

Aszú *(Hungarian)* Wine made from specially picked overripe grapes

Auslese *(German)* Wine made from specially picked overripe grapes

Austere Denotes a powerful but undeveloped wine that will probably be very good

B

Baked Describes strong smell of grapes burnt and shrivelled by hot sun

Balance Satisfactory blend of a wine's physical characteristics such as alcohol, acid, tannin and fruit, and its less tangible elements of character

Beerenauslese *(German)* Wine made from individually picked overripe grapes

Bianco *(Italian)* White

Big Denotes a very powerful, balanced, well-flavoured wine

Bijelo *(Serbo-Croat)* White

Binning The system of laying bottles of wine horizontally in racks

Biser *(Serbo-Croat)* Sparkling

Bite Taste resulting from the mixture of tannin and acid found particularly in a young wine; unpleasant if excessive

Bitter Taste that signifies sickness in a wine; probably due to unwanted acidity or metallic contamination during vinification

Bjalo *(Bulgarian)* White

Blanc *(French)* White

Blanc de Blancs *(French)* Wine made entirely from white grapes; used in particular in Champagne

Blanco *(Spanish)* White

Blend Wine made from a combination of either grapes and/or wines

Bocksbeutel *(German)* Squat bottle originally used for bottling the wines of Franconia; now also used in Portugal

Bodega *(Spanish)* Producer's cellar or warehouse

Body Weight of a wine in the mouth. This is due principally to the alcoholic content and varies with the quality of a wine, its style and origin; it tends to be heavier in southern regions such as the Rhône Valley

Botrytis cinerea Mould which forms on ripe grapes and shrivels up the skins; the juices are highly concentrated in sugar. This mould is not harmful; it is known as *pourriture noble* ('noble rot') in France, *edelfäule* in Germany, and as *muffa nobile* in Italy.

Bottle sickness Temporary ailment lasting a short time after wine has been bottled; it disappears with aeration

Bouchonné *(French)* Wine that is 'corked', i.e. contaminated by a faulty cork; this can be detected by smelling the wine which will have a musty, corky smell. The term is often used incorrectly

Bouquet The smell, aroma or fragrance of a wine

Branco *(Portuguese)* White

Breed Denotes the quality of flavour and texture of wine produced by outstanding vineyards and growers

Brut *(French)* Unsweetened, or very dry; often used to describe Champagne

Butt Large oak cask or barrel

C

Cantina *(Italian)* Wine cellar or winery

Cantina sociale or **cooperativa** *(Italian)* Wine-growers' co-operative

Capsule Metal (sometimes plastic) cap which protects the exposed surface of the cork

Casa vinicola *(Italian)* Wine firm

Cave *(French)* Cellar or wine store

Cep *(French)* Vine stock

Cepa *(Spanish)* Vine stock

Cépage *(French)* Vine plant or variety of grape. Vines are chosen for their suitability to the soil and climate of a wine region; sometimes the same vines are found in different regions but under a different name. It is rare, except in Burgundy, that a wine is made from only one variety of grape

Chai *(French)* Building (above ground) in which wine is stored, particularly in Bordeaux

Chambrer *(French)* To bring a wine slowly to room temperature ready for serving (so it is *chambré*)

Chaptalisation *(French)* Process of adding a controlled amount of sugar to must before fermentation begins so that a wine's alcohol content is increased; it is only allowed under certain conditions in certain areas

Charmat process Modern method of making a wine sparkle by fermentation in closed vats and by bottling under pressure; cheaper and quicker than the *méthode champenoise*

Château *(French)* Literally a castle; name for an estate or vineyard property where wine is made

Château-bottled On a label this means that the wine was made and bottled in the same place. It is written in French as either Mise en Bouteille au Château or Mise du Château

Cherveno *(Bulgarian)* Red

Chiaretto *(Italian)* Very light red

Clairet *(French)* Light *(clair)* red wine. The word 'claret' for Bordeaux red wine is thought to be derived from *clairet*

Clarete *(Spanish and Portuguese)* Light red or dark rosé

Classé *(French)* Officially classified, as in Cru Classé; a term applying particularly to Bordeaux wines

Classico *(Italian)* Describes wines from the central and very best vineyards of a wine region

Clavelin *(French)* Bottle used only for *vin jaune* from the Jura region

Clean Describes a wine's fresh smell in which no foreign odours can be detected

Climat *(French)* Term used in Burgundy meaning a single field or plot in a vineyard

Clos *(French)* Literally enclosure; it refers to an enclosed vineyard e.g. Clos de Vougeot

Coarse Tasting term which may mean a wine is rough and indifferently made or may refer to immature young wine

Colheita *(Portuguese)* Harvest or vintage

Colle, collina *(Italian)* Slope or hillside (where vines are often planted)

Commune *(French)* Village district (where wine is made)

Consorzio *(Italian)* Wine-growers' association

Cooked Describes the smell resulting from the use of excess sugar in a poor vintage

Corked See **Bouchonné**

Cosecha *(Spanish)* Harvest or vintage

Côte, coteau *(French)* Slope or hillside (where vines are often grown)

Coupage *(French)* Practice of blending wine

Crémant *(French)* Semi-sparkling

Crno *(Serbo-Croat)* Red

Cru *(French)* Growth or crop; wine from a specific vineyard. The term may be used in conjunction with other words to give a number of different terms as follows

Cru Classé One of the five official growths of the Médoc in Bordeaux, which refer to the Classification of 1855 (see page 121); this term may appear on labels. It may also describe any classed growth of another district, however classified

Cru *continued*

Cru Bourgeois Supérieur and **Cru Bourgeois** Widely used terms meaning superior bourgeois and bourgeois growths; in the Médoc these are third and fourth ranks below Cru Classé

Premier Grand Cru Classé Widely used term meaning first great classified growth, also the first rank of St Emilion in Bordeaux classed growths (see the 1954 Classification, page 120)

Grand Cru Classé Widely used term meaning great classified growth; also the second rank of St Emilion classed growths (1954 Classification)

Grand Cru First rank of Burgundy vineyards with its own Appellation Contrôlée; also called Tête de Cuvée

Premier Cru Second rank of fine Burgundy vineyards

Crust Sediment found in old port

Cuve *(French)* Vat with a huge capacity made of wood, cement, stone, brick or stainless steel, lined with either glass or silica, and used for fermentation and storage

Cuvée *(French)* Vatting; it refers to the blending of wines from different vineyards but the same vintage

Tête de Cuvée Traditional term used in Burgundy and Champagne for the finest vineyards

Decant, to To separate a wine from the sediment in the bottle by pouring it gently into a glass container or decanter

Dégorgement *(French)* The process in Champagne-making whereby the sediment deposited on the cork is removed from the bottle with minimum loss of gas and wine

Delicate Tasting term which describes a light and pleasant balance of quality and flavour in a wine

Demi-sec *(French)* Describes a wine which is rather sweeter than medium sweet

DOC *(Italian)* Denominazione di Origine Controllata; Italian code of laws which control wine-growing and wine production methods; similar to the French AOC

Distillation Process for making spirits which turns fermented grape must into vapour by heat to drive off the volatile alcohol which is then collected by condensation

Doce *(Portuguese)* Sweet

Dolce *(Italian)* Richly sweet

Domaine *(French)* Property, estate or vineyard. The Burgundian equivalent of *château*

Domaine-bottled On a label this means that the wine was bottled where it was made. It is written in French as either Mise en Bouteille au Domaine (or à la Propriété) or Mise du Domaine

Doux *(French)* Usually means sweet; a term used mostly for Champagne and sparkling wines

Dry Denotes very little sugar present in a wine, i.e. it has been fermented out

Dulce *(Spanish and Romanian)* Sweet

Eau-de-vie *(French)* literally water of life; brandy; usually refers to inferior spirits

Edelfäule *(German)* 'Noble rot'; see **Botrytis cinerea**

Edelzwicker *(French)* Alsatian blended wine made from the noble grapes

Édes *(Hungarian)* Sweet

Égrappoir *(French)* Revolving cylindrical machine which separates grapes from stems and stalks

Eiswein *(German)* Very sweet wine made from grapes frozen during the vintage; rare and therefore expensive

Escogido *(Spanish)* Specially selected

Espumante *(Portuguese)* Sparkling

Espumoso *(Spanish)* Sparkling

Estate-bottled See **château-bottled**

Estufa *(Portuguese)* Heated cellar in which Madeira is placed during the ageing process

Fat Tasting term which describes a full, almost rich, rounded flavour and texture in a wine

Fehér *(Hungarian)* White

Fein *(German)* Fine or excellent

Fermentation Wine-making process of converting natural grape sugar to alcohol by the action of yeasts

Fiasco *(Italian)* Straw-wrapped flask

Finesse Delicacy or elegance in a wine

Fining Process of clarifying a young wine during its stay in cask

Finish   Taste that remains after swallowing a wine. A firm, crisp finish indicates good balance and a reasonable amount of acidity; a watery finish indicates a poor quality wine

Fino *(Spanish)*   Very dry, pale sherry

Flinty   Describes the characteristic smell of gun flint found in dry white wines grown on chalky soils, such as Chablis

Flor *(Spanish)*   Yeast or bacteria which grows naturally on the surface of wine to form a white crust. It is important to sherry-making in Jerez de la Frontera where it determines the type of sherry made; flor can also be cultivated in Cyprus, South Africa and Australia

Fortified   The addition of brandy, either during or after fermentation, which increases the alcoholic strength of a wine. If brandy is added during fermentation this process will stop and a sweet wine will result because only part of the sugar has been converted to alcohol. Port, sherry, Madeira and Marsala are all fortified wines

Foxy   Describes musty, earthy flavour characteristic of native American vines

Frais *(French)*   Chilled

Frappé *(French)*   Iced

Free-run wine   Wine made from the juice that runs from the grapes under their own weight before pressing; held to be the best quality wine

Frizzante *(Italian)*   Slightly sparkling or prickly on the palate

Fruity   Describes a wine full of the flavour of the grape

Full-bodied   Describes a wine with a high alcohol content that feels full and heavy in the mouth

Garrafeira *(Portuguese)*   Special quality

Gay Lussac   French method of measuring strength of alcoholic liquids as a percentage of pure alcohol by volume

Generic   US term for a wine named after a European wine which it resembles e.g. Californian Burgundy

Gewächs *(German)*   Growth

Goût de bouchon *(French)*   See **Bouchonné**

Goût de terroir *(French)*   Taste imparted to a wine by the soil in which the vine was grown

Grand *(French)*   Great, superior; often used unofficially on labels. See also **Cru**

Grand marque *(French)*   Denotes a top-quality Champagne

Grapy   Describes the distinct aroma produced by grapes. All grape varieties have certain characteristic smells: for example the cabernet sauvignon is reminiscent of blackcurrants

Green   Describes a young, raw wine with plenty of acidity

Growth   See **Cru**

Gun flint   In French this smell is called *pierre à fusil*; see **Flinty**

Habzó *(Hungarian)*   Sparkling

Hard   Describes a harshness or severity in wine due to excess tannin and acid, both of which may mellow in time

Heady   Describes wine with a high alcohol content

Heavy   See **Full-bodied**

Hectare *(French)*   Measure of area equivalent to 2.47 acres

Hock   Popular English word for German wines and said to be derived from the town of Hochheim in the Rheingau district

Hogshead   Cask; in Bordeaux it is an official measure of 46 gallons

Hybrid   Vine produced by grafting vine stocks of different varieties; frequently found in the East Coast of the USA

Imbottigliato dal produttore all'origine *(Italian)*   Estate-bottled

Imperial   Bottle equivalent to eight ordinary bottles' capacity

Infiascato alla fattoria *(Italian)*   Bottled in flask at the winery

Iskriashto *(Bulgarian)*   Sparkling

Jeroboam   Bottle equivalent to four ordinary bottles' capacity

Kellerabzug, Kellerabfüllung *(German)*   Estate-bottled

Lage *(German)*   Site of vineyard

Lees   Impurities and solids left at the bottom of a cask or vat after wine has been clarified

Light   Implies a lack of body

Liqueur de dosage *(French)*   Solution used in Champagne-making at the first bottling of cane sugar in Champagne with a little brandy

Liquoreux *(French)*   Very sweet, luscious

Liquoroso *(Italian)*   Very sweet, luscious

Little   Describes a wine's lack of bouquet which can signify either immaturity or lack of character

Lozia *(Bulgarian)*   Vineyards

Luscious   Describes a well-balanced wine that is soft, sweet, fat and fruity

Madérisé *(French)*   Describes a white wine that has aged too long and has oxidized so that its colour is brown rather than white or yellow

Maduro *(Portuguese)*   Old, matured

Magnum   Bottle equivalent to two ordinary bottles' capacity

Maison *(French)*   Firm or business

Manzanilla *(Spanish)*   Pale, very dry sherry similar to a *fino*

Marc *(French)*   Liqueur or brandy made by distilling the last pressings of grapes

Meaty   Describes a wine that is rich and almost chewy in texture

Medium dry   Wine with only a small amount of natural sweetness

Medium sweet   Wine that is definitely on the sweet side but not quite a dessert wine

Méthode champenoise *(French)*   Traditional French process of making Champagne

Methuselah   Bottle of Champagne equivalent to eight ordinary bottles' capacity

Mousseux *(French)*   Sparkling

Muffa nobile *(Italian)*   'Nobile rot'; see **Botrytis cinerea**

Mussante *(Italian)*   Sparkling

Must   Unfermented grape juice

Musty   Describes a stale smell occurring when the cork is drawn; usually due to stale air in the bottle, it wears off after a few minutes

Naturrein, naturwein *(German)* Wine fermented without the addition of sugar

Nebuchadnezzar Bottle equivalent to 20 ordinary bottles' capacity

Négociant *(French)* Shipper

Négociant-éleveur *(French)* Merchant – shipper who buys wines and blends and ages them in his own cellars prior to distribution and shipment

Nero *(Italian)* Black; used to describe dark red wines

Noble rot Mould which forms on ripe grapes, see **Botrytis cinerea**

Non-vintage Describes wine made from blends of different vintages, particularly Champagne and port

Nose See **Bouquet**

Oeil de perdrix *(French)* Literally partridge's eye; type of rosé wine in Switzerland and France, particularly Burgundy, whose colour resembles the pink eye of a partridge

Oenology Science of wine-making

Oidium Mould or fungus; one of the most common wine diseases

Oloroso *(Spanish)* Sweet type of sherry

Ordinaire *(French)* Plain, undistinguished

Originalabfüllung *(German)* Estate-bottled

Ouillage *(French)* The topping up of cask or bottle with wine of the same vintage or blend to prevent oxidation

Oxidation Exposure to air which causes an orange-brown colour and change in taste in both white and red wines

Passe-Tous-Grains *(French)* Inferior type of Burgundy made from a mixture of pinot and gamay grapes

Passito *(Italian)* Sweet wine made from semi-dried grapes

Pasteurization Treatment of wine by heat to kill yeasts and bacteria; only allowed under certain conditions

Pelure d'oignon *(French)* Literally onion skin; describes the pink colour of certain rosé wines

Perlant, perlé *(French)* Very slightly sparkling

Perlwein *(German)* Slightly sparkling wine

Pétillant *(French)* Slightly sparkling

Phylloxera Aphis or louse which burrows into the vine root and destroys it by feeding off the sap. Phylloxera came to Europe in the 1870s and destroyed most of the vineyards, which are now planted with vines grafted onto American vine stocks or roots which are resistant to phylloxera

Pipe Large cask for storing wine, usually associated with port

Piquant Describes a fresh and mouth-watering sharpness in a wine

Polšuho *(Serbo-Croat)* Medium dry

Pourriture noble *(French)* 'Noble rot'; see **Botrytis cinerea**

Press Apparatus for pressing grapes

Proof spirit A system of measuring and expressing alcoholic content; there are two scales. In the British (Sikes) scale proof spirit contains 52.10% alcohol by volume at 60°F; in the American scale proof spirit contains 50% alcohol by volume at 60°F

Propriétaire-récoltant *(French)* Owner-manager of a wine property

Pupitre *(French)* Literally desk; the racks used to hold bottles of Champagne

Puttonyos *(Hungarian)* Measurement of crushed grapes with 'noble rot'; the number of *puttonyos* used indicates the degree of sweetness of a Tokay wine

Qualitätswein *(German)* Superior table wine subject to certain controls

Qualitätswein mit Prädikat *(German)* Strictly controlled top quality wine

Quinta *(Portuguese)* Estate or producer's cellar

Rack, to To draw the clear wine off the lees and run it into new casks

Raya *(Spanish)* Cheaper blend of *oloroso* sherries

Recolta *(Romanian)* Harvest or vintage

Récolte *(French)* Harvest or vintage

Rehoboam Bottle of Champagne equivalent to six ordinary bottles' capacity

Remuage *(French)* The daily turning of bottles of Champagne which encourages the sediment to slide down onto the corks

Reserva *(Spanish)* Specially aged wine

Reservado *(Spanish)* Specially selected

Réserve *(French)* Specially selected grapes or wine

Riserva *(Italian)* Specially selected grapes or wine

Robust Describes a full-bodied wine

Rosado *(Spanish and Portuguese)* Pink or rosé

Rosato *(Italian)* Pink or rosé

Rosé *(French)* Pink

Roseewein *(German)* Pink wine made from red grapes

Rosso *(Italian)* Red

Roşu *(Romanian)* Red

Rotling *(German)* Pink wine made from a mixture of red and white grapes

Rotwein *(German)* Red wine

Ruzica *(Serbo-Croat)* Pink or Rosé

Schaumwein *(German)* Sparkling

Sec *(French)* Dry

Seco *(Spanish and Portuguese)* Dry

Secco *(Italian)* Dry

Sekt *(German)* Type of sparkling wine

Silky Tasting term describing a wine's texture – somewhere between firm and soft in the mouth

Sladko *(Bulgarian)* Sweet

Slatko *(Serbo-Croat)* Sweet

Soft Tasting term which describes a light and agreeable texture of wine in the mouth

Solera *(Spanish)* System of casks arranged in tiers for blending and ageing sherry

Sommelier *(French)* Wine waiter

Soutirage *(French)* Process of racking to remove wine from the lees in the cask

Spätlese *(German)* Wine made from late-harvested grapes

Spicy Describes rich, herb-like flavour in wine

Spritzig *(German)* Slightly sparkling

Spumante *(Italian)* Frothy or sparkling

Spumos *(Romanian)* Sparkling

Stravecchio *(Italian)* Very old, mellow

Suho *(Serbo-Croat and Bulgarian)* Dry

Sulphury Describes sharp smell caused by excessive use of sulphur during cellar treatment or bottling which tends to 'catch' the back of the throat

Supérieur *(French)* Describes wine superior to *vin ordinaire* with a higher alcohol content

Supple Tasting term describing the texture and flavour of a wine – partly silky, partly full in flavour

Sweet Denotes wine with a high sugar content, probably a dessert wine

Száraz *(Hungarian)* Dry

T

Table wine Term describing all unfortified wines which normally accompany a meal; their alcohol content ranges from 9.5–14%

Tafelwein, Tischwein *(German)* Ordinary table wine

Tannin Substance vital to the ageing process of wine, particularly red wines, found in the skins and stalks of grapes. It has a bitter, hard taste and is easily recognized in young red wines

Tastevin *(French)* Literally 'taste wine'; name given to a small metal cup, usually made of silver, which is used for tasting young wines from the cask, notably in Burgundy. (Pronounced 'tutt-vin', the 's' being silent)

Tinto *(Spanish and Portuguese)* Red

Tirage *(French)* Bottling

Trocken *(German)* Dry

Trockenbeerenauslese *(German)* Wine made from specially selected overripe grapes

V

Varietal US term for fine wine named after its predominant grape e.g. Californian Riesling

Velho *(Portuguese)* Old, aged

Vendange tardive *(French)* Late harvest

Viejo *(Spanish)* Old, aged

Vigneron *(French)* Wine-grower

Vignoble *(French)* Vineyard

Vigorous Describes a lively, healthy wine that is developing well

Viile *(Romanian)* Vineyard

VDQS *(French)* Vin Délimité de Qualité

Supérieur – an official wine standard between *vin ordinaire* and AOC wines

Vin *(French)* Wine

  de consommation or **courant** Wine for everyday drinking

  doux naturel Fortified sweet natural wine

  gris Rather inferior rosé wine

  de goutte Wine made from the last pressing, normally of rather poor quality

  jaune White sherry-type wine of the Jura region that is not fortified; made from sun-dried grapes

  de liqueur Lesser sweet natural wine

  ordinaire Plain, undistinguished wine

  de paille literally straw wine; sweet white wine of the Jura region made from grapes which are dried in the sun on straw mats

  du pays Local or country wine

  de presse Wine made from pressed leftover must and grape solids

  de réserve Specially selected wine

Vin *(Romanian)* Wine

  de masa Table wine

  superioare Superior wine

  usoare Light wine

Vinho de mesa *(Portuguese)* Table wine

Vinho verde *(Portuguese)* Literally green wine; slightly sparkling, refreshing wine from the Minho region

Vino *(Italian and Spanish)* Wine

  corriente *(Spanish)* Ordinary wine, not usually bottled

  liquoroso *(Italian)* Very sweet dessert wine

  de mesa or **de pasto** *(Spanish)* Table wine

  da pasto *(Italian)* Table wine

  Santo *(Italian)* Wine made from sun-dried grapes; often labelled and always referred to as Vin Santo

Vinoproizvoditel *(Bulgarian)* Wine-grower

Vintage Grape harvest; if the year of the vintage is given on a label it denotes a wine made only from grapes harvested in that year

Vitis labrusca, riparia and **rotundifolia** Vines native to the East Coast of the USA

Vitis vinifera Common but important European vine used for making wines in many countries throughout the world

Vörös *(Hungarian)* Red

VO Cognac term: very old

VSO Cognac term: very superior old

VSOP Cognac term: very superior old pale

W

Wachstum *(Germany)* Growth; often used on labels to indicate a wine made by the wine-grower himself

Weinkeller *(German)* Wine cellar

Weisswein *(German)* White wine

Winzergenossenschaft *(German)* Wine growers' co-operative

Woody Smell the cask sometimes lends to wine. It is caused by late racking or contact with a poor or fresh new cask

Y

Yeasts Natural organisms which collect on the skin of grapes; they are vital to fermentation of the must and work on the juice by converting the sugar into alcohol as soon as the skins are broken

Z

Zwicker *(French)* Alsatian term for ordinary wine made from blending different grapes

France

Champagne

Champagne differs from all other wines in its ability to sparkle and effervesce. There are various ways of making sparkling wines but none is comparable to the lengthy and complicated *méthode champenoise*. It is the adoption of less costly ways of production – bypassing the correct *méthode champenoise* technique – that has led to the misuse of the term champagne for other sparkling wines. Under French law wine made within a defined area, with specific grapes and by the *méthode champenoise* is the only wine that may be called Champagne.

Exactly when it was discovered that Champagne became effervescent after bottling is uncertain. The English are partly credited with the discovery; during the 17th century they shipped vast quantities of the wine, which was very popular, in cask to England and then transferred it to bottles, whereupon it was noticed that the wine had a 'sparkle'.

Towards the end of the 17th century the Church – and one man in particular, Dom Pérignon, a monk at the Abbey of Hautvillers near Epernay – was responsible for major developments in making Champagne. He and his fellow monks noted that the wine began to effervesce, causing the cork to leap out of the bottle, and proclaimed it a 'mischievous wine'. Under the guidance of Dom Pérignon, stronger bottles were made and the corks were tied down with string, because the pressure of the gas often caused the bottles to burst.

The Church used to buy wine from many proprietors to blend for commercial purposes. The first tentative steps towards the skilled art of blending wines from different parts of the area were taken at this time.

Location of vineyards

The zones which are, under French law, entitled to produce Champagne cover some 44,700 acres of vines. This amounts to only a very small percentage of the wine-growing areas of France. These vineyards are the most northerly in France and are, therefore, subject to colder winters than those elsewhere.

The chief characteristic of the Champagne region is its chalky subsoil in areas where vineyards are planted. The vine thrives in this subsoil which ensures natural and regular drainage but does not drain all the moisture from the topsoil. It also has the advantage of storing the heat of the sun and reflecting it back onto the underside of the vines at night; this speeds the growth of the vines and the ripening of the grapes so that the vintage may be earlier here than in other areas. Autumn comes quickly and the grapes must be harvested before the first frosts.

The principal zones

The major zones are the Montagne de Reims, the Vallée de la Marne, and the Côte des Blancs; they are concentrated around Reims and Epernay, homes of such famous Champagne houses as Veuve Cliquot, G. H. Mumm, Pol Roger, Lanson, Moët et Chandon, Charles Heidsieck, Krug, Irroy, Louis Roederer, Taittinger, and Mercier.

Grapes grown at Chavot in the Côte des Blancs have been sorted and are ready for pressing. All unripe or mildewy berries have been removed. In this area they are carefully packed in huge baskets, called caques, *which hold up to 160 lb*

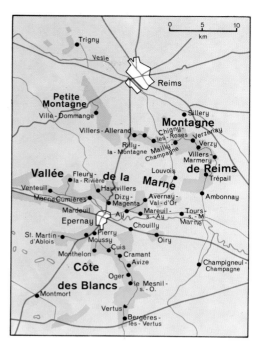

Montagne de Reims

This northern zone lies to the south-east of Reims and is a large, slightly sloping plateau. Pinot noir grapes are planted here and the principal vineyards are located at Ambonnay, Beaumont-sur-Vesle, Bouzy, Louvois, Mailly, Sillery, Verzenay and Verzy.

Vallée de la Marne

This is the central zone and is planted largely with pinot noir grapes. Vineyards are situated principally around Mareuil-sur-Ay and Dizy.

Left: the four major wine-producing zones of Champagne, north east of Paris. (Where kilometres are used map scales are in km; 1 km = 0.6214 miles) Below: modern machines such as this one are now used for ploughing and spraying throughout France

Côte des Blancs

South of Epernay and the Marne river lies the Côte des Blancs so named because it produces almost entirely white chardonnay grapes, the other important grape for making Champagne. The well-known Blanc des Blancs wine, made solely from chardonnay grapes, comes from this area. Vineyards are located around Cramant and Avize.

The Côte de Vertus, the Congy region and the Côte de Sézanne are the southerly continuations of the Côte des Blancs. Here the black meunier grape predominates,

Gently rolling countryside and flourishing vines near Epernay. Such vast stretches of vines give little idea of how small individual holdings may be. It is usual for grape growers to sell their produce to wealthy concerns that can afford to make Champagne

producing a very fruity wine, but it is going out of favour because it is too prone to disease.

One other zone that is relatively minor compared with the other three lies some miles to the south-east of Troyes, around the Aube river. Vineyards are located around Bar-sur-Aube and Bar-sur-Seine.

Care of the vine

The vine is pruned short – a marked characteristic of this region – to comply with the legal provisions drawn up by the Comité Interprofessionel des Vins de Champagne. The purpose of these regulations is to limit the quantity of grapes produced so that quality is guaranteed. The oldest pruning method is the *taille guyot*; other authorized methods are the *chablis* and the *cordon de royat.* The pruning gives the vine the shape that will allow it to derive the greatest possible benefit from the sunshine and so hasten the ripening of the grapes. It also allows the vine to bear the maximum number of bunches of grapes evenly without tiring the plant.

As elsewhere, the vines require constant attention. They flower between the end of May and the beginning of June – a very critical period of some four days – during this short time the quality of the eventual harvest is determined. Rainfall, morning mists or cold nights can cause enough damage to prevent the vines attaining the standard necessary for a great Champagne year.

When the flowering is over, vine branches are trimmed (*rognage*) so that the sap is channelled back to the mature vine stock to concentrate its growth. From July onwards, while the grapes swell and ripen, the soil between the vines is cleared of weeds and ploughed lightly several times (*binage*) until the vintage. The wine-grower may fix the date for the vintage any time between August and October, depending on the weather and how quickly the grapes have ripened. Teams of workers are recruited, traditionally from the mining communities of the north and Lorraine, to gather the grapes quickly and carefully.

Pressing the grapes

Pressing takes place as soon as possible after the vintage; and the selection of grapes made at this stage is very important.

Great care is taken to ensure that the must, the juice from the grapes, is run off untainted by any colouring matter from the grape skins, for both black and white grapes are used. Regulations stipulate the amount of pressing allowed.

In Champagne presses have a large surface area and are very shallow so that the pressing may be carried out as quickly as possible. Pressing takes place in several stages. It is only the *cuvée*, the juice from the first three pressings and the free-run wine, that is used for the best Champagnes. The remaining pressings are called the *tailles* and consist of what liquid can still be drawn from the grapes.

The must then flows into large vats where it remains for 10–12 hours so that any solids, such as pips or skins, can sink to the bottom. Only then is it drawn off into 205-litre casks which are stored in the cellars for the preliminary fermentation at a controlled temperature.

Preliminary fermentation

The first fermentation is called *bouillage* because the yeasts in the must, which is kept at a constant temperature around 20°C, boil furiously. A 'head' or scum is thrown off, purifying the *cuvée*.

At the end of about three weeks, the wine is drawn off and exposed to the cold to stop fermentation and to let any sediment sink to the bottom, thus clearing the wine. It is then drawn off into vats where it stays from April, May or June, depending on when it is bottled.

Blending the wine

So far the wine-making process in Champagne has not differed greatly from that of any other wine-growing region. But here the similarity ends, for while other wine-growers strive to achieve a perfect wine with as little blending as possible, for Champagne blending is the rule rather than the exception.

The wines are blended with other wines of the same vintage from neighbouring vineyards within the Champagne area to give a uniform blend. The proportions must be right to achieve the required balanced qualities that Champagne is famous for, and only experience can give the wine its bouquet, flavour and necessary ageing qualities. Each Champagne firm has its own individual style of wine, based on a formula handed down over the years.

In order to maintain the uniformity of a wine, a special *vin de réserve* may be added to the young wine. This is usually a Champagne kept in cask from a previous very good harvest.

After blending, one more process must take place before the wine is ready for bottling. A solution of pure cane sugar, dissolved in the wine of the year, is added

Top left: grapes enter the press for the first time. In Champagne the bunches of grapes are kept whole; the grapes are not detached from their stalks as they are in Burgundy. The Champagne presses are wide and shallow so that pressing (top right) may take place as quickly as possible

Centre: when the must from the first pressings has been extracted for the best Champagnes the pulp is again pressed
Far left: sediment collected in the neck of the bottle is removed in a swift and skilful operation. The bottle may then have a cork put in (left)
Above: strict rules govern the corks used for Champagne; the stamp on the cork guarantees the wine

to the casks to start the second fermentation that will eventually produce the famous sparkle in the wine. The strength of this solution, which in no way sweetens the wine because the sugar will ferment out, governs the amount of effervescence in the finished wine. When this has been added, the wine is at last ready to be put into bottles.

Making Champagne

The sparkle in Champagne is the natural transformation of the sugar in the wine into alcohol and carbon dioxide. This must by law occur in the bottle, and takes three to five years for vintage wine, two to three years for non-vintage wine.

The wine becomes cloudy and a sediment forms; the pressure of the gas increases, reaching up to 80 lb per square inch, sometimes causing the bottles to burst. While this is happening, the bottles are stacked on top of each other in huge caverns dug out of the limestone rock. Some cellars extend for several miles, and one firm has a train to cover its 15 miles of tunnels under the wine region.

After lying undisturbed the bottles are moved to special wooden racks (*pupitres*), where they are placed at a slight angle with the corks pointing down, so that the deposit left after fermentation will start sliding down and settling on the cork. Every day, each bottle is given a slight twist and its angle of slant is increased.

Left: Champagne bottles are carefully racked so that sediment will fall onto the cork; each bottle must be turned every day until its position is nearly vertical, whereupon the sediment is removed
Right: deep in the limestone rock underlying the region huge caverns have been hollowed out to store the wine at an even temperature while it matures.

This turning of the bottles is called *remuage*.

By the time the bottle is in the near vertical position, the sediment is resting on the cork. Then comes the tricky operation of removing it on the cork without letting precious wine or gas escape; this is called *dégorgement*. The traditional method requires great manual skill, for the cork is withdrawn from the bottle while it stands almost on end; the gas in the wine pushes out the cork, with its clinging sediment, and no more than a small cupful of wine is lost. However, the method favoured now is to chill the neck of the bottle in a vat of brine cooled to −20°C so that the wine in the neck turns to ice. The bottle can then be turned

'Champagne is the only wine which allows a woman to retain her looks after drinking it' – Madame de Pompadour

upright, the cork removed, and the sediment enclosed in ice is ejected. Hardly any wine is lost in this way.

The very small quantity of wine lost in this operation is replaced by wine of the same blend, when a *liqueur de dosage* is added. The *dosage* is made from pure cane sugar dissolved in old Champagne and stabilized with a good brandy to prevent further fermentation occurring. It is the degree of sugar in this *dosage* that determines the final sweetness of Champagne as described on the label. The driest of all is Brut or Extra Dry; Sec or Dry is less dry; Demi-Sec is moderately sweet, and Doux is distinctly sweet.

Corking is very important for all wines but especially so for Champagne, because of the gas in the bottle. The cork must measure from five to six cm in length by three cm wide; it is covered by a capsule and enclosed in a small wire net. The name Champagne has to be stamped on the stem of the cork where it enters the bottle, together with the date if it is a vintage year.

Bottles must remain in cellars for a legal minimum of one year but it is customary to keep them there for at least three years – longer for vintage Champagne. Champagne has an alcohol content of 12% and will keep in bottle for up to 10 years; after that, it may start to deteriorate.

To serve Champagne

Champagne should be drunk cool at a temperature of 6°C–8°C, but not iced or chilled as this tends to dull the wine and spoil its flavour. The best way of cooling the wine is to place the bottle in a bucket filled half with ice and half with water. If a refrigerator has to be used to cool it don't put the wine in the freezing compartment.

Uncork Champagne with great care – the cork is not meant to explode into the air, with the wine spilling out. Remove the wire netting on the cork, tilt the bottle slightly, hold the cork firmly with one hand and turn the bottle, not the cork, with the other. If this is done properly, the gas escapes gently.

Wipe the rim of the bottle with a napkin and pour a little Champagne into each glass before filling all the glasses two-thirds full.

Champagne is best drunk from a slim, high-stemmed wineglass, with a tulip-shaped bowl. If the glass is held correctly by the base, the long stem prevents the warmth of the hand warming the wine. The bouquet is held in the top of the glass because only a small surface area of the wine is exposed to the air. The traditional European Champagne flute is more decorative than practical and the popular saucer-shaped glass allows the bouquet and the effervescence to escape.

Once opened, Champagne should be drunk quickly for the full appreciation of its effervescent qualities. Never use a swizzle stick or stirrer for it kills the bubbles, so wasting the costly efforts and expertise that the Champagne maker has put into his wine.

Alsace

The border province of Alsace, in the north-east of France, has suffered many hardships as a result of war and occupation over the centuries. From 1870 to 1914, Alsace was part of Germany, and its vineyards were converted to producing cheap white wine for the German market. It was not until 1919 when the Treaty of Versailles restored Alsace to France that Alsace was able to return to French ways and concentrate on improving its viticulture. With the advent of World War II, Alsace was again occupied by Germany, yet somehow the majority of the vineyards survived the vicissitudes of war.

Since 1945, Alsatian wines have greatly improved and are today enjoying an increasingly high reputation; this is due to the perseverance and painstaking care of the wine-growers who have immense pride in their wines. They make German-style wines in a French manner — that is to say every ounce of sweetness, a quality much sought after in German wines, is fermented out so that the resulting dry white wines have a strength comparable to a good white Burgundy.

A delightful way of seeing Alsace and its vineyards is to follow the beautiful *Route des Vins* that winds along the foot of the eastern slopes of the Vosges mountains through pretty cobbled-street villages with their timbered, Gothic-style houses, some of which date back to the 15th century; particularly attractive are the towns of Kaysersberg and Riquewihr.

Location of vineyards

The picturesque vineyards of Alsace lie in a thin strip of land, rarely more than a mile wide and some 70 miles long, behind the Vosges mountains. The area falls in the *départements* of Bas Rhin and Haut Rhin; the Rhine river acts as the border between France and Germany.

Vines are planted on every suitable site on the steep eastern slopes of the Vosges, which range from 600–1,500 ft. Owing to the steepness of the slopes, the terraced vines are trained on wires to grow tall so

Throughout the wine region of Alsace you encounter attractive villages, such as this one, surrounded by flourishing vineyards

and clay – ideal for fine white wines. The best wines come from the Haut Rhin area, though they are not necessarily all from the same grape. They become progressively softer, with less acidity, and richer in flavour as one travels south.

The wine trade of Alsace has for generations been a family affair, and some growers are also the shippers. They buy grapes from outside their own vineyards to make wines for sale under their label. There are some 60,000 small wine-growers who are beginning to feel the effects of competition and rising costs as demand for their wines increases. In order to stay in business, many of the small growers have joined together to form co-operatives so that quantity and quality are maintained on a more selective basis.

Types of grapes

The wines of Alsace are always white and the best wines are made from five noble grapes (*cépages nobles*) – the riesling, traminer and gewürztraminer, muscat, and tokay d'Alsace (also known as pinot gris). The Alsatians decided to abandon the usual French practice of labelling a wine with the name of the vineyard, commune or district, grower

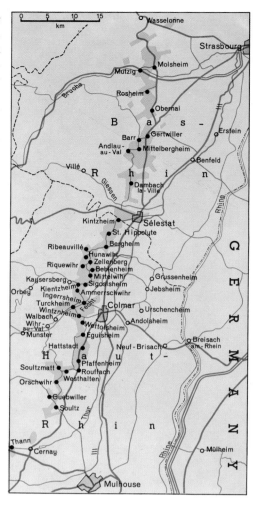

Every member of the family lends a hand when it is time to harvest the grapes

Traditional carved oak casks are still in use in the cellars of Alsace

Above: vineyards of the province of Alsace, close to the German border

that the grapes will benefit from every ray of sun. The high Vosges mountains shelter the vineyards beneath them from much of the cold, wet weather that would otherwise shorten their growing season. However, the northerly situation of the vineyards does have one drawback – the grapes ripen slowly.

The vintage usually takes place in the second week of October or as late as possible to let the grapes have the maximum ripening period. It may not take place until the middle of November if the summer and the autumn are particularly fine, so that the juice in the grapes can become more concentrated. These late pickings produce wines similar to the German wines made from selected overripe grapes; they are labelled Vendange Tardive (literally late harvest) to differentiate them from the usual wines. The wine's strength is highly concentrated, the bouquet almost exotic yet the flavour remains full and dry.

The soil on the slopes is a mixture of limestone and granite, with some chalk

and shipper in favour of the simple method of quoting the grape name only. In 1962 AOC was introduced and accordingly the words Vin d'Alsace indicate wine made from a noble grape produced in the authorized areas; the words Grand Vin or Grand Cru, Grande Réserve or Réserve Exceptionelle all indicate a higher quality wine of more than 11% alcohol content, the minimum legal level.

Gewürztraminer is one of the finest Alsatian wines. Its very fruity, heavily spiced bouquet comes from its reddish-brown grape. *Gewürz* in German means spice and this is a characteristic of this full-flavoured yet mellow wine. The traminer grape is also widely used.

Riesling produces beautifully crisp and clean-tasting wine, fruity and full-flavoured. The riesling is also the noble grape of fine German white wines, but Alsatian wines are different in style to

Below: this enormous press at Hattstadt, dated 1687, shows that the basic method of pressing grapes has hardly changed. Since the Middle Ages Alsatian wines have been highly valued in France

their great German counterparts.

Muscat bears no resemblance to the intensely sweet white wine usually associated with the muscat grape. Here it is a dry, light, fruity wine.

Tokay d'Alsace is a big and rich wine but with a more spicy bouquet than the other wines. It should not be confused with the Hungarian Tokay wine which is made from a different grape altogether, the furmint.

The next category of grapes, known as *cépages fins*, consists of the sylvaner and pinot blanc or klevner. Sylvaner produces a light, dry, fruity wine of the same name with a slight sharpness that sets it apart from the other wines. Pinot blanc has a rather neutral flavour and is more full-bodied than sylvaner, with what one might describe as a slightly earthy tang (*goût de terroir*).

Lastly, the ordinary wine sold by the carafe and drunk as *vin ordinaire* is made from grapes called *cépages courants* — the chasselas, knipperlé, goldriesling and kitterlé. The wine made from a blend of the common grapes is called Zwicker, and Edelzwicker is the name for a wine

blended from noble grapes (*edel* means noble in German).

A little red wine known as Rosé d'Alsace is made from the pinot noir grape, but it is in fact a very pale pink; another rosé wine is sold under the name Vin Gris, meaning literally grey wine.

Making the wine

After pressing, the must is allowed to stand and all the sediment or deposits left to settle out. The wine is lightly sulphured to delay the onset of fermentation for a few days, to allow a further settling out of deposits and to kill wild yeasts.

After this rest period, the wine is again racked to clear it of any remaining sediment, and a yeast culture is added to give a steady and reliable fermentation.

Fermentation lasts from one to three months and takes place in large, wooden or glass-lined cement vats. After fermentation, the young wines may be blended and the ordinary ones are bottled immediately. Better quality wines are racked in January and rested from one to five months. After the rest and if no

Above: harvest at Obernai. Throughout Alsace grapes are transported in the traditional wooden hottes
Above right: grape-picking at Riquewihr
Right: hottes *are loaded onto special lorries to go to the press-house*

further racking has been necessary, the wines are bottled; those that have rested in the wood are usually bottled after about two months.

Alsatian wine is rarely sold in the barrel since the wine-grower attaches great importance to the fact that his wine should retain its original fresh taste, its fruitiness and above all its bouquet. When the wine is bottled a special long cork is used so that as little air as possible is left in the bottle. Under the wine laws, the cork must have the name of the grape printed on it.

The best Alsatian wines are ready for drinking after two to four years in bottle. It is a mistake to drink the good wines very young as they have not had a chance to develop fully but do not keep them for too long. They should be drunk chilled, but not iced, at a temperature between 7°C–9°C. Serve them in long-stemmed, oval-shaped glasses.

The Loire Valley

The wide and beautiful river Loire rises in France's Massif Central and slowly wends its way to the Atlantic some 600 miles away. Along its meandering course are the vineyards of the Loire Valley, and despite the many variations of soil and grapes, the wines retain one common characteristic – they are flowery, light and refreshing. With few exceptions, Loire wines are most appealing when young.

The vineyards cover some 14 *départements* of France, from Auvergne in the east to Brittany in the west, and include the ancient provinces of Berry, Orléans, Touraine and Anjou.

Location of vineyards

There are four main wine-growing zones: Loire Atlantique, which includes Nantes, the region of Sèvre-et-Maine and part of the Coteaux de la Loire; Anjou and Touraine, whose names have officially been used to describe the wines made in these zones, and Pouilly-sur-Loire/Sancerre, in the east near the town of Nevers.

Very different wines are produced in these zones, though most of them are white and rosé; the sweeter wines come mainly from Anjou and Touraine, and the fine dry whites from Sèvre-et-Maine and Pouilly-sur-Loire/Sancerre.

The variations of the soil are partly

Above: Château de Luynes where the vine has been cultivated for centuries

responsible for the versatility of the wines. Often referred to as the garden of France, the Loire Valley, famed also for its *châteaux*, is green and fertile with a generally temperate climate.

Around the coastal region, the soil is rich in minerals and consists mainly of clay with a granitic subsoil. In adjoining Anjou, the best vineyards are situated on the slopes bordering the river (*coteaux*) where the soil is of hard sandstone and quartz rock with a rich, shallow topsoil in the east, and of limestone in the west. The soil of Touraine consists mainly of chalk and limestone, with a mixture of sandy gravel and clay. Around Pouilly-sur-Loire/Sancerre, the soil is mainly limestone and gravel, with some clay.

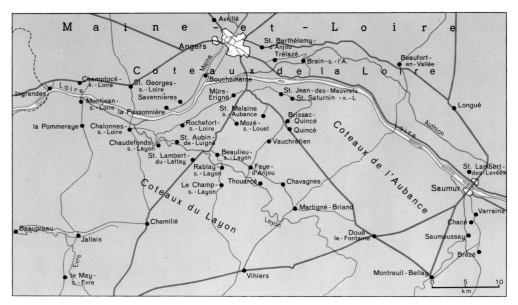

Anjou, south-west of Paris, where the best vineyards are to be found on the slopes leading down to the Loire

The principal zones

Loire Atlantique

The town of Nantes in Brittany dominates this province. Only one wine of importance is produced here – Muscadet – which takes its name from the muscadet or melon grape, not from a district. Muscadet is a comparative newcomer as it only achieved recognition in the last 50 years. The wine is a dry white, pale yellow in colour, soft yet rather acid in taste, with a fine fruity bouquet. It is not a wine for keeping in bottle, being at its best when drunk a few months after the vintage. It has become a very respectable substitute for Chablis and makes an excellent accompaniment to oysters and all shellfish.

Only three wine types (*crus*) have AOC status; they are Muscadet, Muscadet Sèvre-et-Maine, and Muscadet Coteaux de la Loire.

One other wine – Gros Plant – is made here. It is nowhere near so fine as Muscadet which is made from the same grape, and is more acid in taste.

Anjou

Part of the Coteaux de la Loire and the town of Saumur lie in this zone, whose reputation rests mainly on its rosé wines.

However, some 60 years ago, the traditional vintages of Anjou were rich, sweet dessert wines made like Sauternes, using the chenin blanc grape, or pineau de la Loire as it is called locally. The reputation of the Coteaux du Layon is founded on its sweet wines. Although wines of this type are still made today, the demand for them was never very great, so many wine-growers changed to making the more commercial light, medium sweet white and rosé wines that are now associated with Anjou. Nevertheless they continued to use the same grape. The exception to this is a dry light white wine made from the chenin blanc at Rochefort-sur-Loire.

Saumur, lying to the east of Anjou, produces a number of medium dry white wines which are firm in character and very refreshing.

A number of slightly sparkling wines are made using the Champagne method; these are labelled Anjou Pétillant or Mousseux, and Saumur Pétillant or Mousseux.

The principal wines with AOC status are Anjou, Anjou-Coteaux de la Loire (sweet white), Anjou-Coteaux du Layon (sweet white), Coteaux de l'Aubance (medium dry white), Savennières (the best dry whites come from here), Rosé d'Anjou and Cabernet d'Anjou (both sweet rosés), Saumur (dry to medium dry white), Quart de Chaume (sweet white) and Bonnezeaux (sweet white).

A few red wines are made in Anjou; their bouquet is fresh and fruity and they should be drunk young.

Below left: vintage at Bourgueil in Touraine. Red wines entitled to the name of Bourgueil must be made from cabernet franc grapes and reach an alcohol strength of at least 9.5%
Below: Tours on the Loire

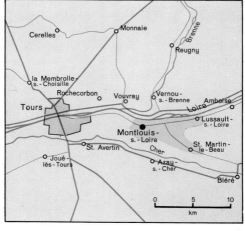

Touraine

The predominant wines produced in this zone are the red wines of Bourgueil and Chinon, and the white and rosé wines of Vouvray and its neighbouring districts.

The red wines are mostly made from the cabernet franc, one of the Bordeaux grapes; at their best, they are comparable to a good claret. They are soft and rather light, with a bouquet reminiscent of raspberries. Bourgueil, St Nicolas de Bourgueil and Chinon are the principal districts although some rosé is made from the cabernet as well. A relatively new red wine is Gamay de Touraine, made from the gamay grape like a Beaujolais which it strongly resembles.

The best known wines of the Touraine are the whites from Vouvray and nearby Montlouis; these may vary from year to year, from dry to sweet, depending on the amount of sunshine. They are at their best when drunk young so that full advantage can be taken of their refreshing qualities. Sparkling wine, similar to that of Saumur, is also made in Vouvray.

Pouilly-sur-Loire/Sancerre

The last zone, lying some 50 miles east of Tours, is made up of a number of districts. The speciality of the area is dry white wine that smells a little like gun flint. Under AOC law only the wines made from the sauvignon grape are entitled to the names Pouilly Fumé and Sancerre.

Pouilly-sur-Loire produces two wines: the lesser one takes its name from the town and is made from chasselas grapes, the other, Pouilly Fumé or Blanc Fumé, is a more illustrious wine and is made from sauvignon grapes. Do not confuse Pouilly Fumé with the very different Pouilly-Fuissé of Burgundy fame.

The wines of Sancerre are usually the better of the two wines of this area, with the same characteristic gun-flint smell and a somewhat earthy taste. The white wines from the vineyards at Reuilly and Quincy are not so distinguished and can be rather acid. Again, wines made from the sauvignon are the only ones that are entitled to use the AOC district name of Sancerre.

All the major wine-growing zones have AOC status but there are a few districts outside them that have VDQS status, namely Coteaux d'Ancenis, lying northeast of Nantes, the area around Orléans (mostly red wines are made here), and the Coteaux du Giennois, north of Pouilly-sur-Loire.

Bordeaux

The vineyards of Bordeaux cover the whole *département* of the Gironde in south-west France. They take their name from the city and port of Bordeaux and extend over some 500 square miles; they produce about 10% of France's wines and more fine quality red and white wines than any other French wine region.

The history of wine-making in Bordeaux goes back to the time of the Romans. However, Bordeaux wines first became popular in England in the 12th century when Gascony, as the south-western province was then known, fell into English hands when Henry of Anjou married Eleanor of Aquitaine; it remained English for some 300 years. Special laws favoured the exporters of local wines to England so that Bordeaux wines grew very popular and won a reputation for quality over all other regions that has never been lost.

The popularity was due to the lightness and subtlety of the red wines, a quality quite rare at that time, when most wines were heavy, coarse and harsh. The Gascons called their wines *clairets* because of their light purple-red colour, and from this the word 'claret' evolved to describe red Bordeaux wines.

Château Yquem in Sauternes; from these vineyards comes Bordeaux's finest white wine

Location of vineyards

The Bordeaux region embraces two rivers – the Garonne and the Dordogne – and where they join a few miles north of the city of Bordeaux, they form the Gironde river that flows on to the Bay of Biscay and the Atlantic Ocean. Most of the vineyards producing the best wines are situated along the banks of these rivers, with lesser wines coming from neighbouring districts.

The climate and soil here are extremely favourable for growing grapes as the proximity of the Gulf Stream brings mild winters, and the westerly winds temper the dry heat of summer with the rainy periods essential for the growth of the grapes.

The soil varies greatly. There are rich, alluvial plains around the mouth of the Garonne where there were once vast tracts of marsh and swamp; here the vines of the Bas Médoc grow profusely and the wines are long-lasting but without great finesse.

In the districts of St Emilion and Entre-Deux-Mers there is a mixture of clay, chalk and limestone that produces wines of exceptional delicacy with a high alcohol level; the gravel and sand of the Haut Médoc and Graves districts give wines which have great distinction in taste,

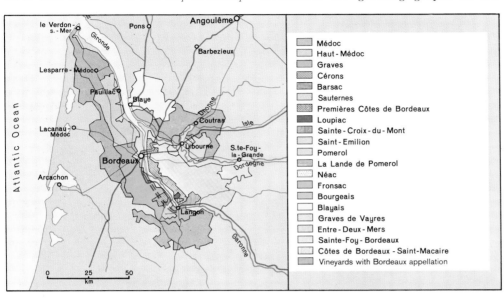

Médoc
Haut - Médoc
Graves
Cérons
Barsac
Sauternes
Premières Côtes de Bordeaux
Loupiac
Sainte - Croix - du - Mont
Saint - Emilion
Pomerol
La Lande de Pomerol
Néac
Fronsac
Bourgeais
Blayais
Graves de Vayres
Entre - Deux - Mers
Sainte-Foy - Bordeaux
Côtes de Bordeaux - Saint-Macaire
Vineyards with Bordeaux appellation

Left: chief wine-producing areas of the Bordeaux region; Bordeaux, in the south-west of France, has for centuries been the centre of a thriving wine trade.
Below: grapes picked and sorted, ready for pressing

colour and body.

Chalky soil gives a wine body; gravel and sand combine to give it finesse and bouquet. The proximity of the rivers ensures a good supply of water and the gravelly soil allows for drainage. Every

Château Lafite-Rothschild, home of one of Bordeaux's greatest clarets. The châteaux of Bordeaux are internationally famous for their distinctive wines

aspect favours the vine, and there is a local saying that sums it up quite well: 'The wine is good when the vine has its roots firmly planted in the gravel and can see the river.'

The principal grapes grown for red wines are the cabernet franc, cabernet sauvignon, merlot, malbec and petit verdot; for white wines, they are the sauvignon blanc, sémillon, pinot blanc, chardonnay and muscadel.

Classification of wines

Most Bordeaux wines are blends. Even when they come from a single vineyard, they are usually a mixture of at least two kinds of grapes. The proportions vary from vineyard to vineyard, and this factor, coupled with the differences of soil and climate, explains why there are such distinctive styles of wine associated with the Bordeaux *châteaux* or estates.

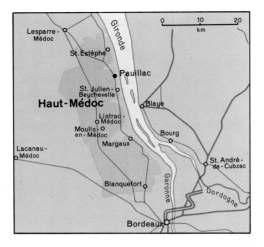

Haut Médoc, north of the city of Bordeaux

In 1855 a special ranking of the best known Bordeaux wines was drawn up by shippers and wine-growers for the Great Exhibition in Paris in 1855. It was based solely on the prices the wines had fetched over a specific period, and it has since become known as the 1855 Classification.

The Classification covered both red and white wines, but only 60 *châteaux* from hundreds of red wine vineyards were selected and listed in five groups known as *crus* or growths. On the whole, this ranking of Médoc wines still holds good today as a guide to the best *château*-bottled wines.

All the AOC wines of the major zones must carry on their labels the words Mis en Bouteille au Château (bottled at the *château*), together with their growth ranking such as Grand Cru Classé, the name of the vineyard, its commune or village, and the vintage date. The cork must also be stamped Mis en Bouteille au Château and sometimes the name of the *château* is used. These are the guarantees of a single vineyard vintage wine.

The principal zones

Bordeaux is made up of 20 wine-growing zones and, except for the zone Vignoble d'Appellation Bordeaux, all have AOC status.

There are five major zones whose wines are outstanding; they are the Médoc, usually divided into Bas (lower) and Haut (upper) Médoc, Graves, Sauternes, St Emilion and Pomerol.

Bordering on these zones are the lesser ones of Cérons and Barsac, Premières Côtes de Bordeaux, Loupiac, St Croix-du-Mont, Entre-Deux-Mers, Lalande de Pomerol, Néac, Fronsac, Bourgeais, Blayais, Graves de Vayres, St Foy-Bordeaux, Côtes de Bordeaux-St Macaire, and Vignoble d'Appellation Bordeaux. Between them, these zones produce some 60,000,000 gallons of red and white wine per annum.

Médoc

This is the most famous red wine district of Bordeaux. It is a narrow strip of land, some 50 miles long, that stretches from the Gironde estuary along the left bank of the Garonne to a point just north of the city of Bordeaux. Bas Médoc lies near the mouth of the Gironde estuary and Haut Médoc, which produces the better wines, lies closest to Bordeaux.

At Château Yquem the grapes are put through an égrappoir *to separate the berries from the stalks*

The principal grape grown here is the cabernet sauvignon, and Médoc wines usually need at least eight years in bottle before they are ready to drink.

Within Haut Médoc, there are four villages whose wines reach such heights of perfection that they have an AOC status of their own, and are allowed to use the village and vineyard names on their labels. They are the villages of St Estèphe, Pauillac, St Julien and Margaux (see map on this page).

St Estèphe's wines are the sturdiest and have the most acidity when young; the wines age very well. Among its vineyards are those of Calon-Ségur, Canteloup, Clos St Estèphe, Haut Marbuzet, Morin, Phélan-Ségur, Tronquoy-Lalande, Montrose and Lynch-Bages.

Pauillac is the home of great clarets and its famous vineyards include Lafite-Rothschild, Latour, and Mouton-Rothschild which has just been awarded the long-deserved status of Premier Cru. This district has the best possible soil, and its vineyards have enjoyed a continuity of ownership and dedication to viticulture which have led to an ever-improving standard of wine-making.

St Julien is the smallest of the villages; its wines have a consistently high standard and their character is one of soft, elegant suppleness – a contrast to the virility of the St Estèphe wines. Its vineyards include Beychevelle, Ducru-Beaucaillou, Lagrange, Langoa-Barton, Leoville-Poyferré and Talbot.

Margaux

In general, Margaux wines are lighter and more subtle than the wines of the other villages. They possess a distinctive and very attractive bouquet. Its outstanding vineyard is Château Margaux whose wines are always in great demand. It has been called *'le roi du Médoc'*. Other vineyards include Boyd-Cantenac, Giscours, Kirwan, Lascombes, Palmer, Rauzan-Gassies and La Tours-du-Mons.

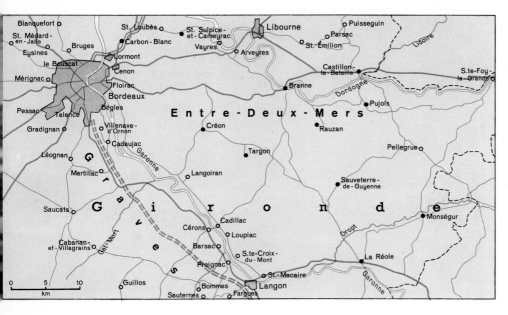

East of the city of Bordeaux lies Entre-Deux-Mers, a large wine area

Graves

The French word *graves* literally means gravel, the type of soil so characteristic of this zone. One of the largest Bordeaux wine districts, it runs south from the outskirts of Bordeaux along the Garonne river to a point just south of Langon, and actually encompasses the zones of Sauternes, Cérons and Barsac.

Graves was once an area renowned for its red wines, but the encroachment of the city of Bordeaux on its vineyards over the years has left few surviving today, and

Fermentation of the must can be slowed down or accelerated by shorter or longer periods in open cuves or vats; here is the surface of one of these vats at St Emilion

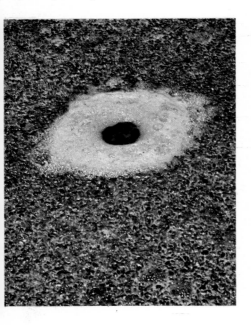

it is now more readily associated with medium dry white wines that are full of flavour and body.

The most recent classification of Graves wines was in 1959 and ranked 12 red vineyards in all, excluding Château Haut Brion which, since the 1855 Classification, has retained its separate ranking of Premier Cru, like Châteaux Lafite, Latour and Margaux from the Médoc.

There are only eight classified growths of white wines and vineyards include Carbonnieux, Olivier, La Tour Martillac and Domaine de Chevalier.

Sauternes

Lying within Graves, Sauternes includes the lesser zones of Cérons and Barsac.

The wines of Sauternes are unique and generally held to be the finest of all sweet white wines. The taste can only be described as lusciously rich, the bouquet intensely flowery. The colour of the wine ranges from pale yellow and amber in its youth to a deep gold as it ages.

What makes Sauternes so different is *la pourriture noble* – the 'noble rot'. This is a fungus, *Botrytis cinerea*, created by the climatic conditions peculiar to the area, that forms on the ripe grapes and shrivels and dries them up almost to the point of rottenness. The fungus breaks the grape skin and attacks the juice, causing the water content to evaporate, leaving a highly concentrated sugar mixture.

Sauvignon, with some sémillon grapes are used for Sauternes. They need more time to ripen than other grapes for they are individually picked as soon as they are overripe and attacked by the 'noble rot'. Should it rain before harvesting is com-

pleted, the grapes are left to dry out; in some vineyards they may be covered over to protect them from rain. Sometimes harvesting can take place over a period of a month.

Fermentation comes to a halt of its own accord when the alcohol level reaches between 14–17%; it is not possible for all the sugar to ferment out which is why the rich golden liquid, often described as *liquoreux*, is so sweet. Most people find one glass of Sauternes is adequate on account of its rich flavour and exceptionally high alcohol content.

The chief communes are Sauternes, Barsac, Preignac, Bommes and Fargues, all with AOC status. The 1855 Classification ranked the wines of Sauternes in three groups: Grands Premiers Crus from only one vineyard – Château d'Yquem; Premiers Crus and Deuxièmes Crus. The full list is given in the back of the book.

Sauternes age extremely well; exceptional wines like Château d'Yquem last as long as 30 years, remaining in prime condition. Most are ready for drinking after 8–10 years in bottle.

St Emilion and Pomerol

These adjoining areas lie to the east of the port of Libourne on the Dordogne river. Not quite on a par with the Médoc, their red wines are still immensely good with plenty of body and flavour. They need at least five years in bottle before their qualities become apparent. Most of the grapes grown are cabernet franc, merlot and malbec.

St Emilion's vineyards fall into two districts: the gentle hills immediately around the town of St Emilion where the choicest wines are made, and along the slopes of the outlying villages known as the Côtes St Emilion.

The vineyards of the first district are concentrated around the communes of St Christophe, St Hippolyte, St Laurent, St Sulpice and St Georges; those of the lesser district are around Montagne, Lussac and Puisseguin. Fine *châteaux* wines come from the vineyards of Cheval Blanc, Figeac, Ausone, Belair, Canon, Pavie and St Georges.

In 1954 there was an official classification of St Emilion wines that ranked 75 vineyards in two groups: Premiers Grands Crus Classés – in which only 12 vineyards were ranked – and Grands Crus Classés.

The tiny area of Pomerol lies to the west of St Emilion. A rather flat, unimposing area, it is almost totally devoted to growing vines. A comparative newcomer, it has no official classification of its distinctive wines and was almost certainly underrated in the past. They are well coloured, have a ripe bouquet and are soft yet rich in taste but not unduly acid, which means the wines mature earlier than those of the Médoc.

The suppleness of Pomerol wines makes them very appealing, and they are a good starting point for anyone unfamiliar with clarets.

There are 44 outstanding *châteaux* with AOC status; they include Pétrus, Vieux-Château-Certan, Gazin, Lafleur-Pétrus, Trotanoy, Clos René, Nenin and Rouget.

The lesser zones

Most of the vineyards in the lesser zones are not entitled to AOC status, even though the wines may come from single *châteaux* vineyards. As mentioned before, the purpose of the AOC laws is to control output so that quality is never sacrificed to quantity. As a result, many wines from the minor districts are very good and worth trying; they are known as 'bourgeois growths' and are usually sold in cask to the shippers and *négociants* of Bordeaux or to co-operatives. The wines are blended and bottled and sold under the name Bordeaux or Bordeaux Supérieur; in the case of the latter, the wines have a minimum alcohol content of 11%.

Sometimes the labels bear the name of a *château*, though the wines have not necessarily originated from a single vineyard – a point to bear in mind when buying claret.

Cérons and Barsac are districts within

Sauternes producing similar types of white wine.

Entre-Deux-Mers is a large area lying, as the name implies, between the Garonne

Here grapes are being separated from their stalks by hand; in Bordeaux the husks are thrown out so that the vegetable acids they contain (which make the young wine acid) are excluded

and Dordogne rivers. It makes an enormous quantity of dry white wine, and a smaller amount of red wine. Although they have been accorded AOC status, many of its wines are sold as *vins ordinaires*.

The area sandwiched between the right bank of the Garonne and Entre-Deux-Mers is called the Premières Côtes de Bordeaux. Mostly medium sweet white wines, with a few ordinary reds, are made here in a belt of vineyards running through some 34 communes from Ambarès in the north to the lesser districts of Loupiac, St Croix-du-Mont and the Côtes de Bordeaux-St Macaire in the extreme south.

Sweet, liqueur-like white wines are made from the sauvignon, sémillon and muscadel grapes, though a few dry whites are made as well. Red wines come mainly from the northerly vineyards around Ambarès.

The St Foy-Bordeaux district is east of Entre-Deux-Mers. It has 19 communes with AOC status making rather sweet white wines, as well as a few dry fruity whites.

The last district situated in the stretch of land between the Garonne and the Dordogne is Graves de Vayres which lies to the south-west of Libourne. Its principal wines are dry, perfumed whites, and well-balanced reds that should be drunk within a few months of harvesting.

The Côtes de Castillon, renamed Castillon-la-Bataille in commemoration of the battle that finally ended the Hundred Years' War between England and France harbour the vineyards of Lalande de Pomerol, Néac and Fronsac, the minor districts of Pomerol and St Emilion respectively. All the red wines are of above average quality in comparison with those from most other lesser zones.

The two zones of Blayais and Bourgeais stand on the right bank of the Gironde estuary. Their red wines are very good and with the growing demand for clarets that mature early, they are becoming increasingly popular. Some dry white wines are also made here.

In Bourgeais 61 vineyards have AOC status; in Blayais 75 red wine vineyards have been accorded the lesser status of Bordeaux Supérieur. Vignoble d'Appellation Bordeaux (Crus Bourgeois) usually denotes existing *châteaux* of lesser standing; Bordeaux Supérieur covers all classes of wine, particularly those of inferior standing, and in some cases those that may exist in name only.

Burgundy

The ancient province of Burgundy has long had a reputation for individuality, and its wines are no exception. With Bordeaux it produces the greatest wines of France, although its vineyards are only one-third the size of those of Bordeaux and its output so much smaller that prices are high and demand exceeds supply.

Vineyards have flourished in Burgundy since the times of the Romans, and the old towns of Dijon and Beaune have always been centres for making, buying and selling wine. The famous Hospices de Beaune is a legacy from medieval times. A hospital and home for old people, the Hospices – today the pride of Beaune–was founded in Beaune in the mid-15th century by Nicolas Rolin, Chancellor of the Duchy of Burgundy, and his wife Guigonne de Salins.

A number of vineyards whose wines were, and still are, outstanding were gifts to the Hospices on its foundation and vine-growers since have continued to bequeath their properties to the hospital.

The Hospices wines are sold by public auction in Beaune's market hall on the second Sunday in November after the vintage, and the proceeds support the hospital and its patients.

Vineyard divisions

The French revolution of 1848 had long-lasting effects on the Burgundy vineyards and led to a complex and often misleading system of naming wines. Most of the properties or estates were owned by the Church and had enjoyed a reasonable continuity of owners well versed in the art of wine-making. The revolutionaries confiscated properties and handed them over to peasants who promptly divided the land amongst themselves, with little thought of what might happen to the wines.

What remains today is a huge number of small plots of vines, ranging from two acres to the tiniest with just ·4 acres, that together make up larger single vineyards or properties, and each plot is owned by a different grower; yet every grower is entitled to label his wine with the name of the same vineyard. For example, Clos de Vougeot has over 60 growers in its 124 acres, and Montrachet has 13 growers in its 17½ acres.

Obviously, some of the wines may not be so good as those from the neighbouring vineyards of the same property, and it is, therefore, important to know the reputation of a vineyard when buying a single vineyard wine. The diversification of properties does not lend itself to easy application of the AOC laws which have only partially solved the problem.

Another point to bear in mind when buying Burgundies is that most properties are too small to handle their own cellaring and marketing.

Their young wines, both great and small alike, are sold to *négociant-éleveurs* (merchant-shippers) who not only distribute the wines but also blend, bottle and age them. As a result, they can greatly influence the wines of the region, unlike *négociants* elsewhere, and it is as important to know the reputation of the *négociant-éleveur* as of the vineyard.

Aerial view of typical Côte d'Or countryside; such villages with patterned-tile roofs are to be found, surrounded by vineyards, throughout Burgundy

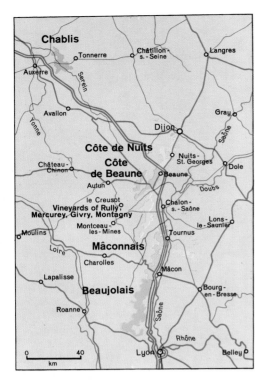

South-east of Paris, the vineyards of Burgundy run from Chablis in the north to Beaujolais in the south of the province near Lyon

Labelling of wines

Several key phrases appear on the labels of Burgundy wines, some so similar that it is very easy to mistake them when buying.

The few vineyards able to make, bottle and sell their own wines from their own properties are known as *domaines* or *clos*, and their labels carry the authorized words Mis (or Mise) en Bouteilles au (or du) Domaine; in a different form the label may read Mise en Bouteilles par le Propriétaire or à la Propriété; similar words are stamped on the cork as well and are the best guarantees of a *domaine*-bottled wine.

The fact that these wines are produced in such limited quantities makes them the most desirable and also the most expensive of wines.

However, some *négociants* may use a similar form of wording for their blended wines that do not come from a single vineyard. The words Mise en Bouteilles dans Mes Caves mean only that the wine was bottled in the cellars of the *négociant*, and sometimes the word Domaine is used, followed by the name of the *négociant*.

Under AOC laws, Burgundies are sold under place names as are most other wines. The best wines may take the name of their vineyard – those are the *domaine*-bottled wines.

As you go down the scale the wines take the name of the village or commune, district, and then the region. This distinction is more clearly shown with the wines from the principal zones that follow.

Standards of assessment

There are further divisions of the wines for although no official classification exists as it does in Bordeaux, the single vineyard wines are usually ranked as Grands Crus or Têtes de Cuvée (best growths) and Premiers Crus (leading growths). District wines are ranked in turn: they may bear the district name only such as Beaujolais, or this may be followed by the word Supérieur.

Regional wines have three rankings: Bourgogne (the French name for Burgundy) which must be made from pinot noir or chardonnay grapes and originate from any vineyard(s) in the Burgundy region; Bourgogne Ordinaire which can be made from a mixture of gamay or aligoté grapes, and has a low alcohol content of about 9·5%, and Bourgogne Passe-Tous-Grains which is made from two-thirds gamay and one-third pinot noir grapes. The latter may also be sold as Bourgogne Aligoté if it is made principally from aligoté grapes.

Location of vineyards

Burgundy lies about 120 miles south-east of Paris. It is made up of five major zones whose wines are both different and distinctive. Running from north to south, these important zones are Chablis, the Côte d'Or that embraces the Côte de Nuits and the Côte de Beaune, the Côte Chalonnaise, the Côte Mâconnaise, and Beaujolais.

Soil and climate

Soil and climate vary tremendously here. The climate is continental, that is to say there are severe, dry winters and hot, humid spring and summer months. The hills of the region give some shelter from cold winds particularly in the fertile river valleys.

Chablis, being the most northerly zone, suffers most from vagaries of weather, particularly from severe frosts in spring. Its south-facing chalky slopes are quite steep in places and are separated from the town of the same name by the Serein river which flows on to join the Yonne. Only here does the chardonnay grape make the superb white Chablis wine which derives its dry, steely qualities from the chalky slopes; and even within this small area there are marked differences in the various vineyards.

The Côte d'Or is a narrow strip of land about half a mile wide and some 30 miles long, that runs along the eastern slopes of a low range of hills. The hill tops are barren except for some woodland, but the lower slopes, with their mixture of clay and sand, are rich in minerals and ideal for the vine.

The Côte de Nuits is the northerly district of the Côte d'Or and its characteristic red clay, rich in iron, produces the great robust red wines of Burgundy from the pinot noir grape. The Côte de Beaune has the milder climate of the two districts but its soil is less rich and its red wines are correspondingly softer and less robust. However, the limestone in the soil and the chardonnay grape combine here to

Vougeot in the Côte d'Or is one of the best-known names of Burgundy although the original estate is now divided

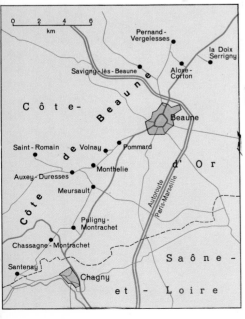

Above: this kind of tractor makes spraying the vines against disease a fast and efficient operation today
Left: south of Dijon, the area around Beaune reveals some famous wine names

produce the great white wines of Burgundy.

The Côte Chalonnaise is situated on a ridge of hills. The vines grow on hillsides facing east and south-east, and the soil is a mixture of limestone, clay and silica. The lower slopes consist of clay and chalk.

The Côte Mâconnaise is a series of hilly valleys running parallel from north to south. The best wines come from the area to the south of Mâcon where the soil is basically limestone and marl; the area north of Mâcon is similar to the Côte Chalonnaise.

Beaujolais, the most southerly zone, lies on a plain that slopes gently down from the hills to the west to the Saône river. This is the home of the gamay grape whose bright red-purple wines are so renowned for their freshness. The soil that suits this grape so well is mainly granite, with some sandy gravel. Beaujolais usually has a good climate, with mild winters, hot summers and warm, rainy springs.

The principal zones

Chablis

Lying midway between Auxerre and Tonnerre, Chablis is so far north of Burgundy's other wine-growing districts it hardly seems part of Burgundy. This is basically due to the after-effects of the phylloxera plague in the 19th century

Vineyards of the Côte Mâconnaise; the 19th-century French poet, historian and statesman Lamartine came from this area and maintained a lifelong interest in wine-growing

and the changing soil structure.

The very dry Chablis has no equal yet it is the most imitated of all white wines. True Chablis has a delicate yet flinty taste, and is free from sweetness; its golden colour has a greenish hue that is most apparent in the young wine.

The AOC laws class Chablis in 4 groups: Grands Crus, Premiers Crus, Chablis and Petits Chablis. Only eight vineyards have the top ranking (Grands Crus) and 24 are ranked as Premiers Crus; between them they make the finest wine with alcohol contents of 11% and 10·5% respectively. The lesser vineyards make the less distinguished Chablis (10% alcohol) and Petits Chablis (9% alcohol).

Côte d'Or

Two areas together, the Côte de Nuits, which takes its name from the town Nuits-St-Georges, and the Côte de Beaune, whose centre is the town of Beaune, make up the largest wine area of Burgundy. It extends from Dijon in the north to Santenay in the south and its red and white wines are amongst the most distinguished of all wines.

To be sure of buying a distinguished Burgundy is difficult, even if you can afford it. But it is possible to choose first-

class wines providing you understand the complex labelling system and have a reasonable knowledge of the growers and their vineyards, as well as the *négociant-éleveurs*, as has been explained before. A tall order perhaps for anyone but the

Côte Mâconnaise, situated between the Côte d'Or and Beaujolais, whose centre is the town of Mâcon

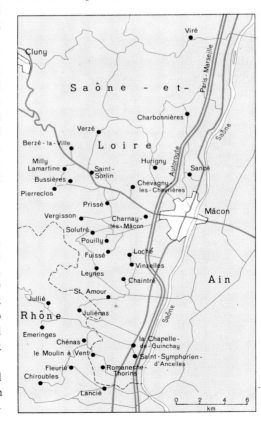

connoisseur, yet if you are armed with a few basic rules, the selection of Burgundy need not be so baffling.

First, since the fragmentation of the vineyards and their varying standards make classification of the wines so difficult, it is generally agreed amongst the wine-growing fraternity to class the wines in two groups: Grands Crus and Premiers Crus, and both terms appear on labels of wines whose vineyards have merited this distinction. The remaining vineyards, and there are many of them, produce the lesser AOC Burgundies which may at their very best equal some of the Premiers Crus.

The second point to bear in mind is that the communes or villages often link their names with that of the best vineyard in their district. As a result, the wine labels show both names with the vineyard last, e.g. Vosne-Romanée. This wine may be very good but a wine bearing the name of the vineyard only, i.e. Romanée, together with a specific plot of vines in that *same* vineyard will be infinitely better, e.g. Romanée-St Vivant.

Once you have mastered the labelling system, the next step is to get to know the reputation of the growers and shippers, a lengthy and rather costly job with today's high prices for good Burgundies, but a rewarding one.

Among the distinguished robust red wines of the Côte de Nuits (with the commune/village name in brackets) are Chambertin (Gevrey), Clos St Denis (Morey

St Denis), Musigny (Chambolle-Musigny), Clos de Vougeot (Vougeot), Richebourg, La Tâche, and Romanée-Conti (all Vosne-Romanée), and St Georges (Nuits-St-Georges). The wines are rough when young and now need to age only three to four years in bottle before they are ready to drink because of a change in vinification; high quality wines, however, still require at least five years in bottle and truly great ones may last up to 15 years.

The Côte de Beaune runs from Ladoix to Santenay, and produces both red and white wines of great renown. The red wines are softer and more velvety and mature more quickly than those of the Côte de Nuits. Among the best red wines (with commune/village names in brackets) are Corton-Charlemagne and Corton (both from Aloxe-Corton), Bressandes and Grèves (both from Beaune), Vergelesses (Pernand-Vergelesses), Duresses (from Auxey-Duresses and Monthelie), Epenots (Pommard), Caillerets and Santenots (both from Volnay), and Les Gravières (Santenay). The wines of the Hospices de Beaune vineyards are very much sought after, consequently prices have been pushed beyond the pocket of the average wine-drinker today.

The powerful, fruity white wines of Burgundy come from vineyards around the towns of Meursault and Montrachet. Important vineyard names to look for are Charmes and Genevrières (from Meursault), and Bàtard and Chevalier (from Montrachet); their wines are frequently 'listed' by wine-merchants.

Côte Chalonnaise

This is the first of the three southern areas of Burgundy whose wines never achieve the greatness of Chablis and the Côte d'Or. Its vineyards are scattered around the town of Chalon-sur-Saône, from which the area takes its name, and they produce large quantities of red, white and sparkling wines that sell at moderate prices. Made from pinot noir and chardonnay grapes, the wines are fresh and fruity, and are best drunk after one or two years in bottle.

Only four villages of the Côte Chalonnaise have AOC status and some of their vineyards are ranked as Premiers Crus. Rully is the most northerly village and is best known for its dry, rather acid white wine. Mercurey is famed for its red wines, while the red and white wines of Givry are growing in popularity. The last village, Montagny, produces mainly white wine.

Côte Mâconnaise

Taking its name from the town of Mâcon, this area covers part of the *département* of Saône-et-Loire. Its wines are mostly reds and whites of average quality, though the exception is the light, dry white wine, Pouilly-Fuissé, from the district of the same name.

Under AOC laws, only the villages of Pouilly, Fuissé, Vergisson, Solutré and Chaintré can sell their wines as Pouilly-Fuissé, and the best vineyards include Boutières, Brulets, Château Fuissé, Clos de la Chapelle, Perrières, and Vignes-Blanches. Pouilly-Fuissé wines are fetching extremely high prices now, particu-

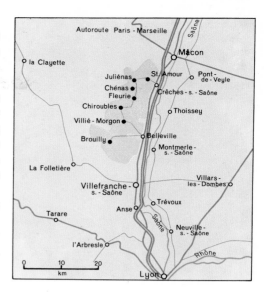

Beaujolais in the south of Burgundy, just north of the city of Lyon

larly in the USA, due simply to their popularity.

A few neighbouring villages are, under AOC laws, able to add their name to Pouilly, e.g. Pouilly-Vinzelles and Pouilly-Loché, but their wines are less distinguished than Pouilly-Fuissé.

The remaining white wines of the Mâconnais are usually sold under district

Left: running fresh and fruity straight from the press the new Beaujolais
Below: wine-grower, tasting his wine from the traditional tastevin. *In Burgundy the new wine can be tasted and tested by the end of November*

names and are in three groups: the best are called Mâcon Blanc or Mâcon Supérieur Blanc and include the name of one of its vineyard towns, e.g. Mâcon Viré; the second group is called Mâcon Villages, and the third is called simply Mâcon.

Red and rosé wines of the area have an AOC status of their own and can carry the village name on the label but none of the wines is outstanding.

Beaujolais

Some 45 miles long, the last area of Burgundy is renowned for one wine – Beaujolais, a fresh, fruity, purple wine made from the quick-maturing gamay grape; it is best drunk cool and fairly young. The gamay grape is grown only in Beaujolais for in the 14th century Philip the Bold outlawed it from the rest of Burgundy, ordering 'the ignominious grape' to be uprooted. Times have changed and the gamay now takes its place alongside the other great wine grapes of France.

So fruity and refreshing is Beaujolais, and so lacking in the customary heady qualities of red wine, that it can literally be quaffed. It was traditionally served in a stone or earthenware bottle or pot,

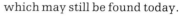

Below: annual wine-selling ceremonies at Beaune have continued since the Middle Ages and today attract crowds of people to Beaune, and Clos du Vougeot

Above: bottles of wine mature for several years in the cellars of Aloxe-Corton; the wine produced by this commune is among the best of the Côte de Beaune

which may still be found today.

The qualities of young Beaujolais have been somewhat exaggerated for, as with most wines, it improves on bottling and, when vinified by the *ancienne méthode*, it can develop extraordinary deep qualities. However, commercial interests have greatly helped to foster the popularity of drinking Beaujolais immediately after the vintage. Every year, the French government set a date – during the first or second week of November – after which the new Beaujolais wine called Vin de l'Année or Beaujolais Primeur can be sold. In recent years an immense rivalry has built up between restaurants, cafés and bars all over France, especially in Paris and now in London as well, to be the first to sell the new wine.

Beaujolais lies mostly in the *département* of Saône-et-Loire, and has two main districts: Haut Beaujolais in the north and Bas Beaujolais to the south, where the ground is less favourable to the vine. Haut Beaujolais is a hilly stretch that runs from Beaujeu, from which the area takes its name, to Belleville, and the best wines of the Beaujolais originate from 35 villages known collectively as Beaujolais-Villages. Nine of these villages produce exceptional

wines and have been given an AOC status of Grands Crus; their labels may also carry the name of the vineyard or grower.

Brouilly

Rising steeply from the village and the centre of its vineyards, Mont Brouilly overlooks the entire district; on its summit stands a chapel, a place of pilgrimage since 1857. The wine of Brouilly is one of the most full-bodied of Beaujolais wines; it is well-balanced, fruity, with a beautiful deep purple colour, and it ages very well.

Côte de Brouilly

North of Brouilly, vines have been planted on the slopes of the hills and wines from here are named Côte de Brouilly. There is little to choose between these wines and those from Brouilly.

Morgon

The village and its vineyards are north of Brouilly and parallel to the village of Beaujeu. The wine is warm, robust, full-bodied and charms the eye with its ruby colour. Known for its keeping quality, it is at its best after five or six years in bottle.

For over 1,000 years this peaceful cellar has housed fine wines while they matured. In Burgundy shippers are usually responsible for making, bottling and selling the wine

Chiroubles and its neighbour to the east, **Fleurie**, produce similar fruity wines; Fleurie has the more flowery bouquet – as its name implies. **Chénas, Juliénas** and **St Amour** all produce typical Beaujolais wines and they are best drunk after two or three years in bottle.

Moulin-à-Vent

This village lies slightly to the east of Chénas and Fleurie and makes the finest of the Grands Crus. It owes its name to an old windmill, the only one of its kind in the region; all that remains of it today is its tower, now listed as an historical monument. Moulin-à-Vent ages well, and in good years has all the qualities of a good Burgundy from the Côte d'Or.

Under AOC laws, the 26 villages not ranked as Grands Crus can add their individual names to the Beaujolais-Villages appellation, and as a result, they are winning recognition in their own right. Village names to look for include Beaujeu, Odenas, Charentay, Romanèche-Thorins, Lancié, Chânes, Jullié and Emeringes.

The wines of Bas Beaujolais are sold either as Beaujolais Supérieur (with at least 10% alcohol) and Beaujolais (with a minimum of 9% alcohol). Some wine called Beaujolais, which hardly resembles true Beaujolais except in colour, is made outside the AOC region, so check the label for the words Appellation Contrôlée.

The Rhône Valley

Scattered along the course of the Rhône river as it hurries south from Lyon to the Mediterranean are the vineyards of the Côtes du Rhône (Rhône Valley). The wine-growing zone is about 150 miles long, starting south of Vienne and extending along both banks of the river as far south as the old city of Avignon, the former stronghold of the papacy in the 14th century.

Once the poor cousins of France's wines, the reds, whites and rosés of the Côtes du Rhône now stand on their own merits and rightly so. The red wines are renowned for their ageing qualities and need at least five years in bottle before they are ready to drink. The classic grape of the Rhône is the syrah which makes a dark, almost black, red wine, robust and hard in its youth but changing to a rich purple-red colour, full of flavour yet soft, with a heady bouquet, and a minimum alcohol content of 11%. The white wines are equally full-bodied and scented, and age well. The rosés are best drunk within two years.

Rhône wines may be a blend of up to 12 different grapes. Principal varieties grown are the syrah, grenache, cinsault, carignan, marsanne, viognier, picpoul, terret, clairette and muscat.

More wine per acre of vines is produced in the Rhône valley than in either Burgundy or Bordeaux and, whereas these two illustrious zones have almost exhausted their stocks of authorized unplanted vine land, the Rhône has thousands of acres available. With a world shortage of fine Burgundies and Bordeaux, people are turning more and more to the less expensive yet equally distinguished Rhône wines. The minimum annual output is in the region of 21,000,000 gallons, of which 20% has AOC status.

Classification of Rhône wines can be confusing. The term Côtes du Rhône is a general one applicable to all the wine-growing districts, communes and villages within its AOC bounds; should their wines not reach the required standard, the growers can then add the name of the *département* to the words Côtes du Rhône, e.g. Côtes du Rhône-Drôme. Only 14 communes are entitled to the more superior ranking Côtes du Rhône-Villages, and they lie in the southern half of the

valley. There are also 15 top-ranking appellations with an individual AOC status, and these include districts, communes and villages, and a single estate. They are Côte Rôtie, Condrieu, Château Grillet, St-Joseph, Crozes-Hermitage, Tain l'Hermitage, Cornas, St Péray, Die, Châteauneuf-du-Pape, Gigondas, Tavel, Lirac, Beaumes-de-Venise and Rasteau.

Location of vineyards

The Côtes du Rhône divides into a northern and a southern region extending over six *départements*: Rhône, Loire, Ardèche and Gard to the east of the Rhône river, and Drôme and Vaucluse to the west. The vineyards of the northern region consist of Côte Rôtie, Condrieu, St-Joseph, Hermitage and St Péray. Then there is a gap of about 30 miles, with the one outlying district of Die, before the start of the southern region below Donzère. Here lie the vineyards of Châteauneuf-du-Pape, Gigondas, Tavel, Lirac, Beaumes-de-Venise and Rasteau.

So varied are the soil, vines and their situation that the differences are reflected in the wines. The northern region is mainly towering granite rocks with patches of sandy soil that make vine cultivation very difficult. Sheltered pockets of vines are literally baked by the sun, giving the Côte Rôtie (literally roasted hillside) its name.

Chalk and clay mixtures are found in parts of Hermitage and St Péray, and as one moves south, the hills are less steep with gravelly slopes, and there are extensive areas covered by large, flat pebbles, particularly in the Châteauneuf-du-Pape district. The vines seem to grow in a desert of stones whose usefulness is threefold: they reflect the heat onto the undersides of the grapes, protect the roots of the vines, and ensure good drainage.

Climatically, the valley has very hot dry summers, mild winters and warm springs, with occasional but violent rainy periods. Strong winds are prevalent at certain times of the year, blowing mostly from the Alps; the valley acts as a funnel, driving the wind along, and the rocky hills help to shelter the vines.

Below left: Châteauneuf-du-Pape vineyards
Below: the northern and southern regions of the Côtes du Rhône. The whole region extends from Lyon in the north to the Mediterranean in the south, and includes much uncultivated land which could be used for vineyards

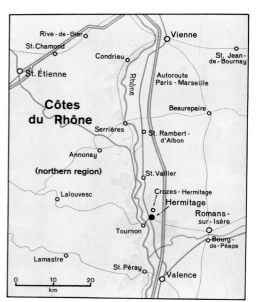

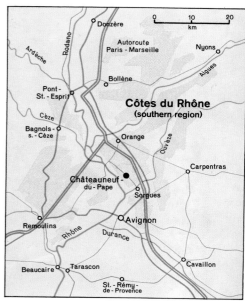

The principal areas

Côte Rôtie

This district lies to the west of the Rhône; it falls naturally into two – the Côte Blonde and the Côte Brune – on account of the light and dark brown qualities of the sandy soil. The wines are predominantly robust reds mostly made from the syrah; the viognier grape is more common on the Côte Blonde and helps to lighten the colour and soften the hard taste of the young wines. Leading communes are Ampuis and Tupin-Sémons.

Condrieu

Just south of the Côte Rôtie, the commune of Condrieu produces highly individual dry white wines from the viognier grape; they are delicate, have a slight hint of spiciness and a good bouquet. Château Grillet is a tiny estate of 2·47 acres whose wines are so exceptional it has an AOC status of its own. **St Joseph** and **Cornas** are districts east of the Rhône and south of Condrieu. Their full-bodied red wines are made mostly from the syrah and resemble Hermitage wines. **St Péray** lies opposite the town of Valence across the river; it produces a magnificent dry white wine and a fine sparkling white wine.

Hermitage

Sometimes spelt Ermitage, this district takes its name from the Hill of the Hermit.

The vineyards in the neighbourhood of Tournon produce some of the finest red and white Rhône wines. The hill of Hermitage is tightly terraced with vines and rises above a bend of the Rhône at Tain l'Hermitage. Its famous red vineyards include Meal, Greffiux, Bessards and Murets, and the most renowned white vineyard is Chante Alouette. Crozes-Hermitage is a lesser district nearby whose wines do not have such finesse as those of Hermitage or Tain l'Hermitage. Grapes grown are the syrah, grenache, carignan, marsanne and roussette.

Die

This district lies some miles south-east of Valence around Die on the river Drôme. Its best wine is a pale, sparkling white called Clairette, made from the grape of the same name.

Châteauneuf-du-Pape

The ancient papal town is the centre of the greatest red wine-growing district of the Côtes du Rhône. Its wines not only have the highest minimum alcohol strength of any French wine – 12·5% – but were also the first to be so regulated.

The finest wines of the district are sold under the name of the vineyard and include Château Fortia, Château de la Nerthe and Château Vaudieu. The wines take at least seven years to mature, developing a round, warm flavour and heady bouquet.

Hermitage vineyards, cultivated on granitic soil. Some 350 acres of vines are cultivated in the folds of the hill; two-thirds of the wine they produce is red and one-third is white. Both red and white wines of Hermitage have a bouquet reminiscent of honeysuckle

Gigondas

The excellent red wines of this district and the nearby lesser districts of Vacqueras, Cairanne and Vinsobres are overshadowed by Châteauneuf-du-Pape, and have only recently begun to have a following outside France.

Beaumes-de-Venise and Rasteau

Lying either side of Gigondas, these districts produce the only dessert wine of the Rhône Valley. The fine sweet white wine of Beaumes is made from the muscat grape, the lighter wines of Rasteau mostly from the grenache.

Tavel and Lirac

These districts are renowned for the quality of their rosé wines. The most famous is Tavel, though the vineyards of Lirac and the lesser districts of Laudun and Chausclan are rivalling its reputation. The predominant grape is the grenache which produces a light, medium-sweet rosé that is pink-gold in colour, slightly sharp and 'winey' in taste; it has an alcohol content of at least 11%.

Provence

Mention the south of France and Provence, and instantly images of pine-clad hills, fields of lavender and thyme, terracotta villages basking in the sun and the sound of cicadas spring to mind. Its seaside resorts have long been a Mecca for holidaymakers. Yet it also has a name for light, refreshing wines from vineyards scattered over an area stretching south from Avignon to Marseille and the Bouches-du-Rhône, from Vaucluse to the Basses-Alpes and Draguignan, and east as far as Nice.

Unhappily, none of the wines are outstanding; at their best they are good but ordinary table wines with a status no higher than VDQS. They are fresh and fruity, have a strong flowery bouquet and the alcohol strength ranges from 9·5–12%. Rosé wines are generally held to be the best, though some reds and whites can be good as well. Red wines must age for at least 15 months before they can be sold; whites and rosés must age for a minimum of eight months.

Most Provence wines are entitled to the appellation Côtes de Provence and those around Aix-en-Provence may also be called Coteaux d'Aix-Provence. Four districts – Palette d'Aix, Cassis, Bandol and Bellet de Nice – have an individual AOC status.

There are six other VDQS wine-growing districts often described as Provence wines although, in fact, all of them except

The sun beats down to ripen the grapes grown in Haute Provence

one should really be included in the Rhône Valley region: Côtes du Ventoux near Carpentras, Haut-Comtat, Côtes du Vivrais and Coteaux du Tricastin all in the *département* of Drôme, Côtes du Luberan, south-east of Avignon, and Coteaux de Pierrevert in the *département* of Var.

The vineyards known as Côtes de Provence are in the *départements* of Bouches-du-Rhône, Var, Alpes-Maritimes and Basses-Alpes. Var makes the largest quantity of wine, followed by the Bouches-du-Rhône.

There are many differences in soil here. As the vineyards run down the hillsides to the plains, so their quality diminishes when the granite of the mountains and hills gives way to sandstone, chalk, clay and marl.

Numerous grape varieties thrive in the different locations and wines are blended from a number of them. The carignan predominates among red wine grapes and gives vigour and alcoholic strength to any blend. The cinsault, grenache and tibourenc grapes add mellowness, softness and bouquet. The mourvèdre grape of the Bouches-du-Rhône nearly died out because of its frailty; it is important for helping a wine to age well.

Nearly all the white wine grapes used are the ugni blanc, clairette, and the rolle of the Alpes-Maritimes. Other permitted varieties include the syrah, cabernet, picpoul, rousanne, pécoui and touar.

Palette d'Aix

This district is to the south of Aix-en-Provence and lies within the general appellation, Coteaux d'Aix-Provence. Its red, white and rosé wines are unmistakably flowery.

Cassis and Bandol

These coastal districts between Marseille and Toulon are separated by a VDQS district centred on La Ciotat. Cassis makes good white and rosé wines (do not confuse them with the very sweet blackcurrant liqueur of the same name made elsewhere in France), and Bandol produces mostly full-bodied strong red wines.

Bellet de Nice

The red, white and rosé wines of this district come from inland vineyards. They are all that remain of the once-flourishing Alpes-Maritimes wine-growing district. A few villages in the surrounding hills still make their local wines for local consumption as they have done for centuries. Very little of this is seen outside the region in spite of the recent increase in the demand for French wines.

Jura

The Jura is a small mountainous area, about 80 miles east of Burgundy, whose range of wines is varied, unusual and very rewarding. Unfortunately, few of them are seen outside France and those that are available are expensive.

The regional AOC name is Côtes du Jura, which covers all types: red, white and sparkling white, rosé, *vin jaune* and *vin de paille,* the last two wines being specialities of the region. There are three outstanding appellations: the districts of Arbois and L'Etoile, and the group of vineyards known as Château-Chalon.

Location of vineyards

The vineyards cover only about 11 square miles, nestling among the foothills of the Jura mountains. They stretch from Aigle-pierre and Arbois in the north to Lons-le-Saunier and Beaufort in the south.

The soil is a mixture of limestone, chalk and clay and is ideal for producing full-bodied yet subtle white wines.

The dry white wines and sparkling whites are made primarily with savagnin

Below: Jura, east of Burgundy, is very near the border with Switzerland
Right: vineyards at Arbois where all types of wine, including vin de paille, *are made*

and melon grapes. The red wines, of which the best come from Arbois, are made from the poulsard, a grape that only grows in the Jura and is known locally as plant d'arbois, the trousseau and the savagnin. Some reds are lighter than others and take on a reddish-brown colour; they are often called *pelure d'oignon* (onion skin). The colour is misleading for the wine is full-bodied and heady.

Vin jaune (yellow wine) and *vin de paille* (straw wine) are the outstanding wines of the Jura. *Vin jaune* is a strong white wine, with a minimum alcohol strength of 11%, made from the savagnin grape by a method similar to that for making sherries in Spain, although it is not fortified.

Fermentation takes place slowly and lasts several weeks; the young wine is transferred to small wooden casks in a cool cellar; by law, the casks are left, uncovered, for a minimum period of six years. During this time, evaporation occurs but the cask cannot be topped up, and yeast growth or flor slowly forms a crust on the surface of the wine. At the end of this time oxidation has made the wine yellow and it is put in special squat

bottles, called *clavelins*, that are used only for *vin jaune.*

Good *vin jaune* is a rarity and therefore expensive. The vineyards of Château-Chalon produce the best, though wines from l'Etoile, Pupillin and Poligny are not far behind. A lesser *vin jaune* is made at Arbois.

Vin de paille, the other unusual white wine of the Jura, takes its name from the straw mats on which the poulsard and trousseau grapes are spread and left to dry for two to three months until they are shrivelled and full of concentrated sugar. Fermentation begins during January or February but the cold temperature and the high sugar content of the grapes makes it a slow process. For a *vin de paille* to have an AOC status, it must have a minimum alcohol strength of 15% – exceptionally high for a white table wine; however, it is most frequently drunk in small quantities as a dessert wine because of its intense sweetness.

A small amount of rosé wine is made and is sometimes known locally as *vin gris* (grey wine); it is pale in colour, rather sharp in taste but quite refreshing. It is seldom seen outside the Jura.

Savoy

The mountainous province of Savoy acts as a buffer between eastern France, Switzerland and Italy. Its wines are light and dry, with a freshness that is as lively as the mountain air. Sad to say, the wines are not readily available in Britain and the USA because production is so small and they are not shipped commercially.

There are basically three wine-growing areas, each consisting of numerous villages whose vineyards produce mostly fine white wines, as well as some good reds and rosés. Some 300 acres in all are under vine, but the steep, hilly terrain and changing mountain weather make wine-growing a hazardous affair and the quantity made is very tiny in comparison with other regions.

Several grape varieties favour the basically chalky ground; the altesse is mostly used for white wines, the mondeuse for reds.

The best white wines come from the areas to the east of Lake Geneva, and down the Rhône, near Aix-les-Bains, and around Lake du Bourget. Here, two communes produce such good white wines that they have their own AOC status – Crépy, from vineyards near Lake Geneva, and Seyssels, near the Rhône.

Crépy is an elegant light dry wine made from the chasselas grape, and is similar in taste to Swiss wines.

Seyssels is made from the altesse grape, and is dry, fruity, rather yellow in colour and has a fine bouquet; a sparkling variety is made as well.

Both Crépy and Seyssels are the Savoy wines most likely to be found abroad.

The traditional aperitif wine of the region is called Blanc de Savoie, and it also makes a fitting companion to mountain river trout and lake fish. Villages producing this wine include Abymes, Apremont, Chautagne, Chignin, Montmélian, Ste Marie d'Alloix, and Cruet.

Some of the white wines made from the local jacquard vine have recently gained VDQS status. The best come from districts near Ayze, which produces a sparkling wine, Apremont and Abymes.

Wines sold as Roussette de Savoie come from the grape of the same name and the best come from Frangy, Marestel, Monthoux and Monterminod.

The highly perfumed red wines, often

called Mondeuse de Savoie after the grape variety, come from vineyards around Chignin, Cruet, Arbin, Montmélian and St Jean-de-la-Porte. A few vineyards at Chautagne on the Rhône make a light pleasant red wine from the gamay grape.

Above: vintage in Savoy, where vineyards are overshadowed by mountains and climatic conditions are often hazardous to the growth of the vine
Below: Savoy wines go well with fondue, a local speciality

Languedoc and Roussillon

The great arc of France's coastline from the mouth of the Rhône down to the Pyrenees and the Spanish border embraces the vineyards of Languedoc-Roussillon. The largest wine-growing area of France, it is also the least distinguished. Its fertile land gives an abundant harvest of grapes but their quality is low, so the bulk of the wine is no more than good *vin ordinaire*, the everyday drink of the Frenchman. This region now meets a large percentage of France's annual demand for *vin ordinaire*.

Nevertheless there are several districts whose wines merit attention although, like the wines of Jura and Savoy, many of them are not readily available abroad.

With so few wines of distinction, however, the controls over wine production are more relaxed than elsewhere. A few districts have an AOC status, although they do not meet the standard of the rankings in regions like Bordeaux and Burgundy. On the whole, the best districts have a VDQS status.

Corbières-Roussillon
This district is in the south-west of the area and extends southwards from Narbonne. It makes a quantity of VDQS red, white and rosé wines that are known collectively as Corbières de Roussillon; they are light and refreshing when young.

Fitou
This is a small district within Corbières that lies south of Villeneuve. Its fine red wines, made mostly from the carignan grape, have their own AOC status. Its best communes include Tuchan, Paziols, Villeneuve and Cascastel.

Blanquette de Limoux
This is a small AOC area a few miles south of Carcassonne. The best sparkling white wine comes from here and is made by the *méthode champenoise*. The name Blanquette comes from the white underside of the leaves of the mauzac grape from which the wine is made. A light, dry, still wine, called Limoux Nature, is also made here.

Minervois and St Chinian
These are red wine districts to the north of Corbières. Their best communes are St Chinian and St-Jean-de-Minervois.

Two districts in eastern Languedoc are renowned for white wines called Clairette after the grape variety used. Clairette de Languedoc is a full-bodied white wine, with a powerful flavour, and is best drunk young; it has an AOC status, and is often used as a base for vermouths. The principal communes include Aspiran, Ceyras, Péret and Paulhan.

Left: autumn in Corbières after the grapes have been harvested
Above: vineyard flooded with rain

Clairette de Bellegarde comes from the vineyards near the village of Bellegarde, which is midway between Nîmes and Montpellier. The Clairette made here is best drunk young.

Costières du Gard is a district surrounding Bellegarde, near the mouth of the Rhône, whose wines are ordinary reds.

The south-west

The wines of the far-flung wine-growing areas of south-west France rarely reach Britain and the USA, though their unusual qualities make them well worth seeking out. The bulk of the wines from this region are good *vins du pays* but many growers now produce VDQS wines, which in some cases have AOC status. There are four major areas.

Bergerac
The sweet white wines, with their luscious, delicate flavour similar to the Sauternes of Bordeaux, have made the reputation of this area. The best wines come from Monbazillac, whose vineyards are crowned by a picturesque hill, just a few miles from the town of Bergerac on the right bank of the Dordogne river. As in Sauternes, the grapes are only harvested after they have the 'noble rot'. The golden wines have an alcohol strength of 13–14% and are ready for drinking only after six years in bottle.

Other white wines, some quite dry, are made in the districts of Montravel, Rosette and the Côtes du Duras. The dry whites are fruity, light in colour and soft, with a minimum alcohol strength of 12%; the best come from the Côtes de Saussignac and Côtes de Bergerac.

A little rosé wine is made; its slightly acid taste makes it pleasant and refreshing to drink. The red wines of Bergerac are light and pleasing and the best come from the district of Pécharment, north of Bergerac.

Cahors
The vineyards of this town have made remarkable progress in recent years; once recognized as the leading VDQS wine of France, its red wine now has AOC status. The powerful reds, made almost entirely from the malbec grape of Bordeaux, are almost black due to their exceptional ability to withstand the action of oxygen. They develop well in cask and bottle, often taking longer than a fine Bordeaux though never developing its subtlety and finesse. Cahors seems to be the rising star of French wines and one to look out for.

Gaillac
Wines entitled to the appellation Gaillac-Premières Côtes come from vineyards situated along the Tarn river, between Montauban and Albi. Principal villages making the dry white wine include Rabastens, Salvagnac, Castelnau, Cordes and Cadalen. A quantity of sparkling wine, called Gaillac Mousseux or Perlé is also made here.

Jurançon
Crouching in the foothills of the Pyrenee Mountains near the Spanish border, these vineyards once produced great sweet dessert wines that were the equal of Sauternes. Over the years, however, the standard has declined and wine production is now only a fraction of what it used to be. The trend today is to make dry rather than sweet wine, partly because the nearness of the mountains brings variable weather making the late harvesting necessary for sweet wine too hazardous for commercial success. The leading villages are Aubertin, Jurançon, Gan, Laroin, Monein and St-Faust.

Château Monbazillac where excellent sweet rich white wines are made from sauvignon and muscadel grapes

Corsica

The vineyards of the island of Corsica are similar to those of Provence, but the pebbly, rocky soil, and local vines produce their own characteristic wines.

Although the island is very mountainous and covered with scrub called *maquis*, there are great viticultural possibilities, yet because of poor conditions and lack of wine-production expertise, wine-growers have only recently begun to exploit them. With modern technology, government aid and greater experience, Corsica now produces very good rosé wines, red, white and sweet dessert wines. Many quality wines have the appellation Vin de Corse; lesser wines have VDQS status.

There are four main wine-growing districts: Bastia in the north including Cap Corse, Calvi and Ajaccio on the west coast, and Sartène in the south. There are a number of vineyards on the south-east and east coasts but, except for Porto Vecchio, they produce nothing more than *vins ordinaires*.

Bastia

The vineyards of Patrimonio produce the finest of the island's wines. They are full-bodied, perfumed white, rosé and red wines, all with AOC status. The vermentino grape is used for white wines, the alicante for reds, and their wild country bouquet makes them intriguingly different. At Cap Corse, the most northerly point of the island, sweet dessert wines called Muscat du Cap Corse, with an aroma of liquorice, are made by blending the muscat grape with the genoese.

Calvi

White wines and rich, fruity reds and rosés are made in this area.

Ajaccio

The town of the same name is both the capital of the island and the centre of its vineyards. On the hills of Ajaccio, the vineyards at Bastelicaccia produce the wines Paviglia and Pisciatello, the Capitoro comes from Cauro, and Sposata is Ajaccio's own wine. All the red, white and rosé wines have the appellation Coteaux d'Ajaccio.

Sartène

This VDQS district is chiefly known for strong reds and rosés. The more southerly vineyards of Bonifacio and Figari also produce good red wines.

Vineyards near Patrimonio where white, rosé and red wines are produced. These are the best of the island's wines and, as the tourist trade continues to expand, they are beginning to enjoy increasing popularity and to be exported in larger quantities

Sweet natural wines

There are special types of sweet natural wines peculiar to France that are called *vins doux naturels* and *vins de liqueur.* By law they are made from a must that is particularly rich in sugar — 252 g per litre — and only from certain grapes, the grenache, malvoisie, maccabeo and muscat. To the must, a strictly controlled quantity of alcohol is added: 5–10% for *vins doux* and 15% for *vins de liqueur* which are made from less good wines and are not so sought after.

Sweet natural wines improve very much with age in cask or bottle. When they achieve the required taste and colour of old wines by maturing in cask, the word Rancio may be used to describe them in much the same way that tawny is used to describe port.

Location of vineyards

Languedoc-Roussillon
The wines from the districts around Perpignan were once called 'Spanish wines' and they make up no less than 95% of the French sweet natural wines. Rich in

Top: Coteaux de Banyuls where the sweet natural white, red and rosé wines entitled to bear the name Banyuls are produced. Banyuls is a dessert wine of exceptionally high alcoholic strength so it should be drunk in moderation. It is made from mainly muscat grapes; they are so rich in natural sugar that a certain amount is retained when fermentation has finished
Above: Banyuls is one of the few wines left to mature out in the open
Left: large, modern bottling-plant used for sweet natural wines

natural sugar and with an alcohol strength of 21·5%, they are primarily dessert wines although they make a good aperitif when drunk cool. The best of these wines come from vineyards along the Mediterranean seaboard between Marseille and the Pyrenees.

Grand Roussillon is the collective AOC name for sweet natural wines from four districts: Banyuls, Maury, Côtes d'Agly and Rivesaltes. The wines of Banyuls and Maury are garnet-red and have a good bouquet, while the wines of Côtes d'Agly and Rivesaltes are a gleaming red-gold. The area is important for, in a good year, about 8,000,000 gallons of Grands Roussillons may be produced.

Other districts in Languedoc-Roussillon renowned for their *vins doux naturels,* called Muscats, are Frontignan, Lunel and Minervois.

Côtes du Rhône
The districts of Beaumes-de-Venise and Rasteau produce distinguished sweet natural wines as well as the reds for which the area is more famous.

Cognac
This region of south-west France, famous for its brandy, also makes a very good *vin de liqueur* called Pineau des Charentes that has brandy added to the must.

Brandy

Brandy means any spirit distilled from wine. The brandies of Cognac and Armagnac in France are famous throughout the world. Only spirit distilled in authorized areas has the right to bear the names Cognac and Armagnac.

The process of distillation is basically a simple one but sophisticated techniques and modern equipment have made it more complex so that the purity and quality of fine brandy is assured. After fermentation, the young wine is heated in a still, traditionally a copper pot still, to separate the water from the alcohol. The alcohol rises as a vapour and is collected and condensed into a pure, white, harsh liquid, about 70% proof, which is the young brandy. It is then run off into barrels of white oak for ageing, a sophisticated process that, together with the addition of controlled amounts of sugar and caramel, gives brandy its flavour and colour.

The forest of Limousin, some 80 miles east of Cognac, supplies the oak for the barrels; its wood is very porous and low in natural tannin. Some 10 barrels of wine are needed to make one barrel of brandy and an enormous quantity of spirit is lost through evaporation as it matures. The barrels are stored in huge, low, dark, earthen-floored cellars known as *chais*; the moist but airy atmosphere is carefully controlled so that the rate of evaporation is slow and the spirit absorbs moisture over the years to dilute the alcohol strength. Most firms hold large stocks of old brandies that are mainly used either to top up barrels when excessive evaporation occurs or to improve the type of brandy being made.

Since brandies are blends of spirits of varying ages, every shipper has his house style. Among the best known firms in Cognac are Hennessy, Martell, Delamain, Salignac, Hine, Rémy-Martin, Courvoisier and Bisquit. The shippers' practice of keeping stocks of unblended vintages made it difficult to control the age factor when labelling brandies, so five years is now the maximum age a firm may legally claim on its Cognac label.

Armagnac does not have large and famous shippers like Cognac, and its business is almost entirely in the hands of small growers based on the towns of Auch, Condom and Eauze.

Cognac

The old French provinces of Angoumis, Saintonge and Aunis formerly made up Cognac and produced inferior wines until the late 17th century when the wines were transformed by a crude distillation process into a fiery spirit. Now the vineyards extend from the north of the Gironde estuary between Royan and La Rochelle, and as far inland as Angoulême. The Charente river runs through the region and gives its name to the *départements* of Charente and Charente-Maritime in which the majority of the vineyards are situated. Some 250 square miles are under vine and the principal grape for Cognac is the folle blanche.

Owing to the great variations in the chalky limestone soil and the consequent variations in the quality of spirit produced, the zone is divided up into six districts in order of decreasing merit.

First come Grande Champagne and Petite Champagne, the central zones surrounding the town of Cognac. They produce the finest brandies which are sold under the appellations of Grande Champagne and Petite Champagne respec-

tively. Fine Champagne brandy is a blend of the two and must contain at least 50% Grande Champagne brandy.

Then come the lesser districts of Les Borderies, on the right bank of the Charente river, Fins Bois which surrounds the Petite Champagne district, and last, Bons Bois and Bois Ordinaires which are the furthest limits of the zone.

VSOP (Very Superior Old Pale) brandy must spend at least five years in barrel before it can be sold.

Armagnac

Once the ancient province of Gascony, this remote hilly region lies about half-way between Bordeaux and the Spanish border.

The brandy of Armagnac is similar to Cognac but lacks the mellow subtlety of flavour; it has a stronger flavour and bouquet than Cognac and its black colour is due to the use of black oak barrels for ageing it. It is made mostly from the Cognac grape, the folle blanche, which is known locally as the picpoul.

Control of production is strict and no spirit sold is allowed out of the district under an alcohol strength of 40% (70% proof in British measurements, 80% in American, or roughly the same strength as a bottle of whisky).

The principal wine-growing districts are Bas-Armagnac and Tenarèze, the flatter areas of the north where the finest Armagnacs are produced, and Haut-Armagnac, a hilly area in the south.

The French also make a less distinguished and much coarser brandy called Marc. It is made by distilling the watered and refermented grape must left over after the juice for wine has been pressed out. The quality of Marc varies considerably, though the best is a very acceptable substitute for Cognac.

Other countries produce brandies similar to Marc that are sold under the names of Grappa (Italy), Trestebranntwein or Trinkbranntwein (Germany), Aguardiente (Spain) and Agurdente (Portugal).

Finally, do not confuse grape brandies with fruit brandies for the latter are quite different. They may be made from fruits such as apples (Calvados), cherries (Kirsch), plums (Prunelle or Slivovitz) and strawberries (Fraises).

Above: tasting the brandy, known the world over as eau-de-vie (water of life) Left: a copper pot still is always used for distilling Cognac

Germany

The northern limit of wine-growing in Europe is reached in Germany on the same latitude as Newfoundland in Canada. It is, therefore, a tribute to her growers that she makes some of the world's finest white wines from an area of only 250 square miles in the most difficult viticultural conditions.

The vineyard areas are situated on the slopes along the valleys of the Rhine, in the Rheingau, Rheinhessen or Hesse, Rheinpfalz or Palatinate, and its tributaries the Mosel or Moselle, the Saar, the Nahe, the Ruwer and in the districts of Franconia and Baden-Württemberg.

Germany's wine history dates back many centuries. The vine is believed to have grown in the Rhine Valley before the Roman occupation, but it was the Romans who organized the planting of vineyards and establishment of towns like Trier and Neumagen in the Mosel Valley. Later the Church, in particular the monasteries, influenced wine-making by maintaining the vineyards through the difficult times of the Dark Ages, and it is a bishop, Bishop Fulda, who is credited with the discovery of the technique of making sweet wines from overripe grapes with the 'noble rot' instead of discarding them as unsuitable for wine-making. For centuries German wines were exported all over Europe.

In the Middle Ages, Germany was split into principalities and under the feudal system, tithes (taxes) were paid for the use of vineyards, often in the form of wine. Evidence of this period of history can often be found on German wine labels today in the form of intricate heraldic coats of arms belonging to families who once held important posts in Germany's former princedoms.

Many vineyards were secularized by Napoleon in 1803, when he needed to reward Germans who had served him in his campaigns and had helped him raise armies on German soil.

Recent wine history in Germany has seen the unification of the small vineyards and a general simplification of nomenclature, combined with great advances in the science of wine-making.

Types of grapes

Unfavourable climate and difficult terrain result in German wines bearing the highest production costs in the world. German viticulture is, therefore, closely controlled in order to make the best possible wines from such a very limited area.

German production, which represents only 3% of the world total, is smaller than the total output of the Bordeaux region in France; 85% of German wines are white and are made from the following grapes.

Riesling

The aristocrat of all white grapes, the riesling makes the majority of the top-quality wines, and is used almost entirely in the Mosel, Saar, Ruwer and in the majority of Rheingau wines. The berry is small and hardy and develops late in the year therefore yielding less juice than other German vine varieties. The further south it is grown from the Rhine Valley, the more disappointing the wine it produces – proof of the old adage that the

Below: riesling grapes, which produce Germany's finest white wines, growing along the banks of the swift-flowing river Rhine (opposite page)

vine gives of its best in the most difficult conditions.

Wines made from the riesling have an unmistakably fragrant bouquet and surpass all other vine varieties with their fine fruity flavour.

Sylvaner
Germany's most prolific grape, the sylvaner, is soft in character and never develops the subtleties of the riesling, but yields double its volume. Although grown in many districts, it is most commonly found in the Rheinhessen and the Rheinpfalz.

Traminer or Gewürztraminer
This vine is losing favour in Germany because it is difficult to grow. The bouquet and flavour are distinctively spicy and used to be contributing factors to the richness of Pfalz wines.

Müller-thurgau
This is a cross of the riesling and sylvaner, named after its biologist creator. The vine has been widely accepted in Germany because it combines the quality of riesling with the generous fruiting of the sylvaner. The grapes are mostly used for com-

mercial wines, especially in the Hesse and the Pfalz, and the wines are clean and unobtrusive.

Scheurebe
This is another cross of riesling and sylvaner, although under the new wine laws, it is only permitted to make up a small percentage of any blend. Its noticeable characteristics are a distinctive, pungent nose, an ability to yield well on poor soil and an early development some weeks before the riesling. It is planted widely in the Rheinpfalz but is also used in the Rheinhessen and Rheingau.

Rulander
Also known as the pinot gris or tokaier, this grape has a full, rich flavour but is only used in small quantities in the Saar, Upper Mosel, Franconia and Baden.

Other vines used for white wines in small quantities include the cutedel, elbling, and muskateller.

Only 15% of German wines are red; they are made from the spätburgunder (pinot noir), portugieser, trollinger and the müller-schwarz riesling at Assmanshausen and Ingelheim in the Rheingau, the Ahr valley south of Bonn, and in Württemberg.

Location of vineyards

The wine-growing regions lie between the latitudes 48°–51°N and stretch from Koblenz to the Franco-Swiss border; there are 10 principal districts.

The Rheingau
The wines of the Rheingau are considered by many to be the finest white wines in the world. The vineyards stretch along a south-facing slope on the right bank of the Rhine as it turns westward from Wiesbaden to Rudesheim, 20 miles downstream.

The micro-climate of the district is well suited to the vine: the river gives reflected heat, light and humidity, while to the north the wooded Taunus mountains provide the necessary protection from northerly winds.

This area is only about 5,500 acres — small when one considers the reputation of some of its wines, which may come from any one of the following villages: Rudesheim, Geisenheim, Johannisberg, Mittelheim, Oestrich, Hallgarten, Kiedrich, Erbach, Eltville and Rauenthal.

Within the limits of these villages are found some world-famous vineyards:

Schloss Johannisberg, Schloss Vollrads, Steinberg, Kloster Eberbach, Markobrunn, and Schloss Eltz are just a few of them.

Over 70% of the wines are made from the riesling, 15% from sylvaner and 8% from müller-thurgau grapes.

Just 15 miles further east on the north bank of the Main river lie the vineyards of Hochheim, from which the term Hock is derived; the wines produced here can often equal those of the Rheingau.

Rheinhessen or Hesse

This 34,000-acre area is one of the biggest vine-growing areas in Germany. The region has its southern limits on the border with the Rheinpfalz and then follows the Rhine northwards, passing

Mosel vineyard in winter; the vines have been pruned and trained ready for the next year's crop

through some of the best-known wine villages on the Rhine front until it reaches Mainz, the capital city of Hesse. Here the river turns westward and the vineyards follow its south bank to Bingen at the mouth of the river Nahe.

Generally speaking, the wines lack the subtle qualities of those from the Rheingau, partly due to the high percentage (65%) of sylvaner planted, a vine which gives a large volume of soft wine which drinks well in youth but benefits little from ageing.

The exceptions to this rule are the beautiful wines made from the riesling on the rich red soil of the Rhine front. The villlages from which these wines come are Nierstein, Oppenheim, Bodenheim, Laubenheim, Nackenheim and Guntersblum. The label may also be marked with the vineyard name such as Niersteiner Hipping and may be followed by added definitions of quality in good years.

Rheinhessen is also the home of Liebfraumilch, a popular wine named after the small Liebfrauenstift vineyard which adjoins the Liebfrauenkirche in Worms, but now used to describe any wine from the Rheinhessen district.

The Rheinpfalz, Pfalz or Palatinate

This is Germany's largest wine-growing area and is situated at the foot of the Haardt mountains on the border with Alsace. Here, in the south-west, the climate is the warmest and driest of all the German districts, and the grapes, therefore, develop better than those further north and give wines with more body and sugar.

The most enjoyable way to visit the district is to take the *Weinstrasse* (wine route) from the French border at Schweigen and travel 50 miles north through picturesque villages which give their names to fine wines.

Rheinpfalz is divided into three sections: Unter (lower), Ober (upper) and Mittel (middle) Haardt. The last section, Mittel Haardt, has a soil of chalk and basalt on which the riesling grape makes some distinguished wines, particularly in the villages of Deidesheim, Forst, Wachenheim, Dürkheim, Ungstein and Kallstadt. The best vineyard sites, called *lagen* in German, in the Mittel Haardt are owned by three well-known families: Burklin-Wolf, Bassermann-Jordan and von Buhl.

Apart from these top-quality wines, the Pfalz produces a large quantity of wine sold under the local village name, or used in the more commercial blends of the Hesse and the Rheingau.

The Mosel

Without doubt, this is one of the most beautiful wine-growing districts in the world. The vines are planted on precipitous south-facing slopes of shale, overlooking the narrow, ever-twisting river valley with its scattered villages, which have changed little since medieval times.

The vineyards are found over the entire length of the river from the Roman city of Trier in the south to its confluence with the Rhine at Koblenz in the north, but the finest Mosel wines come from the middle sector, known as Mittel Mosel, between the villages of Zell and Trittenheim.

The most famous of these vineyards is Bernkastel, which is overlooked by the small but legendary Doktor vineyard. Other vineyards famed for their wines are Trittenheim, Neumagen, Dhron, Piesport,

Brauneberg, Wehlen, Graach, Zeltingen, Urzing, Erden, Traben-Trabarch and Enkirch.

The riesling grape is used exclusively for the fine wines of the Mosel and has a pale greenish colour, an exquisite bouquet, and a crisp, delicate palate. As in other areas, the village name may be followed by the vineyard, such as Wehlener Sonnenuhr and Graach Himmelreich.

The Nahe

This is a small tributary of the Rhine which meets it at the town of Bingen. The vineyards are to be found along the hilly slopes of the valley. The wines have a distinctive flavour due partly to the porphyry rock in the soil; their style falls between the light, acidic freshness of the Mosel and the more supple, fruity Rhine wines. The best known vineyards are around the towns of Schlossbockleheim, Bingen, Kreuznach, Bad Münster and Niederhausen.

The Saar

This is a small tributary of the Mosel which it joins at Konz near Trier. There are only about 1,500 acres of vineyards that have a similar slate soil to that of the

Characteristic view of the Mosel Valley in West Germany; here vines are being grown on the steep slopes leading down from the castle to the river

Mosel, with which it is often classed.

In good dry years, the wines of the Saar often outclass the Mosel, and their honeyed riesling bouquet and fine steely palate asks to be savoured over and over again. In average years, these wines are light, low in alcohol and rather acid for the normal palate.

The vineyards of note are found on the south-facing slopes around the villages of

Niedermennig, Filzen, Kanzem, Wiltingen, Oberemmel, Wawern, Ockfen, Ayl, Saarburg and Serrig.

The Ruwer

This small stream joins the Mosel five miles east of Trier. There are 500 acres of steep, south-facing slopes of slate soil that make wines similar to those of the Saar, listed as Mosel-Saar-Ruwer.

In the Avelsbach corner of the valley, the riesling vine will, in good years, give exceptionally fine wines which have established the Ruwer on the wine lists of the world. Like the Saar, the wines of less good years are noticeably acid and are often used in blends or for the production of Sekt, a sweet German sparkling wine. The best vineyards are found around the villages of Kasel, Mertesdorf, Eitelsbach, Avelsbach and Waldrach.

Franconia

The majority of the wines from this 6,000-acre district are white, and come from the vineyards around the fine old town of Würzburg, 70 miles east of Wiesbaden. The sylvaner is the predominant grape, although wines are also made from the riesling, müller-thurgau and mainriesling.

The two characteristics which separate these wines from those of other German districts are first, the lime soil which gives the wines a certain *goût de terroir*, or earthy flavour, and second, the *bocks-beutel*, the flat-sided bottle in which the wines are normally sold. The label description of the wine will vary, the better quality wines showing their local town names, for example, Escherndorf, Iphofen and Randersacker, but the more commercial wines are sold as Steinwein, although this should in fact refer only to one particular vineyard in Würzburg.

Baden

This is a predominantly white wine district, lying on Germany's south-west border with France and Switzerland. The vineyards are scattered over a wide area and the various districts are best described as Bodensee, the *seewein* or lake wine from the shores of Lake Constance, Markgräferland, Kaiserstuhl, a hill of volcanic orgin near Freiburg, and Ortenau, an area of wine villages scattered along the foothills of the Black Forest, overlooking the Rhine. The wines from these areas are mostly consumed on the home market and seldom seen abroad. The vines used are riesling, rulander (pinot gris), elbling, gutedel (chasselas) and traminer.

Württemberg

This district is a few miles north-east of Baden and its vineyards lie on the slopes along the valleys of the Neckar river and its tributaries, near the city of Stuttgart. This is the only German wine region making a sizeable quantity of red and rosé wines, for which trollinger and spätburgunder vines are used. White wine grapes are riesling, sylvaner, traminer and rulander.

Wine label terms

The Germans are very precise when it comes to describing wine on a label; in fact, they have sometimes been accused of being so precise as to be confusing. However, once one masters the names of the villages and the terminology, the labels become interesting and informative.

The more common, blended wines only use simple descriptions and perhaps the best example of this is the word Liebfraumilch which may describe any blended wine from the Rheinhessen.

As the quality of the wine increases, the label becomes more explicit and gives the description in the order of importance: e.g. Region: Rheinhessen, Vintage: 1966, Village/Town: Niersteiner, Vineyard: Pettenthal, Grape: Riesling, Grower: Franz Karl Schmitt, Quality: Spätlese.

When the quality of a wine is superior to that of a normal year, it is described on the label as: Spätlese (late-picked grapes), Auslese (selected bunches), Beerenauslese (selected berries) and Trockenbeerenauslese (selected overripe grapes) – the highest category. Eiswein is an exceptionally rare and fine white wine, made from overripe grapes that were frozen during the harvest and pressing.

Apart from these descriptions, other details may appear on the label. Some of the most common ones are: Mein Eignes Wachstum (grower's own wine), Gewächs (growth), Naturrein or Naturwein (pure unsugared wine), Originalabfüllung, Kellerabzug or Kellerabfüllung (estate-bottled and bottled in the merchant's own cellars), Feine or Feinste (fine), Kabinett or Cabinett (originally the grower's own reserve, but now used to describe his choice of superior wines), and Winzergenossenschaft or Winzerverein (wine co-operative).

In 1971, Germany passed new wine laws that give more precise definitions for labelling. The names of the areas, villages and estates remain but further qualification may be used on labels, such as Tafelwein (ordinary table wine), Qualitätswein (superior table wine) and Qualitätswein mit Prädikat (strictly controlled, top quality wines).

Vineyards in the Mosel – one of the most picturesque of wine regions

Austria

Austria has a long history of wine-making, though it is only recently that her wine-growers realized the potential of their wines and sought markets abroad. Consequently, a number of Austrian wines are beginning to appear on wine lists.

The finest Austrian wines are dry, white and clean tasting although they are sometimes sweet in the tradition of Trocken-beerenauslese and Sauternes wines, made from overripe grapes. Although similar in style to German wines, they never achieve the same perfection and richness of flavour. The principal vines used are riesling, sylvaner, Hungarian furmint, muskat-ottonel and the indigenous veltliner.

The small quantities of red wine produced are soft, pleasant and fairly full-bodied; they are made from the blaubur-gunder (pinot noir) and portugieser vines.

The wine laws of Austria are straightforward and control of the various stages of wine production is quite lax, relying greatly on the wine-growers' integrity. Labels may either carry a full description of the wine like those found on German labels, or they may carry only a brand name such as Edelfräulein. In the case of the latter, the wine may be either a blend of ordinary wines or top quality, and the reputation of the shipper is the only reliable guide to quality.

Location of vineyards

Only in the east of Austria is wine made. There are about 135 square miles of vineyards that extend westwards from the borders with Czechoslovakia, Hungary and Yugoslavia to a point about 50 miles west of Vienna.

Viticultural conditions are similar to those found in Germany and many of the vineyards cascade down steep shale slopes, where forests and hills offer protection from winds.

Weinvertel

The name of this district means 'wine quarter'. Its wines are light, dry and fruity, with almost a spicy flavour. They are made mainly from the veltliner grape, and the green-gold wine is most appealing when drawn straight from the barrel.

The Wachau

Lying about 40 miles east of Vienna along the steep slopes of the Danube, the Wachau is Austria's best-known district. Schluck is its most famous product, a dry wine made mostly from the sylvaner grape; other good wines are now being made from the riesling and veltliner vines.

The wine-growers of Wachau mostly belong to a large co-operative in the scenic town of Dürnstein, and the vineyards have been regrouped into sections called *rieds* to simplify the marketing of their wines.

The leading villages of the district are Loiben, Dürnstein and Rohrendorf, where Austria's most famous wine-grower, Lens Moser, has his cellars.

Vienna

The beautiful capital city is flanked by vine-clad hillsides which produce distinguished white wines. The best of the villages near the city are Grinzig, Nussberg, Nussdorf and Neustift.

Further south, around Baden, lies the district of the Sudbahn whose best wines are made from late-picked veltliner,

Harvesting along the banks of the Danube where Schluck is the best-known wine

riesling and gewürztraminer grapes. The vineyards are situated at Baden, Gumpoldskirchen and Bad Voslau.

Burgenland

This district is close to the border with Hungary and her vineyards around Sopron. Sweet white wine, made from the riesling, furmint and muskat-ottonel grapes, are the speciality and leading vineyards are grouped along the eastern shores of Lake Neusiedler around the villages of Apetlon, Illmitz, Podersdorf and Neusiedl. The western shores of the lake produce red and white wine near Deutschkreutz, Rust and St Margarethen.

Styria

Austria's most southerly vineyards lie close to Yugoslavia, and are concentrated to the south-east of Graz. Both red and white wines are produced here around Hitzendorf, Stainz, Deutschlandsberg, Leibnitz and Ehrenhausen.

Switzerland

The Swiss have a healthy appetite for wine; they produce about 25,000,000 gallons per annum and are one of the largest importers of Burgundy, especially Beaujolais. Most Swiss wines are white so the readily available French red wines are very popular.

Undoubtedly Switzerland's geographical position has much to do with her attitude to wine. Surrounded by wine-producing countries of the calibre of France and Germany, she could hardly fail to be influenced by her neighbours.

Swiss wine production is nothing like uniform because of the climatic variations in so mountainous a country. The best wine districts are located on south-facing slopes and around lakes and rivers where plenty of humidity and protection from the cold are to be found. Nevertheless, Switzerland can claim the highest vineyards in Europe at Visperterminen, near Zermatt, where the terraced hillsides rise to almost 4,000 ft above sea level.

The higher Alpine valleys have a continental climate – long, hot dry summers and extremely cold, wet winters. Conditions such as these, where spring frosts often occur, make viticulture hazardous and vines are chosen to give a high yield of quick-ripening grapes. The resulting wines are often heady with an alcoholic strength that is several degrees above the normal 10–11% for dry, white wines.

On the whole, soil conditions are very favourable to producing white wines, as is shown by the fact that almost 80% of Switzerland's wine is white, and most of it is very good. Rich in minerals, the alluvial soil of the mountains is mixed with shale, granite, chalk and limestone – the best possible combination for white wine.

Wine label terms

Swiss wines are usually named either after their village or district of origin, or the grape variety used, or they may be given a 'type' name, rather like a brand name. For example, Fendant is a 'type' name for light dry white wines made from the chasselas grape in the canton of Valais.

The Swiss do not use complicated terms on their labels which are, consequently, very easy to understand; sometimes the name of an estate or vineyard is shown as well as the vintage, name of the wine, its place of origin and the name of the producer.

The chasselas is the principal white wine grape. In the canton of Valais it is called the fendant and in Vaud, the dorin. Other white wine grapes grown are the sylvaner, which is called the johannisberger, the marsanne of France's Rhône Valley which is called the ermitage, the pinot gris, which is called malvoisie, and a number of local grapes, the amigne, arvine and humagne which seem to be less frequently used now.

The principal red wine grapes are the pinot noir and the gamay, the great grapes of Burgundy, and the merlot.

Location of vineyards

Switzerland's largest and best wine regions are the cantons of Valais, Vaud and Geneva; between them they produce three-quarters of her wine. Lesser regions are Neuchâtel in the north-west and Ticino in the south on the Italian border.

A number of districts are scattered along Switzerland's borders with Germany and Austria but their wines, which are mostly white, are rarely seen abroad; centres of wine production are Basle, Baden, Zürich, and the Thurgau and Herrschaft districts.

Valais

In this canton, the mountain slopes of the upper Rhône Valley have been won from nature for cultivation by sheer determination and hard labour. Every favourable slope has been turned into terraced vineyards and because very little rain falls in this part of Switzerland, the wine-growers of the Valais have devised a system of wooden irrigation canals called *bisses* which carry the melting Alpine snows and streams down to the vines during the dry summer months.

The best white wines of the district are Fendant and Johannisberger. The only red wine of any note is Dôle; it is made from pinot noir and gamay grapes and is soft

Left: vineyards in Valais where every slope that can be cultivated is used

and highly scented, resembling Beaujolais in character though not in flavour. If the red wine is not up to the standard required for Dôle wine, it is called Goron. Wine centres are Sion, Vétroz and Ardon.

One of Switzerland's rare sweet dessert wines is Malvoisie, made from grapes of the same name.

Vaud

The canton adjoining west of Valais, Vaud stretches from St Maurice where the Rhône broadens out to Lake Geneva, along the northern shore of the lake as far as Nyon. The principal districts are Chablais at the eastern end of the lake, Lavaux in the middle, and La Côte running down towards Geneva. The slopes are gentler here and not so difficult to cultivate.

Lavaux produces the finest white wines which are light, dry and fruity. The best vineyards are east of Lausanne at Epesses, St Saphorin, Vevey and Dézaley.

The white wines of La Côte are less distinguished than those of Lavaux and the centre of its wine trade is Nyon. The success of the gamay grape here has led to an increase in the production of pleasant red wine.

Chablais produces pleasant enough white wine though it lacks the finesse and balance of the other districts. Centres of wine production are Aigle and Yvorne.

The tiny, isolated district of Mont Vully lies in the northern end of the canton, just south of Lake Neuchâtel. Its white wines are gradually becoming known.

The best red wine made is Salvagnin, the equivalent of Dôle wine from the Valais and made from the same grapes.

Geneva

Here there are a number of villages producing a good white wine called Mandement which some people claim tastes of hazelnuts. The best vineyards are near the villages of Satigny, Peissy and Russin; a village name often appears on the label.

Other wines to look for are Perlan made from the chasselas grape and the light red wines made from the gamay.

Neuchâtel

The vineyards here stretch along the west and north sides of Lake Neuchâtel, which lies in the shelter of the Jura Mountains, and as far as Biel on the lake of the same name. The district's best white wine is the light dry Neuchâtel, made from chasselas grapes. It is very often slightly sparkling or *pétillant* because the lees or sediments are not always racked off. The most famous Neuchâtel wine is a fresh tasting, pink rosé with a pleasant bouquet called Oeil de Perdrix (partridge's eye) – a term also used in Burgundy for a rosé wine made from pinot noir grapes.

Red wines are made mostly from pinot noir grapes which give a pale red, light wine usually named after its village.

Ticino

This is the Italian-speaking part of Switzerland. A number of its wine-growers emigrated to America and helped to found the Italian Swiss Colony vineyards in California many years ago. Vineyards are located around Lakes Maggiore and Lugano where the merlot vine is the most successful and produces a soft but fairly strong red wine. The best Ticino merlot wines are called Viti to distinguish them from the others. The local bondola vine is still grown and is used to make Nostrano, a typical red wine of the region.

Italy

To the wine-lover, Italy is something of an enigma. Here is a country whose wine history dates from classical times when the Ancient Greeks called it Oenotria, the land of wine. Although Italy is the world's greatest wine producer, this status refers simply to quantity rather than quality because Italian wines are, in general, not top quality.

Numerous species of vine are cultivated, including the classic French and German ones, and consequently the variety of wine is astonishing. Red, white, rosé, sparkling, fortified and flavoured – the Italians make them all. Yet only a few merit the term great and only a surprisingly small number of them are either available abroad or as internationally famous as they ought to be. The reasons for this are many.

Until recently, the Italians have preferred to ignore the economic potential of their wines and keep them for home consumption. The wine industry was, until recently, utterly disorganized and operated on a very local basis: there were no legally defined wine regions or districts; grape varieties were neither controlled nor specified, methods of vinification went unchecked and were therefore often unreliable; in fact viticultural conditions were so archaic and chaotic that while they prevailed, there was no chance of Italy improving her international standing.

Another factor to bear in mind is that wine-lovers all over the world have come to accept the classic wines of France and Germany as the yardstick by which all other wines should be judged. Italy's wines have therefore been handicapped right from the start in their efforts to achieve international recognition on their own merits.

First wine laws

Fortunately for Italy, the government took this situation in hand and in 1963 the first wine laws were passed. These laid down basic rules for wine-growing and vinification and introduced three standards of controlled denomination (DOC): Denominazione Semplice, Denominazione di Origine Controllata and, the highest ranking, Denominazione Controllata e Garantita.

Application of the code of laws was entrusted to the National Italian Committee for the Protection of the Denomination of Origin of Wines, a council composed of growers, wine-producers and shippers, state experts and officials whose task is that of submitting to the government the necessary rules for production of wines worth recognition. This is a major step towards clarifying the bewildering variety of wine names which may be derived from the grapes, places – some of which can be non-existent – villages and districts, as well as families.

Any wine-maker who wants his wine to be recognized and accorded DOC status can request that the controlled denomination laws be applied and, once this procedure is completed, he must follow precise rules for the production and sale of his wine.

The task of bringing Italy's wine industry into the 20th century is not an easy one. Old ways die hard and defining wines in terms of their places of origin is extremely difficult, especially when certain place names on labels have been borrowed from districts with no connection with the area where the wine was actually made. There is also the problem that some wine-makers do not accept the laws; they resent interference in and attempts to supervise their traditional practices and have not therefore applied for DOC status.

Their reaction is understandable and the wine laws as they stand cannot cover the entire Italian output; meanwhile reputations can be damaged by cheaper products of a different and sometimes questionable origin within the legally defined areas. It is to be hoped that in time the DOC endorsement of a bottle of wine will be so desirable that winemakers will have no choice but to accept the laws in full.

However, a start has been made and the 20 ancient provinces have been accepted as the basic wine zones; within these a number of districts and sub-districts have been defined.

Other post-war developments have been the growth of *consorzii*, winemakers' associations, who have made it their business, independently of the wine laws, to keep up standards and therefore maintain the reputations of the wines of their districts; the growers of Chianti Classico are the forerunners of these associations. More recent trends are the co-operative wineries which are making wine on a large scale and encouraging the small peasant holdings to sell them the grapes and leave vinification to the experts; viticultural stations have been set up to experiment with different species of vines.

The DOC laws have already encouraged wider production of good quality wines and ensured a greater degree of consistency than ever before, especially in the middle range of wines which make up the majority of Italy's exports. Today, Germany is the largest market for Italian wines, taking over half her wine exports, and she is followed by Switzerland, the USA, Britain, France and Austria.

Types of wine

The countless varieties of vines cultivated all over Italy produce an equally wide range of wines. There are red, white and rosé table wines (with an alcohol content of between 10–14%), natural sweet wines like Passito di Caluso (15–17%), which are made from sun-dried grapes in the style of the *vin de paille* in France's Jura region, fortified wines like Marsala, and flavoured aperitif wines like vermouth.

The noble grapes for red wine are the nebbiolo, sangiovese, barbera and brunello, and for white wine the trebbiano and moscato. Common grapes grow profusely, many of them having different names from district to district, particularly local, indigenous grapes. Foreign vines are well represented too and are increasingly used by growers to improve the quality of their wines. Varieties of *Vitis vinifera* used include the malbec, merlot, pinots, cabernets, riesling, gewürztraminer and sylvaner.

Here are some of the great grapes of Italy where the vine has been cultivated since classical times. Top left: moscato; many varieties of this grape are grown all over Italy. Top right: barbera, the most common vine in Piedmont, which produces red wines that vary in quality but share the characteristic of being harsh when young and mellowing with age. Centre left: nebbiolo which produces outstanding red wines in many areas – the greatest is Barolo. Centre: grignolino which gives its name to a light red wine. Far right: trebbiano, used for 'white Chianti'. Right: grillo grown in Sicily to make Marsala

Wine label terms

The lack of adequate control of wine production means that simple property names like the *châteaux* of France are very seldom found on labels. This makes it difficult to identify wines other than by the names of shippers or established firms – so it pays to be familiar with their names.

In addition to names for wines made and marketed by growers' co-operatives, firms and private individuals, there are those given by the *consorzii*. These bodies give a place name after the wine name and add a special neck label to indicate that the wine has met the necessary standard. As long as the rules of the *consorzio* are strict and are enforced, this, together with the DOC stamp, now provides a reasonable guarantee of quality.

Again, many ordinary wines carry a regional name only, such as Bianco Secco dell'Oltrepo, although a *consorzio* label may still be used. In general, wines are named after the many grape varieties, which can cause confusion, and may or may not be linked with village or brand name; a description of the type of wine – sweet or dry etc. – is usually carried as well.

Helpful terms to know are Riserva (better quality wine), Classico (from the best district of its region), Imbottigliato all'Origine or Messo in Bottiglia del Produttore nel'Origine (estate-bottled), Infiascato alla Fattoria (bottled in flask at the winery), Cantina Sociale or Coopertiva (wine-growers' co-operative), Casa Vinicola (wine firm); and Gradi Alcool or Grado Alcoolico followed by a number gives the alcoholic strength – the percentage of alcohol by volume.

The more usual descriptive terms for colour and style of wine are Bianco (white), Rosso (red), Nero (very dark red), Chiaretto (very light red), Rosato (pink or rosé), Secco (dry), Amaro (bitter or very dry), Amabile or Abboccato (medium sweet), Dolce (very sweet), Vino Liquoroso (natural sweet wine), Stravecchio (old, very mellow), Spumante (sparkling), Frizzante or Mussante (slightly sparkling), Vin or Vino Santo (sweet dessert wine) and Passito (sweet wine which is made from sun-dried grapes like the French *vin de paille*).

Province of Cuneo, south-east of Turin in the north of Italy, where the famous Barolo wine is made; the wine has been made here since the 13th century

Location of vineyards

Italy's best vineyards are in the northern half of the country where climatic and soil conditions favour the production of high quality wines. Vineyards in the hot, dry south give very high yields of grapes but the resulting wines are mostly poor quality, strong and very coarse; there are no truly distinguished wines.

The 20 basic wine zones as defined by the DOC laws are Piedmont, the Aosta Valley, Liguria and Lombardy in the north-east, Trentino, Alto Adige, Veneto, Friuli-Venezia-Giulia in the north-west, Emilia-Romagna, the Marches, Tuscany, Umbria and Latium in central Italy, and Campania, the Abruzzi, Molise, Apulia, the Basilicata, Calabria and Sicily in the south. The island of Sardinia is an additional wine zone.

The greatest wine-producing zones in sheer volume are Apulia, followed by Veneto and Piedmont.

Piedmont and the Aosta Valley

These areas have two specialities: full-bodied dark reds and delicate sparkling whites. No province of Italy produces finer or more varied wines.

The most distinguished red of Piedmont and of Italy is Barolo, a powerful fruity wine similar in style to Châteauneuf-du-Pape of the Rhône Valley, made entirely from the noble grape, nebbiolo. A very harsh wine when young, it must be kept in cask for at least three years before it can attain DOC status; it improves even more with a further three to five years in bottle, and ages as well and as long in bottle as a good claret. It is advisable to draw the cork a couple of hours before serving a Barolo so that its potency is reduced by aeration.

The history of Barolo goes back to the

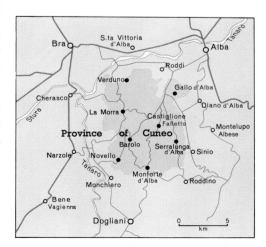

13th century when a Marquis Falletti bought the Barolo estate and planted the first vineyards. Since then, they have never looked back, winning many royal patrons over the years.

The wine, which is known as the 'king of wines', takes its name from the village of Barolo, one of a number of communes in the DOC district near Alba, which lies south-east of Turin, the capital of the province and the seat of the Kings of Savoy until the unification of Italy over 100 years ago.

The nebbiolo is also used to produce other red wines, some of which closely rival Barolo and include Gattinara, the best, Ghemme, Barbaresco and Bonarda. Gattinara and Ghemme take their names

from the villages towards Lake Maggiore, north-east of Turin. Both wines are kept three to five years in cask before bottling. The superior Gattinara wines have a neck label showing a tower standing among vineyards.

Barbaresco, Bonarda, Carema and Donnaz are lighter than Barolo and usually less harsh when young although they are made from the same grape only a few miles away. Ordinary wines are labelled simply Nebbiolo.

Other good red wines named after their grapes are Grignolino, Freisa, Dolcetto and Brachetto d'Acqui.

The most popular red wine of the region is the full-bodied Barbera which is made from the grape of the same name. However, its quality varies not only from district to district but from grower to grower and, to date, only three Barbera wines have DOC place names – d'Asti, del Monferrato and d'Alba. The better wines, grown chiefly around Asti, bear a *consorzio* neck label showing blue grapes overprinted on the city of Asti's medieval tower, in red. Lesser wines are simply called Barbera Riserva or Extra, or they may carry other district names. Take care not to confuse these Barberas with the very ordinary wine called simply Barbera which is slightly sparkling and rather sweet.

The outstanding white wine of these zones is Asti, a delicious naturally sweet sparkling wine made entirely from the moscato grape; by law no sugar may be added to it. Served very cold, it is a most refreshing drink either before a meal or with the dessert. The finest quality wine is called Asti Spumante and bears a *consorzio* neck label showing San Secondo, the patron saint of the town of Asti, in blue on a gold background. Moscato d'Asti is the cheaper, sweeter version whose centre of production is the nearby town of Canelli.

Most Asti Spumante is made by the Charmat process rather than the more costly and lengthy *méthode champenoise;* this means that fermentation takes place in huge closed vats and the bottling is done under pressure.

A recent innovation in the Asti region is a dry sparkling wine called Gran Spumante which is made from pinot and riesling grapes.

Dry light wines are made in several places and include the fragrant Cortese dell'Alto Monferrato made from the cortese grape in the Monferrato hills, Gavi, a sparkling version of Cortese, and Castel Tagliolo.

Blanc de Morgex has a hint of herbs in its bouquet and taste and is made from local varieties of grapes in the highest vineyards of the Aosta Valley.

Several Passito wines, made from moscato grapes, are found here and some have DOC status, notably Caluso Passito and Erbaluce di Caluso. These golden wines have a pronounced bouquet and come from a number of vineyards high in the mountainous country south of Ivrea.

Vineyards in the Aosta Valley where the vines have been trained to grow on trellises to make the best possible use of soil on slopes that are too steep to terrace. French influence on viticulture is pronounced in this border area

Liguria

This is the smallest wine zone of Italy for production and seems likely to decrease further as more and more vineyards are replaced by commercially-grown flowers. It is a narrow strip of land, which follows the coast from the French border to La Spezia, and is one of Italy's most popular holiday areas.

Mostly white wines are made here and the best known is Cinqueterre, made from the vernaccia grape, which comes from five villages – Corniglia, Biassa, Monterosso, Vernazza and Tiomaggiore – all on an almost inaccessible mountain slope west of La Spezia.

The full-flavoured Cinqueterre Bianco is a dry, almost salty wine and the sweet Passito version is usually called Sciacchetra. Other white wines are Vermentino, named after its grape, which comes from a district between Savona and

Imperia, and Polcevera and Coronata, which are made near Genoa.

The best red wines of the region are Dolceaqua, also known as Rossese after its grape, which comes from the hill country around Ventimiglia and Bordighera.

Lombardy

This is a highly industrial region whose capital city is Milan. Its hillier areas in the north and south produce the best red and white wines.

The Valtelline district in the north lies between the Alps and the mountains behind Bergamo. The finest of its distinguished red wines come from terraced vineyards on the lower, south-facing slopes along the right bank of the Adda river; they are Sassello, Grumello and Inferno which are all made principally from the great grape of Piedmont, the nebbiolo. In style, the wines closely resemble the Piedmont nebbiolo wines although they lack their finesse and fullness of flavour. The ordinary wines of the Valtelline are called Valtelline Rosso.

The south-western shores of Lake Garda in the north, especially between Brescia, Desenzano and Mantua, produce numerous light wines, often more rosy than red, as well as one exceptional white. The reds include Colline Mantovane, Colline del Garda, Chiaretto del Garda, Franciacorta and Colline Rocciose which is also known as Botticino.

The best white wine of this district is undoubtedly the white Lugana which is made from trebbiano grapes. A dry wine, it acquires a pale golden colour by ageing in cask for as much as four years before

Below: southern shore of Lake Garda, east of Milan in the north of Italy

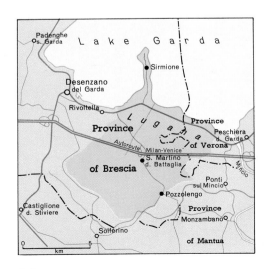

bottling – a very unusual practice for white wine.

Oltrepo Pavese, meaning literally Pavia beyond the Po, is the wine district south of the town of Pavia and the Po river. The vineyards, which are in the foothills of the Ligurian Alps, are well organized and run for the most part by co-operative wineries, a handful of small, dedicated proprietors and a very active, conscientious *consorzio* whose neck labels are numbered and show a tapped and flowing wine butt. Between them, they produce consistently high quality wines – white, red, rosé and sparkling as well – from a mixture of grapes.

Casteggio is the centre of the Oltrepo Pavese wine industry and the nearby village of Frecciarossa is one of the rare instances of a village having a DOC status. All its vineyards belong to a single proprietor, Dottore Odero, who is a distinguished oenologist; he bases his cultivation and fermentation on French principles. In addition to the village name, his four Frecciarossa wines have French brand names: La Vigne Blanche, a dry white, Sillery, a white demi-sec, the rosé Saint-Georges and the red Grand Cru.

Less distinguished wines are the red Buttafuoco, dry and slightly sparkling, Barbacarlo and Sangue di Giuda, which are slightly sweet and frothy and similar to Barbera, and Clastidio, the name given to several Casteggio red, rosé and white wines.

Trentino and Alto Adige

These are possibly Italy's most beautiful wine regions. The Alto Adige stretches from the Alps on the Austrian border as far south as Bolzano and virtually all its wine-growers are German-speaking. Trentino is the southern region; it includes most of the Dolomites and extends as far as the northern shores of Lake Garda.

The affinity between Alto Adige and Germany, Austria and Switzerland is strong; not only do they have a language in common and historical ties but also these countries account for nearly all the wine exports from the two regions. So much so, that even Italians find it difficult to buy their own wines, and the labels may be in either Italian or German. The dedicated

wine-growers of the regions take tremendous pride in their trim, tidy vineyards where the vines are trained onto pergolas at an angle of about 45°.

The Alto Adige wines are finer and more varied than those of Trentino which produces the greater volume; in both regions, the emphasis is on red wines.

The outstanding red of Alto Adige is Santa Maddalena made mostly from varieties of schiava grapes in the hills to the east of Bolzano. Full-bodied and ruby-red in colour it is ready for drinking after about three years in bottle.

Caldaro and Lago di Caldaro are also known as Kalterer and Kalterersee, the German names for the town and lake of Caldaro south of Bolzano where they

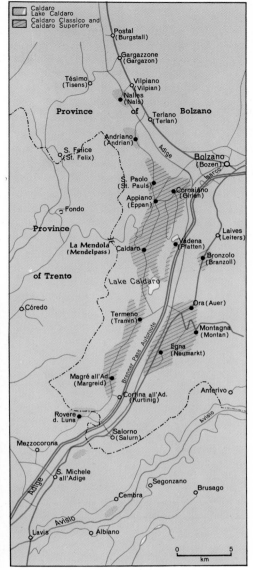

Lake Caldaro, high in the Alps near Italy's border with Austria

are grown. Pleasant, lightish wines made mostly from schiava grapes, they can be drunk young although they will improve with two years in bottle.

Lagrein or Lagarina is also called Lagrein-Kretzer in German. The lagrein vines which give the wine its name are grown around the towns of Gries and Bolzano, and the deep pink rosé is the distinguished wine of the district; its refreshing dry qualities are so popular that less and less red wine is being made there.

Terlano or Terlaner, in German, is named after the village of Terlano on the Adige river between Merano and Bolzano. There are both red and white Terlano wines, made from a mixture of grapes. The best are the dry, fruity whites.

Trentino has fewer varieties of wine

than Alto Adige and the mainstay of its wine production is Teroldego or Teroldico Rotaliano, a big red wine made from the grape of the same name in a district north-west of Trent, the region's centre of commerce.

Cabernet and Merlot, made from French grapes of the same names, are strong full-bodied reds reminiscent of their French heritage; the Merlot is by far the better wine.

Other good wines are the red Marzemino, chiefly found around Isera, south of Trent, Val d'Adige and Vallaganira, and the rosé Casteller. Garda Trentino is the generic name for a number of red, white and rosé wines from the vineyards around the northern shores of Lake Garda.

Veneto

Noted not only for its vast output but for the consistently high quality of its wine, Veneto stretches from the Austrian border and the foothills of the Dolomites almost to Ferrara in the south, and from the eastern shores of Lake Garda to Venice and the Adriatic coast. The principal wine districts are around Lake Garda, Verona, Vicenza, Padua and Treviso.

Quite the finest white wine of Veneto is Soave, a light, slightly flowery wine, naturally pale with a hint of green, which is made largely of garganega and trebbiano grapes. The vineyards of this sub-district are around the old walled town of Soave which lies at the southern edge of the hill country between Verona and Vicenza. The Soave Classico is the better, more expensive wine.

Lake Garda specializes in light red wines, the most famous of which are Valpolicella and Bardolino. Made from

Below: the fine white wine district of Soave near Verona in northern Italy

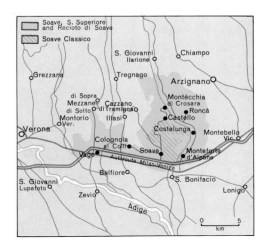

corvina, negrara and molinara grapes, they are often called the Italian Beaujolais because of their fresh, fruity flavour. Like a true Beaujolais they are delicious drunk cool and young. Both these wines and Soave are protected by the Veronese *consorzio* whose neck label shows the Roman arena at Verona.

There are also special dessert Valpolicellas called Recioto. The name is derived from the word meaning 'ear' and is used to describe wine made from the 'ears' or the finest, ripest outer grapes of a bunch; these are left to dry to increase their sugar content and the wine is then made like a Passito. The most popular Recioto is called Amarone, almost dry and very

powerful; it should not be drunk for at least six years and may easily last 20.

Valpantena, another light red wine, is similar to Valpolicella and comes from the nearby valley that runs north of Verona. Breganze red and white wines come from a small district near Bassano di Grappa, just north of Vicenza.

The hill districts between Padua and Vicenza specialize in light, fresh-tasting white wines like Colli Berci, Colli Euganei and Gambellara; several types of Moscato, one of them a sparkling version, are also made here.

Treviso, north of Venice, is mostly a white wine area; some of the wines are sparkling, the best being Verdiso

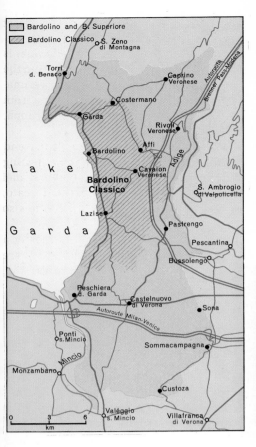

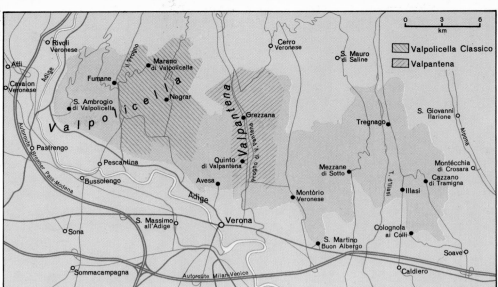

Above: eastern shore of Lake Garda and the Bardolino wine district
Above right: north of Verona lie the Valpolicella and Valpantena districts

Sylvaner, Prosecco, Colli di Valdobbiadne, Colli di Conegliano and Colline Trevigiane. The only reds of note are the Cabernet and Raboso.

Friuli-Venezia-Giulia

Tucked away in the north-eastern corner where Italy meets Austria and Yugoslavia is a region with wines noted more for consistency than for anything else. A high proportion of foreign vines are used.

Udine and the surrounding Friuli hills, Gorizia and Trieste are where the vineyards are concentrated. The white wines are generally better than the reds; white wines to look for are Sauvignon, Verduzzo, Riesling, Collio Goriziano, Collio Friuliano and Tocai, the latter wine having no connection with the Tokay of Hungary.

The best of the red wines is the Cabernet, thought by some to be better than the Cabernet of the Alto Adige and needing at least three years in bottle before it starts to lose the harshness of a young wine. The other red of note is Gamay, from a comparatively new vine, the success of which promises well for the future.

Emilia-Romagna

Famed for its cuisine, especially in the principal cities of Bologna and Modena, this area also produces some very good wines.

The wine district around Modena produces an exceptional dry red wine called Lambrusco. Although it has a sparkle, there is nothing more than a slight tingle left on the tongue after it has been poured out and drunk. This unusual aspect of a red wine does not always endear Lambrusco to foreign tastes but Italians regard it as one of their finest wines.

The DOC Lambrusco wines are called di Sorbara, the best, di Castelvetro, Salamino di Santa Croce and Reggiano. The best

Modena wine district in Emilia-Romagna where Lambrusco is produced

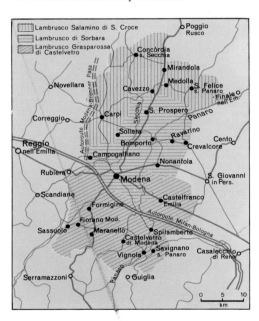

wines carry one of a number of *consorzio* neck labels, for instance, the Romagna one shows a white cock and grapes, and if made at a local co-operative winery, the label shows a man and woman treading grapes.

The Bologna-Rimini vineyards cover the slopes of the hills that rise above the autoroute. The outstanding red wine is the Sangiovese di Romagna from the district around Forli; full-bodied and robust, it is made from the sangiovese grape. White wines include the slightly sweet Albana or Albana di Romagna and Trebbiano, which may be dry or slightly sweet and sparkling.

The Marches

A sparsely populated hill region on Italy's east coast the Marches produce a number of red and white wines, but its most popular and distinguished wine is the white Verdicchio, which is widely sold abroad and easily recognized by its green bottle, shaped rather like an hour-glass. Named after the verdicchio grape, it is full-bodied and delicious when served lightly chilled.

Two Verdicchio wines have DOC status, the well-known dei Castelli di Jesi from vineyards in the Esno river valley around Jesi, and di Matelica from a district further up river and lying south of Fabriano.

The best of the Marches' red wines are Rosso Picena and Rosso Conero from the district between Ancona and Ascoli.

Below: east coast of Italy; vineyards lie between Bologna and Rimini

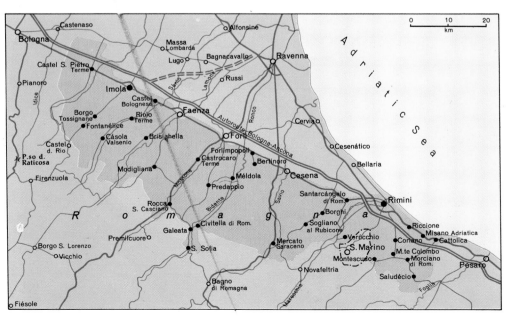

Tuscany

The countryside so beloved of painters of the Italian Renaissance is undergoing the greatest changes in viticulture in Italy. The old pattern of scattered plots of mixed vines, crops and olive trees is yielding to spacious, well arranged vineyards where the vines are kept low on the ground, as they are in France, instead of climbing high among the trees.

Italy's most famous wine abroad is Chianti and it is one of Tuscany's finest red wines. Up until 1963 and the new wine laws, Chianti was made just about everywhere in Italy and the reputation of the genuine wine from the area in the hills between Florence and Siena was sorely damaged. Although white Chianti is made under DOC law it may only be called Vino

Bianco di Toscana; the red is the distinguished wine.

Chianti is made from varying proportions of sangiovese, the predominant variety, black canaiolo, malvasia and trebbiano grapes. It was Baron Bettino Ricasoli, Cavour's successor in 1861 as Prime Minister of the newly united Italy, who first created the wine. In the hills north-east of Siena, the Baron experimented with vines on his Brolio Castle estate until he found a successful formula using the above-named grapes. Other

for Chianti. The finest wine is Chianti Classico the central sub-district whose *consorzio* was, as mentioned earlier, the founder of the growers' associations; their neck label shows a black cockerel on a gold background. The other DOC names are Chianti, Colli Aretini, Colli Fiorentini, Colli Senesi, Colline Pisane, Montalbano and Rufina; each has its own *consorzio* and they carry their respective neck labels which range from a centaur to Romulus and Remus with the she-wolf, the badge of Siena as well as of Rome.

Nobile di Montepulciano, another distinguished red, which is smooth and well-flavoured; both need five years in cask.

Vernaccia di San Gimignano is the outstanding white wine from the hills to the north of Siena; it is best drunk after one or two years in bottle.

Quite a lot of Vin Santo, Italy's rich, sweet dessert wine, is made throughout Tuscany.

The island of Elba off the coast of Tuscany makes several good wines, notably the white Procanica, Elba Spumante, Riminese and the sweet dessert wines Aleatico and Moscato; the best red is Sangiovese. Dry and semi-sweet white wines of only moderate interest come from the island of Giglio.

Tuscan estates followed in his footsteps which is why many Chianti wines outside the Classico sub-district have family names.

There are two types of red Chianti: the classic wine which is aged in claret-type bottles and the less fine, young wines which are only bottled in the familiar straw-covered flasks. The poorer Chianti wines undergo a process of secondary fermentation called the *governo* system which helps to soften them and make them more appealing. Briefly, a controlled amount of rich must from sun-dried grapes is added to the racked young wine after its first fermentation; this sets up a second fermentation which lasts 15–20 days.

At present there are eight DOC names

Tuscany, where, round the cities of Florence and Siena, Chianti is produced

Apart from these named Chiantis, many reputable firms like Melini, Bertolli, Antinori and Frescobaldi, make similar wines but use Chianti as a secondary name on their labels. Ones to look for are Brolio Riserva, Castello di Meleto, Nippozzano, Villa Antinori, Stravecchio Melini and Ruffino Riserva Ducale.

Tuscany offers several other fine wines which tend to be overshadowed by Chianti. South of Siena are two small hill towns which give their names to Brunello di Montalcino, which is made from the brunello grape (a variety of the sangiovese grape that is used for making Chianti and is one of Italy's great reds) and Vin

In the Tuscan countryside both small and extensive vineyards are to be found

Umbria

In central Italy one of the smallest wine regions lies between Tuscany and the Marches. Its wine production is modest and has only one wine of distinction, Orvieto. This famous white wine is named after the beautiful city of Orvieto which stands on a high volcanic rocky outcrop near the regional boundary with Latium. Here the vines are trained to hang over trellises up the rocky slopes.

Both dry and medium sweet versions are made from varying proportions of trebbiano, the predominant variety, verdello, malvasia, procanico and verdicchio grapes, and they are kept two years in cask. Orvieto is usually bottled in squat flasks called *pulcianelle* and the local *consorzio* give both types of wine numbered neck labels.

The semi-sweet or Abboccato Orvieto is unusual because the grapes are left to rot after harvesting and not while they are still on the vine as in France and Germany; the Italian term *muffa nobile* is the same as the French *pourriture noble*

and the German *edelfäule*. The grapes are left to rot before pressing in open casks which are kept in the caves peculiar to the district; the resulting wines are not sweet and cloying but light and delicate.

A sweet, golden Passito wine called Orvieto Vin Santo and a small quantity of red Orvieto are made as well but the latter wine never matches the quality of the white.

One other Umbrian wine deserves a mention, the red Torgiano from a small DOC area around Perugia and Assisi.

Latium

Less wine is made here today than in ancient times, even though the region, dominated by the splendid city of Rome, has remained largely agricultural with tiny hill towns virtually unchanged.

There are two main districts of wine production: south of Rome between Anzio and the Alban hills, and in the north around Lake Bolsena.

Aprilia lies in the flat country between Anzio on the coast and the Alban hills. Where there were once marshes, vines now flourish and produce a number of red, white and rosé wines under the generic

name Aprilia; the district's DOC wines are Merlot, Sangiovese and the white Trebbiano.

Castelli Romani covers about 50 square miles of the Alban hills. Most of the dry and medium sweet white wines made here have specific names, either of villages or brand names of co-operatives, and among the best are Frascati, Marino, Colli Albani and Velletri, all of which have DOC status.

Frascati, the most famous of the Castelli wines, is clear gold in colour, fragrant and quite capable of ageing in bottle; its sweeter version is called Cannellino. The Frascati *consorzio* was formed as long ago as 1949 and their neck label is only given to the authentic wines from the districts of Frascati, Grottaferrata, Monteporzio and a tiny suburb of Rome itself.

Lake Bolsena and its surrounding vineyards lie on a parallel with the nearby Orvieto district in Emilia-Romagna, and its chief claim to fame is the popular Est! Est! Est! wine. Legend has it that the name was derived from a travelling bishop's servant who chalked the word *'est'*, an abbreviation for the Latin *vinum bonum est* (wine is good here) on the doors of those inns he thought suitable for his master, who in fact found some of them triply good. Only the inns of Monte-fiascone, a small hilltop town overlooking the lake, were selected and the town is the present defined area. Both dry and sweet versions of the white wine are made.

Campania

Probably better known for its holiday resorts – Naples, Amalfi and Positano and the islands of Ischia and Capri – than for its wines, Campania marks the start of southern Italy. As one travels south so the quality of the wines decreases; modern methods are improving them but it is a slow process. Much of the Campania wine is sold to the north for blending or making vermouth and little is exported.

The wine-growing districts are concentrated around Naples and the slopes of Mount Vesuvius, Benevento and Salerno.

Certainly the best known wine of Campania abroad is Lacrima Christi, the generic name for the light red and white wines of Mount Vesuvius. Their quality can be variable, however, for in the absence of a local *consorzio* poor imitations can be marketed.

The district north of Naples and around Benevento makes Conca, a purplish-red wine, rather sharp in flavour, Falerno, a dry, full-flavoured red or white, Solopaca, which may be red, white or rosé and is best drunk cool, and Taurasi, a robust red with DOC status, which is one of the many wines made from the aglianico grape (it is called Avellino when it comes from the hills north-east of that town).

Two good white wines are Greco di Tufo, a DOC wine with a strong bouquet, made both dry and medium-sweet and Fiano, a slightly sparkling wine made from the grape of the same name.

Several red and white wines are made on the islands of Capri and Ischia. The wines of the latter have DOC status.

The Abruzzi and Molise

These highly mountainous regions adjoining Campania where some of the peaks are as high as 10,000 ft, have little land available for viticulture, except for a coastal belt on the Adriatic. Most of the grapes are grown for the table. Apart from Montepulciano d'Abruzzo, a DOC red wine that is almost rosé in colour, the wines are poor and mostly for local consumption.

Apulia, Basilicata and Calabria

More wine is produced in Apulia than any other part of the country but none of it is up to the standard of the northern wines. The fierce sun and heavy, poor soil gives coarse wines best suited for blending.

The wild, rugged countryside of Basilicata and Calabria grows straggling vines; the only district of any consequence in Basilicata is around the extinct volcano, Mount Vulture.

The vines thrive on the rich volcanic slopes and produce one of southern Italy's best red wines, the full-flavoured Aglianico del Vulture; there is a sparkling version as well called Aglianico Mussante. Two sweet sparkling wines from the same district are Moscato and Malvasia di Vulture. Further south, the Potenza district produces Asprinto, a dry, slightly sparkling white.

Apulia's best wines are the natural sweet Aleatico, Capo di Leuca which is a generic name for the red and white wines in the bottom of the heel of Italy, and Locorotondo, Martina and Martina Franca which are similar white DOC wines.

Calabria can boast one DOC district to date – Ciro north of Crotone on the coast, where adequate dark red, rosé and white wines are made. An excellent dessert wine made on the east coast is Greco di Gerace which is amber-gold in colour and smells of orange blossom.

Sicily

The island's livelihood comes from citrus fruits and wine in that order. More and more co-operatives are springing up and they are slowly changing the old peasant tradition of farming small plots, the vines mixed with the crops; the new vineyards are spacious and lend themselves easily to mechanization.

The most important wine districts are Trapani in the west, Catania in the east, Messina in the north and between Gela and Siracusa in the south.

Trapani produces the island's most famous wine, Marsala, and as with sherry, port and Madeira, the English influence is strong. John Woodhouse, a Liverpool merchant, set up a family firm in Marsala in 1773 and exported the wine to England. The wine quickly became very popular and a second English firm was established there by Sir Benjamin Ingham. The third English name in Marsala, Whitaker, was Ingham's descendant.

Marsala is a fortified wine and resembles Madeira to some extent because a part of it is 'cooked'. It is made by adding to the dry white wine of the district a controlled amount of liquid made up of one-quarter brandy and three-

Above: Sicily, the island at the foot of Italy where the rich volcanic soil of Mt Etna (right) nourishes and adds character to a variety of wines. The lower and middle slopes of the volcano are covered with vineyards and form a DOC district

quarters of a local sweet wine made from semi-dried grapes. To this is added another controlled amount of young, unfermented grape must that has been heated until it becomes thick, sweet and like caramel in colour, texture and flavour.

The blended wine is then matured in huge oak casks called pipes, each of which holds 93 gallons, and the best of the young Marsalas are matured in a *solera* system like that for sherry. The wine takes on a deep brown colour, the sweetness diminishes with age and the original dry white wine gives the Marsala its characteristic touch of dryness.

Marsala production is carefully controlled and the grades made are Marsala Fine (aged at least four months), Marsala Superiore (aged at least two years), Marsala Vergine (the original wine, without additions but aged, often by the *solera* system; it must be at least five years old) and Marsala Speciale (aged at least five years and the finest of all the wines).

Outside Italy, Marsala is thought of as a wine for cooking with rather than for drinking, although if the top quality Marsala wines were available, people would probably try them. One particular advantage Marsala has over other wines is that it does not deteriorate after the bottle has been opened.

The red Corvo, light and dry, is the best wine from Palermo.

Catania is known principally for wines from the vines grown on the slopes of Mount Etna, which is a DOC district. The ordinary red, white and rosé wines are sold under the generic name of Etna, but the more superior ones are sold under individual names like Ciclopi, Ragabo, Ragalna, Biancavilla and Mascali.

Messina's best wines are the red Faro, the red and white Capo and Milazzo. Southern Sicily produces several Moscato wines as well as a heavy red called Pachino.

Sardinia

Here the speciality is strong sweet wines. Vernaccia is a strong, dry white aperitif wine, something like a natural unfortified sherry, and Nuragus is a good dry white named after its grape. The finest dessert wines are Cannonau and Oliena, though they are also made as dry reds and, in the case of Cannonau, there is a rosé version as well.

Spain

Although Spain has more land under vine than any other country, she produces only one-third of the quantity of wine that comes from Italy. Her vineyards are not so well organized, mostly on a small scale, and often grow side by side with cereals, fruit and olives. The bulk of the wine made is *vino corriente*, ordinary wine of little character. If it is not drunk locally, it is used for blending.

The most famous wine of Spain is sherry which comes only from the region around Jerez de la Frontera (the word sherry is derived from Jerez, the name of the town). More recently, however, Spain has begun to gain a reputation for good quality table wines, especially the reds from Rioja.

The vines grown for making wine in Spain are indigenous, and although attempts were made by French wine-growers at the beginning of the 19th century to plant French vines such as the cabernets on a large scale, none were successful and methods of fermentation and ageing wines are virtually the sole reminders of their efforts.

The principal grapes used are the graciano, mazuela, viura, tempranilla, pardillo, torrentes, huelva, garnacha (the grenache of the Rhône valley), together with the pedro ximenez and palomino, the latter being the great sherry grape.

Labelling of wines

Wine laws corresponding to those of France and Germany are non-existent in Spain. Some labels carry a semi-official stamp that does denote the wine's place of origin. The words to look for that provide the best guarantee of good wine are Denominación de Origen, together with the name of a reputable shipper or wine-maker.

Other terms found on labels are Reserva, meaning wine matured for five years, Cosecha, meaning a vintage year and usually followed by 4°Año or 6°Año which means the wine has spent so many years in barrel and bottle before it was sold. Spanish wine-growers do not have good and bad vintage years like most other wine countries; instead, they award a vintage to their individual wines only when they have been in barrel for several years – long enough for them to assess the wines' merits.

In general, Spanish wines are not labelled with vineyard or regional names as in France but with trade or house names put on them by their producers. Top quality wines may carry the following terms: Vino de Cosecha Propria (wine made by the owner of the vineyard); Criado y Embotellado por . . . (grown and bottled by . . .); or Engarrafado de Origen (estate-bottled). Among the leading *bodegas* for table wines are Compañia Vinícola de Norte de España, La Rioja Alta, Lopez de Heredia, Ignacio Palacios, and Frederico Paternina.

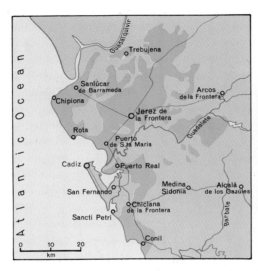

Location of vineyards

Although vines grow almost everywhere in Spain, most regions suffer from insufficient and spasmodic rainfall so that harvests vary considerably. Only a handful of regions have the right climatic and soil conditions: the districts surrounding Jerez de la Frontera, Montilla-Moriles, Rioja and Catalonia. Lesser regions are La Mancha, Valencia, Galicia and Malaga.

Jerez de la Frontera

True sherry comes only from Jerez in Andalusia; countries like Cyprus and South Africa only produce sherry-type wines that have been fortified and made in a similar way.

Unlike most other wine districts in Spain, here the traditional methods of making sherry have always been strictly controlled and kept to a very high standard. The vineyards fan out from the town of Cadiz on the south-west coast and Jerez de la Frontera is the centre of the sherry trade. Here the leading sherry producers like Williams & Humbert, Garvey, Pedro Domecq, Gonzalez Byass, Sandeman, and Fernando A. de Terry have their *bodegas*.

All sherry is made from the juice of white grapes, the most important of which is the palomino. The wine is fortified and blended; and wines from different vineyards and different vintages are blended together so that there is a continuity in style and character. Consequently, there is no such thing as vintage sherry.

The strata of chalk soil called *albarizas* are the sites of the best vineyards, producing the classic sherries called *finos*; vineyards planted on a clay and sandy soil produce lesser wines.

Left: south-west coast of Spain where Jerez de la Frontera, the centre of sherry production, is situated

How sherry is made

At vintage time, around the end of September, the grapes are gathered and spread out on straw mats for at least 12 hours to dry in the sun. Then they are put into mechanical presses or, in a few areas where the old-fashioned method of pressing still survives, into large troughs and trodden by men wearing special hob-nailed boots so that the pips and stalks are not crushed as well. After pressing, the juice, or *mosto*, is run off into casks which are taken to the *bodegas* where the *mosto* is left to ferment for about three months. The first spell of cold weather starts the clearing of the young wine which is then racked off; it is then racked again into casks containing a quantity of spirit for its first fortification.

The next stage in the process is very important and unique to sherry for it determines the basic type of sherry – *fino* or *oloroso.* The casks are only filled two-thirds full with wine so that the action of a rather unpredictable· but vital yeast called *flor* can take place. For reasons unknown, white flor only grows on some of the wines and its presence clarifies the colour and adds dryness to the wine; its growth period on the surface of the wines takes several years and they are carefully watched at all times.

The wines that develop flor are the *finos*; they become pale in colour, delicate and very dry. The wines that do not develop flor are the *olorosos* which are richer and fuller in flavour, though not necessarily sweeter, than the *finos.*

Finos are used for making the Amontillado and Manzanilla sherries. Manzanilla *finos* are the driest and come only from the district around the coastal town of Sanlúcar de Barrameda; its wines have a characteristic tang said to be derived from the salt in the air.

Olorosos are the basis for the best sweet, dark sherries, usually called milk or cream sherries because of their smooth, full flavour. The poorer quality *olorosos* are used for cheaper blends called *rayas.*

Maturing sherry

For many years, sherry shippers have built up a system of maturing butts of identical wine, called the *solera.* These butts are supplemented by more casks of similar wines in different stages of maturation which are known as *criaderas* or nurseries.

There may be any number of *criaderas*, the last holding wine young enough to be refreshed with any wine from nine months to several years old.

When a wine is wanted, it is drawn from the cask of its particular *solera*, which is in turn refilled from the first *criadera*; the first *criadera* is refilled from the second and so on. Each of these separate stages is a scale and the number of scales and number of casks in each scale tell the shipper to what extent the wine has matured.

It is the shipper who governs the frequency and quantity of withdrawals from the *solera.*

Unlike most other wines, sherry acquires sweetness by manufacture for all sherry is dry after fermentation as all the sugar in the *mosto* is converted into alcohol. Medium sweet or sweet sherries have sweetening as well as colouring agents added to give them their characteristic flavour and appearance.

Montilla-Moriles

This tiny district in the province of Cordoba, about 100 miles north of Jerez de la Frontera, is now becoming more widely known. Its chalky soil, similar to that of Jerez, on which the pedro ximenez grape is planted produces very high strength natural wines that require little fortification; these wines also encourage the growth of the flor yeast and make a palatable alternative to sherry.

In the north of Spain near the Pyrenees Rioja is a major wine district

Rioja

This north-eastern region is in the province of Aragon and produces the best Spanish table wines, most of which are red. It takes its name from the tiny Oja river which joins the Ebro as it nears the Mediterranean.

Some of the red wines produced here are comparable to good Bordeaux wines; they tend to have more body and alcoholic strength and are quite capable of ageing at least 10 years. Viticulture here draws on French techniques, brought into Rioja at the end of the 19th century when French vineyards were badly hit by phylloxera.

The vineyards of Rioja follow the Ebro river between Haro in the north and Alfaro in the south, and fall into districts according to their climate and terrain conditions. The best vineyards are in Rioja Alta (upper Rioja) between Haro, the chief wine town, and Logroño, and in Rioja Alavesa which takes its name from the province of Alava. Rioja Baja (lower Rioja) continues to follow the Ebro river and extends to the towns of Calahorra and Alfaro.

The first two districts are cooler and wetter than Rioja Baja and have the better soil; they are also well sheltered by the mountainous Sierra de Cantabria to the north and consequently produce the lightest and finest wines. The light, very pale red wines are called Clarete. Both dry and medium sweet white wines are made and they are best drunk after one year; however, the custom in Rioja is to age them for four or five years which tends to make them rather flat in taste.

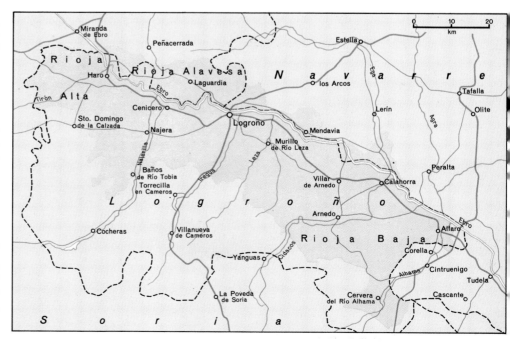

Catalonia

Spain's second largest wine-producing region, the vineyards of Catalonia run parallel to the Mediterranean coast from Barcelona down to below Tarragona. Its districts, Alella, Panades, Priorato and Tarragona, produce between them nearly 20% of Spain's red and white table wines.

Alella, just north of Barcelona, makes a fine light white wine, the best of which is called Marfil, meaning ivory. Panades is best known for its sparkling wine and the centre of the industry is San Sadurní de Noya; Priorato, a small area within Tarragona, specializes in strong, dry red wines. Tarragona is known for its fortified sweet wines and lends its name only to wines of this type. They were at one time very popular in Britain.

La Mancha

This vast vineyard region extends from Toledo, south of Madrid, to Valencia on the Mediterranean coast. It is the largest wine-producing area in Spain and its most popular red wine is Valdepeñas after the town of the same name. Other wines such as Manzanares, Alcazar de San Juan and Ciudad Real take the name of the districts where they are made.

Valencia

South of Valencia, down as far as the town of Alicante, there is another concentration of vineyards. Sweet red table wines predominate and are made from bobel, garnacha and crujidera vines; one wine, Alicante, has a very powerful, flowery bouquet; when it has aged for some time it is called Fondillon.

Galicia

The wine districts of Ribeira and Ponte-vedra in the north-western province of Galicia are close to Spain's border with Portugal. The vineyards here produce a 'green' white wine similar to the Portuguese *vinho verde.*

Malaga

The old town of Malaga lies on the southern coast of Spain surrounded by hills on which pedro ximenez vines are grown. Malaga wine is dark, sweet and strong and is made in various types like sherry. Most of the wines are fortified and live very well in bottle – some have been known to last for 100 years.

Wines in these huge vats are carefully watched as they mature

Portugal

Like Spain, Portugal is best known for her fortified wines, port and Madeira, but she also produces good table wines, particularly rosés, and the *vinhos verdes* of the Minho region. Portugal also contributes to the wine industry in another way – her forests of cork trees provide most of the corks for European wines.

The vine has grown in Portugal since the days of the Romans, and many species are unique to the country. The modern wine industry is relatively new and is expanding rapidly with a strong emphasis on exports. With the assistance of the government, the Junta Nacional do Vinho (national wine board) was set up to supervise wine production, select the most suitable grapes and educate wine-makers; the board also runs state-owned co-operatives. There are a large number of private wine firms as well and viticulture is now run on a very organized and strictly controlled basis.

Apart from the island of Madeira described in the next chapter and the Douro region producing port, the Junta Nacional officially recognizes six other regions for the production of table wines, each of which has strict vinicultural rules and standards similar to the AOC laws of France. Wines from the authorized regions bear the words Região Demarcada (officially demarcated area) or Denominacão de Origem (similar to AOC status); they can also carry the insignia of their respective União Vinicola Regional (UVR), or vinicultural union.

However, there are a number of other unofficial districts whose wines are varied and interesting and well worth trying.

Portuguese wine-makers, like their Spanish counterparts, award their wines a *colheita* or vintage after the wine has been in barrel for at least two years. After that time, the best wines are called Reserva and kept for a longer period before bottling; the remainder are bottled immediately and sold as *vinho de mesa* (ordinary table wine).

Again, as in Spain, wines carry brand or regional names instead of vineyard names, and among the leading names of firms or *adegas* are Real Compania Vinicola do Norte de Portugal, José Maria da Fonseca, Carvalho, Ribeiro and Ferreira, Sociedado Comercial dos Vinhos de Mesa de Portugal.

Other terms found on bottle labels are Garrafeira (best quality wine), Engarrafado na Origem (estate-bottled); and Branco (white), Tinto (red), Clarete (pale red), Rosado (rosé), Seco (dry), Doce or Adamado (sweet) and Espumante (sparkling).

Location of vineyards

North and west Portugal is the land of the vine. Here the climate is ideal for there is ample rain and long, sunny summers. The fertile land is well supplied with rivers. The southern half of the country is unsuited to the vine, although there is a small wine-growing district in the Algarve. Numerous local grapes are used and wines are usually blended.

The principal authorized zones are Minho, Dão, Douro and around Lisbon, Bucelas, Colares, Carcavelos and Setúbal. Douro makes only port and is discussed last. The lesser wine districts are Lafões and Pinhel in central Portugal, Bairrada, Torres Vedras and Ribatejo on the coast north of Lisbon, and Lagoa in the Algarve.

Minho

One of the most beautiful wine-growing areas of Portugal, Minho stretches from the Spanish border in the north-west down to Oporto on the Douro river. The way in which the vines grow here is peculiar to this region, although it is comparable to the way the vines grow in Orvieto in Italy. Vines are trained overhead along trees and trellises to form shade-giving pergolas. In this area of intensive agriculture the soil beneath the vines is planted with crops.

The best Portuguese red and white wines, called *vinhos verdes*, are made here. The whites are the better known. All the *vinhos verdes* are made from local grapes; the reds are made mostly from the vinão, borracal, espadeiro, azal tinto,

Below: Douro vineyards tightly terraced on an inhospitable hillside

cainhos and brancelho vines, and the whites are principally made from the azal branco and dourado vines.

Literally meaning 'green wine', the name *vinho verde* describes the fresh qualities of the slightly underripe, green grapes which are picked early and fermented for only a short time then racked, filtered and bottled so that the wine contains residual carbon dioxide. As a result the wines that are produced are slightly sparkling and very refreshing.

Carcavelos, close to the seaside resort of Estoril, produces rather sweet red wines with an almond flavour. Although it is an authorized wine zone production is limited with little new development.

Setúbal
Just south of Lisbon, this area is famous for the rich Moscatel de Setúbal, the best of the dessert wines made from the muscat grape. Every part of the grape, pips and stalks included, is pressed to extract the maximum flavour; the resulting wine is richer and more fragrant than the muscats of Beaumes-de-Venise in the Rhône Valley. It improves greatly with age.

Lafões and Pinhel
These are districts to the north and north-east respectively of the Dão region. Lafões produces red and white wines similar to the *vinhos verdes* of Minho, and its vines are also trained on trellises. Pinhel on the river Coa, together with Agueda on the river of the same name, produce mostly light, fragrant red wines.

Bairrada
To the west of the Dão region lies Bairrada on the coastal plains. It produces full-bodied red and white wines; the white are used mainly for sparkling wine.

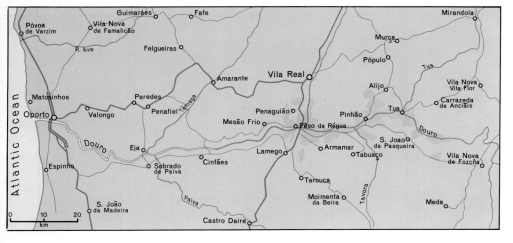

*Left: in the north-west of Portugal the Douro region is the home of port
Below: wine lodges at the mouth of the river Douro. No wine is more strictly controlled than port which may only be matured in these long, low warehouses*

Dão
This large vineyard region of central Portugal lies between the Serra do Marão and Serra da Estrela mountains; it is interspersed with the rivers Dão, from which it takes its name, Mondego, Ceira and Alva. The centre of the wine trade is the old town of Viseu.

The hot, dry climate of this inland region, with its hillsides of granite rock and sandy soil, produces soft red and white wines that are best drunk young. Dão vineyards produce most Portuguese table wines. The principal vines planted are the arinto, pinta pinheira, tourigo and preto mortágnua.

Bucelas, Colares and Carcavelos
These are all coastal vineyard districts around Lisbon. Bucelas produces mostly very dry, light white wine that has a special bouquet; sometimes it becomes slightly sparkling with age.

Colares, just 20 miles from Lisbon, is unique in that its vines have never suffered from phylloxera because they grow on the beach, low along the ground, deeply rooted in the sand – such conditions discourage the phylloxera louse. The red wines, made from the ramisco grape, are almost black in colour, very strong, high in tannin and mature slowly.

Torres Vedras and Ribatejo

These large wine-growing areas to the north of Lisbon stretch from the coastal town of Alcobaça inland to Santarem on the Tagus river. Most of the red wines are full-bodied and used mainly for blending.

Lagoa

From the southern region of the Algarve, comes a pleasant dry white wine.

Portugal is also renowned for its rosé wines the best of which are: Mateus Rosé from the district around the town of Vila Real within the Douro region, Lancers from Setúbal, Lagosta and Moura Basto, both from Minho.

Douro

This area superbly illustrates the adage that the vine gives of its best in the poorest conditions of terrain and in a harsh climate. For sheer inhospitality to the vine the Douro is hard to beat. Port is the only wine made in the official region of the Douro, named after the river that wends its way from Spain through Portugal to the Atlantic Ocean.

It was the British, who, with their taste for sweet fortified wine, were responsible for the development of the port industry during the 18th century. They established *quintas* or estates high in the hills of the Upper Douro. This is why there is a prevalence of English names among the leading port shippers – such as Cockburn, Graham, Dow, Burmester, Croft, Taylor, and Mackenzie.

The unique feature of the Douro vineyards is their terracing. At first, there was not enough soil on the slate and granite mountainsides to give the vines a footing so low walls were built across the slopes to keep in the precious soil and retain water. As a result, the slopes, which appear from a distance to display the contour lines of a map, are rich in fruit trees and olives as well as the vine.

The making of the wine is very strictly controlled and the region falls into two main districts: the Upper Douro which has the best vineyards and the Lower Douro near the coastal town of Oporto (which gives its name to port) and Vila Nova de Gaia, its port and suburb, where the all-important blending and maturing takes place in the port lodges.

In the fertile Minho region in the north of Portugal vines are trained on trellises to leave the ground below free for cultivation of other crops

How port is made

Unlike sherry, port is fortified during fermentation, not after, and it is not deliberately exposed to air during ageing. Most port is blended and made from both red and white grapes and blended from wines of different vintages; only when conditions are near perfect are the wines of that harvest declared by the shippers to be a vintage port.

Harvesting takes place around the end of September; the grapes are gathered and carried to the press-houses where they are trodden by relays of bare-foot men in large stone troughs called *lagars.* Most of the modern *quintas* have replaced men with modern presses and fermentation takes place in sealed vats, but the traditional treading of the grapes can still be found.

The grape juice and pulp are left together so that the maximum flavour and colour can be extracted from the skins; fermentation starts quickly and after about four days so much sugar has been converted into alcohol that fermentation is stopped by running off the young wine into huge 115-gallon barrels known as pipes, which contain a controlled amount of Portuguese brandy. This stops further fermentation and leaves the necessary amount of sweetness in the wine; by law, no sugar may be added.

The pipes are then taken to the port lodges in Vila Nova de Gaia under close supervision where they lie for at least two years, depending on the type of port to be made. The young wines may be blended with similar wines of the same vintage before they are left to age.

Traditionally, the pipes of wine would be shipped down river in the picturesque local high-prowed river boats, *barcos rabelos,* that have now been superseded by the more efficient and reliable trains.

Types of port

Vintage port is the very best wine and consequently expensive. Dark red in colour, it is bottled after two years in barrel and then matured further in the bottle for anything up to 50 years. During ageing, it throws a sediment or crust so it must be decanted before serving. A pipe of young vintage port (about 750 bottles) was once very popular as a christening gift for a boy because 21 years is the ideal time for port to mature.

Late-bottled vintage port is a vintage wine kept for five or six years in cask before bottling. This way it matures more rapidly than in bottle and retains the character of a true vintage port, although it is lighter in body and colour. Shippers have developed this method to meet today's heavy demand for vintage port.

Crusted port is wine not quite up to the high standard of vintage port. It is, therefore, blended. Nonetheless it is still a very fine port and takes only seven to 10 years to mature in bottle; it too helps to meet the demand for vintage-type ports.

Tawny port is a blend of fine wines that are matured in cask for about 15 years. The wine becomes very light in colour, can develop a fine flavour and bouquet, and has a velvety taste. However, not all tawny ports sold are aged like this; the less expensive ones are a blend of young, poor quality wines. Pleasant enough to drink, they cost much less than a true tawny port.

Ruby port does not benefit from a long stay in bottle; instead it is matured in cask (for about two to three years). The deposit is thrown before bottling. The ruby red colour is distinctive and these less expensive wines have all the softness and generous flavour of port.

White port is made only from white grapes fermented out to give a very dry wine, and then fortified. It is best drunk chilled as an aperitif.

Labels on vintage port are a comparatively modern innovation. Formerly bottles were merely marked with a smudge of white paint to indicate which way up they should lie; the name of the shipper was embossed on the metal capsule or wax seal, and branded on the cork, which also provided a means of identifying the wine in the bottle. Since the corks usually began to disintegrate after 20 years in bottle, the wines were often recorked, a practice frowned upon today. Stocks of vintage port are such a rarity now that this problem hardly occurs. Recent port vintages are 1970, 1967, 1966, 1963, 1960, 1958, 1955, 1950, 1948 and 1945.

It is now compulsory for a bottle to be labelled to show the country of origin and the shipper or bottler. Port comes only from the Douro region and must be shipped from Oporto; in the old days it had to cross the harbour bar at the mouth of the Douro river. This definition of port is protected by international law. Ports other than vintage wines are labelled with a brand name of either the shipper or bottler and a description of the type.

Madeira

The island of Madeira lies some 400 miles off the north-west coast of Africa. Its mid-ocean position just to the north of the Tropics gives it a fine and constant climate favourable to many types of tropical plants, fruits and especially the vine, which produces the incomparable wines responsible for the fame of the island.

Approached from any direction, the island is spectacular, appearing as a vast volcanic outcrop reaching 6,000 ft at its highest point, Pico Ruivo. Terraced vineyards are planted over much of its 285 square miles, and so rich is the vegetation that the vines grow on pergolas, leaving valuable space beneath for other crops.

The early seafaring nations – particularly the Phoenicians, Genoese and Portuguese – knew Madeira as the Enchanted Isle, and later as the Island of Trees. It was not until 1418 that Prince Henry the Navigator of Portugal sent two captains, João Gonsalves Zarco and Tristão Vaz Teixeira, to the island to claim it as a Portuguese possession which it has remained until today.

At that time Madeira was covered by dense forest and thick undergrowth that made settlement almost impossible. Zarco therefore decided to burn the forests and, according to legend, they burnt for seven years, leaving a deep deposit of wood ash and humus. So fertile was the soil that many varieties of tropical plant quickly became established.

There is no record of the first planting of vines on the island but it is assumed they arrived from various parts of Europe with the early settlers. The malvasia from which Malmsey is made is reputed to have come from Candia in Crete; Sercial, the driest of Madeira wines, from the German riesling; Verdelho from a cross of the Spanish pedro ximenez and the Italian verdea grapes; Bual from Portugal.

Madeira's position on the trade routes to the East and the Americas made the island a popular re-victualling call for merchant ships and navies alike. Captain Cook, on his famous voyage of exploration, visited the island and so, later, did Admiral Nelson before sailing to the West Indies. The island's wines were usually included in ships' provisions to supplement the water supply and were found so palatable that their reputation soon spread to many

and gradually heated to 29°C, then allowed to cool over a six-month period. This system is still used today. After this *estufa* process, the wine is rested for 18 months, then blended by the *solera* process used in Jerez de la Frontera in Spain.

Types of wine

Although much has been done in the last few years to streamline the production and quality of Madeira wines, there remain four basic types.

Sercial (pronounced sir-sheal) is an amber-gold wine. The best of Madeira's dry wines, it may be served as an aperitif or with soups, particularly turtle soup. Stored under the right conditions, this wine will mature in bottle over a long period.

Verdelho (pronounced verday-lio), now becoming less common, is normally sweeter and darker than Sercial. In its driest form it may be drunk chilled as an aperitif or as an accompaniment to soups or highly-flavoured foods.

Bual (spelt Boal in Portuguese) is sweeter still than Verdelho, has a distinctive bouquet and is classed as a dessert wine for end-of-dinner drinking. Like other Madeiras, it also lives to a great age in bottle.

Malmsey is probably the best known of all Madeiras due, perhaps, to the fact that the unfortunate Duke of Clarence, the brother of England's King Edward IV, was reputedly drowned in a barrel of Malmsey. It is the sweetest and richest in this range of wines. Ideally, this wine should be served with the dessert at dinner or, as in the last century, with a mid-morning cake or biscuit.

Apart from these main types of wine, other names do appear on the label. Rainwater is a dry or medium wine blended specially for the American market, but now also used as a generic name. True Rainwater wine is made from the vineyards on high ground, which are watered only by rain and not by the traditional water courses or *levadas* of the lower vineyards.

Solera wines are particularly fine, and may be from a *solera* started a century ago. Dates appearing on the label indicate the first year the blend was started. Do not confuse this with the date appearing on vintage Madeiras, which are now rare and expensive wines, and therefore the domain of the dedicated wine-lover and collector.

countries, adding an impetus to exports.

Until 1753 the wines were sweet and not particularly distinguished; after that date they were fortified with grape spirit, giving them a cleaner palate and a greater longevity in bottle. Unlike many European wine-growing countries, Madeira remained unscathed during the period of the Napoleonic wars, and enjoyed her greatest prosperity and peak wine production in the 18th and first half of the 19th centuries. However, in 1852 she experienced the first of two setbacks: oidium, a form of mildew which reduced wine production and exports. Hardly had she recovered from this when in 1872 the vineyards were struck by the infamous phylloxera, making many of the shippers, particularly the English, return home, leaving the families which make up the Madeira wine trade today.

Making the wine

The grapes are harvested from August to October, depending on the development of the different vine species. They are then taken to the press-house where they may still be trodden in wooden troughs (*lagars*) by human feet, or crushed by modern mechanical presses. The juice, or *mosto*

Ponta Delgada on the island of Madeira where vineyards slope dramatically down to the sea; the vineyards have now recovered their past glory

as it is now called, is run off into vats where fermentation starts immediately.

The sweeter Madeiras are stopped in mid-fermentation by the addition of brandy spirit, but the drier varieties are allowed to continue their fermentation which is eventually stopped by the gradual addition of brandy.

After fortification, the wines undergo a process unique to Madeira – the *estufa*. Shippers had noted how, in the 18th century, wines that had made long sea voyages in the Tropics had been greatly improved by the higher temperatures and, it was believed, by the rolling motion of the ships. Some companies sent all their wines on voyages to mature but as they gained popularity, it soon became clear that for economic reasons this treatment of the wine was no longer practicable.

The Madeirans therefore designed a system of hot rooms to give the wine the same, much sought-after flavour that maturing at sea gave them. The pipes or barrels of wine were put in these rooms

Hungary

Prior to the phylloxera plague that devastated Europe's vineyards in the late 19th century, Hungary was the fourth largest wine-producing country in Europe. Her vineyards, which go back many centuries, became what the Hungarians call the historical wine regions where numerous vines were indigenous, notably the kadarka, kövidinka, szlankamentha, sarfehér, furmint, hárslevelü, szürkebarát, leányka and kéknyelyü. These historical regions have changed slightly in recent years and some were redefined in 1959.

Most of the country makes good table wines: rosés, a few sparkling wines, but mostly reds and whites. The latter are the better quality wines. The dry, slightly fiery taste of the white wines acts as a perfect foil to the rich, spicy Hungarian food. The red wines tend to be softer and lighter, with the exception of Egri Bikavér, the famous Bull's Blood wine.

The modern wine industry of Hungary is controlled by the state monopoly, Monimpex. The existing wine laws primarily govern the labelling of wines; you find few descriptive phrases on labels of the kind associated with French and German wines because nearly all Hungarian wine is bottled in the state cellars, the Magyar Allami Pincegazdaság, which are found throughout the country and in Budafok, near Budapest. Wines do, however, carry the name of the district where they were made together with the grape name, which is often the wine name as well. The exception to this rule is Hungary's most famous wine, Tokay.

The most common terms found on labels are Minösegi Bor (best quality wine), Borkülönlegessége Szölögazdáságanak (a specialty from the vineyards of the region named), Asztali Bor (table wine), Palackozott (bottled), together with Fehér (white), Vörös (red), Száraz (dry), Edes (sweet) and Habzó (sparkling).

Location of vineyards

About half of Hungary's 250,000 acres of vineyards are situated on the central Great Plains along the Danube river but the vines are rapidly being replaced with tobacco plants. The remaining vineyards are scattered among the hills that run across the country, roughly south-west to north-east, and end up in the Tokay hills near the border with the USSR. Although local vines are grown, foreign ones flourish as well, such as the Italian riesling (olaszrizling), sylvaner, the pinot gris of Alsace, the pinot noir of Burgundy and the muscatel.

Great Plains
Copious amounts of pleasant red and white wines, the *vins ordinaires* of Hungary, are made here mostly from the common grapes. The best wines of the region are Leányka, Olaszrizling, Ezerjó, Kövidinka, Mézesfehér and Kadarka.

Szekszárd, Pécs, Vilany and Mecsek
Mostly light, fruity red wines like Nagyburgundi and Kadarka are produced in these southern districts. The predominant grapes are the kadarka and the pinot noir.

Lake Balaton
A number of wine-growing districts are to be found along its northern and southern shores, producing the best Hungarian table wines, notably Szürkebarát, Kéknyelyü, Furmint, Olaszrizling and Szilvani.

Mór
This is another historical wine region, north of Lake Balaton, which grows ezerjó grapes. The distinctive white wine of the same name is dry and highly flavoured.

Somló
An isolated hill district, north-west of Lake Balaton, Somló is sited on an extinct volcano. One of the historical wine regions, it grows predominantly furmint and Italian riesling vines which produce white wines of the same name. There was once a family tradition in the House of Habsburg that princes and dukes should drink Somló wine on their wedding night in order to procreate a son and heir.

Sopron
This historical wine region extends to the Austrian border; its vineyards are very near the Burgenland wine district. Their best wines are the red Kékfrankas and the white Veltellini and Tramini.

Barsonyos-Csaszar
This is a new district formed in 1959; it lies west of Budapest, close to the Czechoslovakian border and is best known for its dry white wine.

Eger
The second largest wine region, it was created by the combination in 1959 of the historical wine regions of Gyöngyös-Visonta and Debrö. It lies north-east of Budapest along the southern range of the Matra mountains. The best known wines of the Debrö district are Hárslevelü, Olaszrisling and Kadarka.

The town of Eger gives its name to the region and is the centre of the wine

industry for the full-bodied Bikavér or Bull's Blood wine which may have been so named because it is alleged to have given strength to Magyar armies which successfully defended the town of Eger from invasion by the Turks during the 16th–17th centuries.

This wine is made from a blend of kadarka, the Bordeaux merlot and the Burgundy pinot noir grapes. In Hungary the merlot is called the médoc noir and the pinot nagyburgundi.

Tokay

A tiny village on the Bodrog river in northeast Hungary, Tokay gives its name not only to the surrounding wine district but also to the almost legendary sweet white wine that was once so esteemed and coveted by the Czars of Russia because it was held to possess marvellous therapeutic qualities.

The volcanic hills of the region are covered with a rich lava soil in which the furmint and hárslevelü vines flourish, and although these same vines grow elsewhere, only in Tokay are the grapes attacked by the 'noble rot' fungi as they are in Sauternes. The wines made from these *aszú* grapes, as they are called in Hungary, make the finest of all Tokay wines, which are sweet, intensely flavoured and very strong.

The ordinary dry Tokay wine is made in the usual way from ripe grapes but the fine Tokay is made differently. The *aszú* grapes are crushed to a pulp in special wooden tubs called *puttonyos*. These are added to 35-gallon barrels called *gönci* which hold a one-year-old wine. From three to six *puttonyos* of pulp may be added, depending on the amount of sweetness required and the number of *puttonyos* determines the quality of the Tokay wine. If none have been added, the wine is called Szamarodni or dry and is the most common Tokay available. The finer, lush dessert wines are made entirely of *aszú* grapes (that is, with five *puttonyos*) and labelled Tokay Aszú.

The famous golden Tokay Eszencia of the Czars was made only from the undiluted juice that burst from the *aszú* grapes of its own accord. It was so rich in sugar that it hardly fermented at all and its ageing qualities were tremendous. Wine of this type is still made today but is used mostly for sweetening purposes; existing stocks of the rare Eszencia are known to be at least 200 years old and fetch extremely high prices.

Bulgaria

Vines have always grown in Bulgaria, particularly around the Black Sea and the region bordering on Greece which was once part of Thrace; some of the wines are in fact called Trakia, meaning Thrace.

The marks of the centuries-long occupation of Bulgaria by the Turks can be seen in the food and dress of the country and in its architecture; Muslim laws forbad the consumption of alcohol. During the last 30 years, however, Bulgaria has made a rapid recovery, bringing the wine industry out of obscurity and making the export of wine a valuable earner of foreign currency.

This remarkable growth is due to the massive modernization and development programme introduced by the state, which nationalized the wine industry in 1949. The state monopoly, Vinimpex, handles the export and import of wines and spirits. Bulgaria's best markets are the USSR, Czechoslovakia and Germany, and her wines are now available elsewhere, notably the Bulgarian Cabernet and Riesling, Mavrud and Trakia.

Since no peasant tradition of wine-making survives in Bulgaria, her vineyards are planted on a large scale, suited to cultivation and harvesting by machinery. The mass-produced wine is quickly fermented and blended to give consistently good *vins ordinaires*. However, high quality wines are produced and so favourable are conditions that there is every reason to believe Bulgaria will soon be capable of fine quality wines.

Bulgaria's best wines are white, like those of Hungary and Romania; grapes used are the riesling, sylvaner and furmint, as well as the local misket or muscat, dimiat and rczaziteli. A semi-dry sparkling wine called Iskra is also made.

Bulgarian red wines tend to be soft, light and sweet; grapes used are the cabernet sauvignon, alicante-bouchet, kadarka, the local pamid, mavrud and gamza. The few full-bodied reds like Tirnava and Melnik are made mostly from the common

Below: central Bulgarian wine district

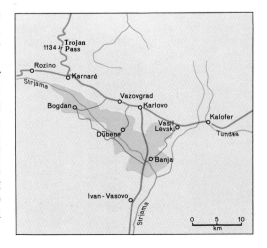

ilicante-bouchet and mavrud vines.

Like other eastern European countries, Bulgaria produces huge quantities of Cabernet and Riesling wines, and to cater for the German market, many of them are given special German names. Bulgaria names her wines after either the district of origin or the grape name or a combination of both. Common terms found on labels include Vinoproizvoditel (wine producer), Butiliram (to bottle), Naturalno (natural), Bjalo Vino (white wine), Cherveno Vino (red wine), Suho Vino (dry wine), Sladko Vino (sweet wine), Iskriashto Vino (sparkling wine). Often these words appear in the Cyrillic alphabet.

Location of vineyards

Vine-growing districts are scattered all over Bulgaria: along the banks of the river Danube and the shores of the Black Sea, in the plains on either side of the Balkan Mountains, and in the west.

Pleven/Vishovgrad and Plovdiv/Asenovgrad

Lying north and south respectively of the Balkans these are the largest red wine districts.

Karlovo and Sungurlare

These are the centres for making Misket, a highly perfumed white wine made from the muscat grape. This wine differs from the usual muscats in that it is completely dry; all the sugar is fermented out and the resulting wine is similar to the Alsatian muscat. The Karlovo vineyards lie in the central Balkans in the Valley of the Roses. Sungurlare, which grows the rczaziteli vine, lies to the east.

Ruse and Silestra

Situated on the Danube, together with some other eastern districts, and the vineyards around Varna and Burgas on the Black Sea, these areas produce mostly white wines, both dry and sweet. Popular wines are Hemus, a medium sweet white, and Tamianka, which is very sweet.

Melnik and Kyustendil

Producing red and white wines respectively these are the principal districts in the south-west and west.

There are a number of small districts in the north-west, some of which are on the Danube, which make undistinguished red wines from the tamianka, gamza and cabernet vines.

Romania

Of all the eastern European wine countries, Romania appears to have the greatest potential for making important wines. She has a long history of wine-making; the Ancient Greeks are thought to have introduced the muscat vine. Many vines are indigenous and soil conditions are very favourable in some areas so that more research and wider education of wine-growers should lead to better wines in years to come.

Romania's modern wine industry is expanding fast and the state is encouraging the planting of experimental vineyards to determine the best vines for the country and the grapes most suitable for its wine-making. Wine production is on a tripartite

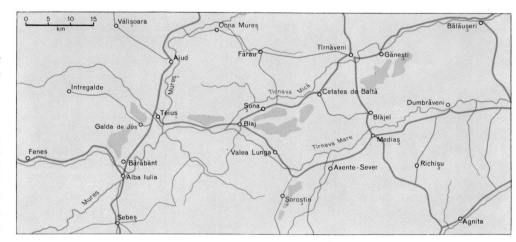

Tirnava in the centre of Romania where Romania's best dry white wines are produced

basis: there are the state agricultural enterprises or the IAS (Intreprinderile Agricole de Stat), regional co-operatives and a number of private firms, all of whom are working towards improving the quality of their wines. The government agency Fructexport handles the expanding wine exports.

Vines are grown in most areas; common native varieties are the feteasca, grasă, galbena and tămîioasă and foreign ones include the noble western European varieties of the cabernet sauvignon, riesling, traminer, pinot noir, chardonnay and aligoté, as well as the Hungarian furmint and kadarka.

White wines predominate in Romania

and range from light dry ones to the rich sweet wines made from grapes with the 'noble rot'. The red wines tend in the main to be soft and rather dull on the palate and, like the few rosé wines made, suffer from over-sweetness.

Wine label terms

Like the Hungarian, the Romanian wines are named either by their place of origin or by the grape variety, or by a combination of both. The place name usually precedes that of the grape.

The most common terms found on labels are Recolta (vintage), Vin Superioare (superior wine), Vin de Masa (table wine), Vin Usoare (light wine), Imbuteliat (bottled) as well as Alba (white), Roşu (red), Rose (rosé), Sec (dry), Dulce (sweet), and Spumos (sparkling).

Location of vineyards

Romanian wine regions are scattered all over the country, from the foothills of the Carpathian Mountains in the north-east and east to the shores of the Black Sea in the south-east, a newly planted area in the south to the western region of Banat and the central plains of Transylvania.

Soil conditions vary greatly; for example, the Black Sea area has a chalky soil and the eastern districts have a rock and lime soil. The northern half of the country has a temperate climate while the southern half is more continental with long, hot, dry summers.

Cotnari

This Moldavian district is renowned for its dessert white wines made from grapes with the 'noble rot'; grape varieties grown are the grasă and muscat. Cotnari wine was once as famous as the Hungarian Tokay.

Iasi and Husi

These are small districts near the USSR border producing red and white wines respectively.

Focşani, Odobeşti and Nicoreşti

The centres of the biggest wine district in Romania, these towns produce good, light wines, mostly red. The red Babească Neagră has a fresh taste reminiscent of cloves. The ordinary wines are usually called Moldavian red or white.

Dealul Mare

This district south of Focşani produces mostly white wine and comprises the largest experimental state vineyard, Valea Călugărească (which means Valley of the Monks).

Murfatlar

Near Constanza on the Black Sea, Murfatlar has vineyards producing sweet white wines rich in sugar and alcohol similar to those of Cotnari.

Drăgăsani, Piteşti and Segarcea

These districts are best known for red wines which tend to be on the sweet side. Grapes used include the cabernet sauvignon, pinot noir, riesling and fetească regală. In the past in Drăgăsani it was the custom for a jug of wine to be left at the gate of every vineyard for passers-by to sample.

Banat

Extensive state vineyards are to be found here concentrated around Arad. A strong Hungarian influence can be seen with the use of the kadarka grape for red wine. The wines of this district are used mostly for blending.

The central plains of Transylvania

Here the best dry white Romanian wines are produced in the district of Tirnava. The vineyards are on the slopes bordering the rivers that rise in the north in the Transylvanian Mountains, and the vines are mostly the finer western European varieties, as well as the furmint and the muscat.

Yugoslavia

The vineyards of Yugoslavia are amongst the oldest in Europe; they grow a great number of vines, many of them indigenous, which produce an incredible variety of white, red and rosé wines. Yugoslavia is at present the tenth largest wine producer in the world; several of her wines, notably the Ljutomer Riesling, Zilavka and Prokupac, are popular in Britain and the USA. One of her biggest export markets is Germany.

The current trend in Yugoslavia's wine industry is towards large co-operatives and, while they do not produce wines of the quality and elegance of the western European vineyards, they do offer consistently good, low-priced wines to meet the demands of the mass market.

Yugoslavian wines are mostly named after their town or district of origin, followed by the grape name, but as there are so many grape varieties, particularly local ones, the labels can be a little confusing. Common terms found on labels are Visokokvalitetno (high quality), Cuveno Vino (selected wine), Stolno Vino (table wine), Punjeno u . . . (bottled by), Proizvedeno u Viastitoj Vinariji Poljoprivedne Zadruge (made in the co-operative cellars of the place named), Prirodno (natural), Bijelo (white), Crno (red), Ruzica (rosé), Biser (sparkling), Suho (dry), Polšuho (medium dry), Slatko (sweet) and Desertno Vino (dessert wine).

The coast of Yugoslavia, with its islands, is an important wine region

Location of vineyards

The major wine regions are Slovenia in the north, parts of Croatia and along the border with Hungary, Dalmatia and central Serbia; lesser regions are Kosovo, Macedonia, Bosnia-Hercegovena and Montenegro.

Slovenia

This area produces the most reliable and best known of Yugoslavia's wines. The dry whites are very similar to those of her neighbours Italy, Austria and Hungary. The Ljutomer, Maribor and Brda districts in the north-east of the province produce notable wines, namely the Lask and Renski Rizlings made from the Italian riesling which is known in Yugoslavia as the graševina. Other grape varieties grown are the sauvignon, traminer, pinot blanc, malvasia, muscat and sipon. The overripe grapes of a local vine, the ranina, are used to make a sweet dessert wine with the unlikely name of Tiger's Milk (Radgonska Ranina).

Croatia

A rapidly expanding region, Croatia produces the largest amount of Yugoslavia's wine. Its wines are similar in style to those of Slovenia, with the addition of a few local wines.

Dalmatia

The vineyards of Dalmatia are scattered along the Adriatic coastline, many of them

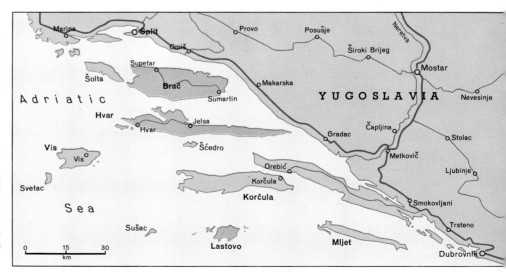

on the islands lying offshore. The emphasis here is on red and rosé wines which vary in colour from dark red to pale pink. Plavac and Dingač, made from local grapes of the same name, are good examples of this region's wines; however, many of them, particularly the island wines like the white Grk of Korčula, Vugava of Vis and Bogdanuša of Hvar, as well as the mainland ones Prošek and Postup, are almost unknown abroad.

The old Turkish town of Mostar, north of Dubrovnik, is the main centre for Zilavka, a dry, fruity white wine.

Serbia
Predominantly a red wine region, Serbia has vineyards concentrated between Smederevo and Vlasotinci. Prokupac, made from the grape of the same name, is the most common red wine of Yugoslavia and is found throughout this region and further south. Light and pleasant to drink, Prokupac can, however, vary and may be dark in colour and almost bitter in taste. A well-flavoured rosé is also made from the same grape. Wines with local names like Zupsko are made from blends of prokupac and plovdina grapes.

Kosovo and Macedonia
These are prolific red wine regions in the south. Kosovo is experimenting with imported vines in an attempt to produce wines after the style of classic French wines for western European markets. Macedonia's best wines are Prokupac and the white Zilavka.

Bosnia-Hercegovina
Yugoslavia's central provinces produce only one wine of note, Zilavka, from a tiny district around Banja Luka.

Montenegro
The province south of Dalmatia has a small wine district around Kotor. Its wines are mostly red and made from the local vranac and plavka grapes.

Vineyards in Slovenia, the most important province in Yugoslavian wine production

Greece

Greece can trace its viticulture back to ancient times, but it was during the 8th and 6th centuries BC that the vine underwent its greatest development.

Unfortunately there are no specific laws for Greek wines today, and so interwoven are the various wine types that defining them is almost impossible.

The principal ancient wine-making zones – and most have survived until today – were located in **Macedonia**, **Thrace,** along the shores of the **Black Sea** and the **Aegean Sea**, **Thessaly**, **Attica** – the area around Athens – and the **Peloponnese**. The islands renowned for their wines included **Crete**, **Samos** and **Rhodes**.

Possibly the best known of Greek wines is Retsina, the resin-flavoured wine which may be red or white. Practised principally in Attica, the ancient method of adding a quantity of resin from a local pine tree, *Callitris quadrivalvis*, to the grape must during fermentation is still in use today. This is what gives Retsina its characteristic bitterness, which increases rather than decreases with age. The addition of resin helps to improve a wine that would be unlikely to survive the extreme heat of a Greek summer.

The other aspect of Greek wines follows the European tradition, and the largest wine-producing zone is the **Peloponnese**. Here there are three regions: the central zone around the ruins of **Mantinia**, the northern zone around **Patras**, and the eastern zone of **Nemea**. Although several white and red table wines are made here from phileri, aghiorghitico, and red and white muscat grapes, two of the best being Demestica, a light red, and Mavrodaphne, a sweetish red, the traditional wines are sweet and white, and are made from muscat, malmsey and a few saviatano grapes.

From the other regions, come wines like Naoussa, an excellent Macedonian red, Ambelakis and Rapsanis, two reds from Thessaly, and Pallini, a white made from saviatano grapes found around the ruins of the temple of Apollo in Delphi.

From the Greek islands comes an assortment of wines: Lindos from Rhodes, the sweet white Muscat of Samos, Verdea from Zakinthos, and Malvazia, Creta and Minos from Crete.

Cyprus

Cyprus has one of the oldest traditions of wine-making in the world and the mixed fortunes of its wine industry are due to the fact that the island has changed hands so many times over the centuries. Britain's association with Cyprus dates from the Holy Crusades of the 11th and 12th centuries when Richard the Lionheart, King of England, captured the island from the Turks. Later, in the reign of Elizabeth I, a flourishing wine trade grew up between the countries and Cypriot merchants established themselves at Southampton.

The Turks subsequently re-occupied the island and under their rule the wine industry began to diminish although it did not die out completely.

The revival of Cypriot vineyards began in 1878 when Britain took over the administration of the island; then in 1956 a commission was set up to report on ways of modernizing the ancient vinification and cultivation methods of the islanders and of bringing the wines more into line with the tastes of northern export markets. Today, one-fifth of the population is engaged in the wine industry which is run by four firms: the family shipping concern of EKTO, founded over a century ago, the co-operatives of KEO and SODAP, also founded several years ago, and Haggipavlu, a family firm which makes about 55% of the island's brandy.

Now that well-organized co-operatives and firms are making the wine and it is no longer at the mercy of the press-houses of badly equipped vineyards, considerable progress has been made in improving wines that were basically very sweet and strong. The greatest advance is in the sherry-type wines that make up nearly 80% of Cyprus's wine. KEO recently produced an excellent *fino* sherry made in the traditional Jerez style by using a native flor; it is a very fine aperitif wine and bodes well for the future. Table wines still have far to go and although they are good, they are unlikely ever to be great.

Like other Commonwealth countries, Cyprus has enjoyed a preferential duty on wine imports to Great Britain for many years and as a result her wines have been substantially cheaper than those of her competitors. However, Britain's entry into the European Economic Community

Cypriot vineyards in the west of the island near Platres

meant that to comply with EEC rules and policy, this preferential duty had to end and Cyprus is now anxiously watching market trends to see how her wine industry will be affected.

Most Cypriot wine is produced from three local grapes: the black mavron, the white xynisteri and the muscat; very few vines have been imported for fear of phylloxera which has never struck the island's vineyards. Although most growers now sell their grapes direct to the shippers or co-operatives who are based on Limassol, the commercial centre and port on the southern coast, there are still growers following the peasant tradition of vinification; they store their new wine in stone amphorae, which are wrapped in goat hair, vine ash and resin, then planted in the ground and left to mature for many years. Such archaic methods are obviously inadequate for a modern industry.

Location of vineyards

Although the hot, arid climate and poor soil conditions are far from favourable to the vine, viticulture is made possible by the Troodos Mountains in the west of the island which attract rain. The vineyards follow the course of the rain and lie on high south-facing slopes.

The most famous Cypriot wine is Commandaria, a sweet red dessert wine of the port type that has great ageing qualities. It has been known to last at least 30 years. The name is derived from the Knights Templar; during the Crusades they established estates on the island at the Grande

Commanderie, Kolossi (now preserved a[t] Kolossi Castle), the Phoenix at Paphos an[d] Templos at Kyrenia. The Knights Templa[r] and their successors the Knights of St Joh[n] made their wine in the classic traditio[n] and the vineyards were planted with re[d] and white grapes; to this day, Comma[n]daria is still made from a mixture of th[e] two grapes.

Although they are no longer intense[ly] sweet, Commandaria wines reminiscen[t] of the legendary flavour of the past can sti[ll] be found. Cypriots usually drink Comma[n]daria as a liqueur and sometimes dilute [it] with a lighter wine or even water.

Other wine villages are Platres, know[n] for its reds and rosés, and Paphos an[d] Pitsilia, centres for white wine.

The white wines are dry and ful[l] bodied, and have an unmistakable flavou[r] of their own; red wines are also ful[l] bodied, very dark in colour and fruity b[ut] they are on the sweet side. The rosé win[e] called Kokkineli because they are coloure[d] with cochineal or similar colouring matte[r] are quite heady and they are unusual[ly] dark and full in flavour.

The wines most likely to be foun[d] abroad, apart from the Cyprus sherrie[s] are the white Kolossi, Aphrodite an[d] Arsinoe; a new wine very popular i[n] Cyprus is Bellapais, a slightly sparklin[g] white which may soon be produced in bul[k] and exported. Red wines include Koloss[i] Othello and Afames, as well as Rosel[la] rosé which is light and fairly dry.

Turkey

One of the many birthplaces of European viticulture was probably the vast region of Anatolia in Turkey, for it was here that the sylvestris variety of *Vitis vinifera* grew wild. It later spread northwards to Russia and central Europe and southwards to Syria, Greece, Italy and throughout the whole of the Mediterranean basin. The Turks may have been responsible for introducing the vine into China.

Although Turkey is one of the largest grape-growing countries in the eastern Mediterranean, only a tiny proportion of the grapes is made into wine; most grapes are eaten. The reason for this is that Turkey is a Muslim country so there is no domestic market for wine.

The recent growth of tourism in Turkey has led the Turkish government to encourage the development of the wine industry but progress is slow. The state monopoly has several wineries and controls the export of wine; there are also a number of private firms.

The north-west region around **Istanbul** and **Tekirdağ** on the shores of the Marmara Sea produces several white wines, the best known being Guzel Marmara, dry and sweet, Marmara Incisi, and Beyaz which is also sweet. Trakya, made from the sémillon grape, is a dry white wine.

The other notable Turkish wines are red, the best being Trakya, Buzbag and Izmir – all dry, light and fruity.

Turkish brandy is surprisingly good, coming closer to Cognac than the brandies of most other European countries.

Below: though much is being done in Turkey today to modernize agriculture, methods are still largely primitive; here is a group of workers in the north of the country
Right: northern Israel where the Binyamina wine district is situated

Israel

As in other countries of the eastern Mediterranean, wine was known in Israel many thousands of years ago. According to students of the Old Testament, Noah's planting the vine, drinking its wine and his subsequent intoxication as related in the Book of Genesis took place in 2347 BC; and the scouts whom Moses sent ahead of the children of Israel to spy out the Land of Canaan returned with bunches of grapes.

What was a thriving industry was suddenly abandoned almost to the point of extinction in the 8th century with the Muslim occupation, and it was not until the late 19th century that vineyards began once more to flourish.

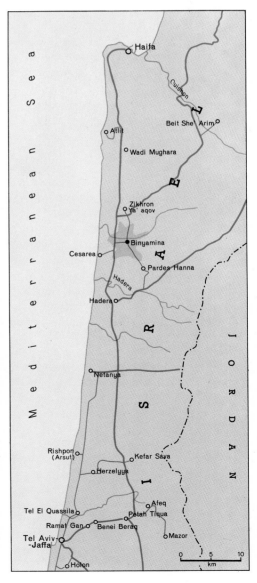

end of the last century.

The best known red wines are Ashkelon (also a white wine), Mikwe Israel from Rishon-le-Zion, Adom Atic and Château Richon, a sweet wine. Binyamina, on the slopes of Mount Carmel, produces a light dry red.

White grapes grown are the sémillon, clairette and muscat. The best known white wines are Avdat White, Carmel Hock, made from blended wines from the müller-thurgau grape, and Muscatel; the first two wines are dry and the Muscatel is a sweet dessert wine. Binyamina is also renowned for several white and rosé wines. The white wine is straw-yellow in colour, becoming amber with age; its bouquet is marked and reminiscent of its vine, and its taste is dry but delicate and pleasant.

Vermouth and some sherry-type wines are made and exported.

Above: carignan grapes, imported from France in the last century, are now grown in vineyards throughout the country to produce light red wines

Location of vineyards

Baron Edmond de Rothschild, of Bordeaux fame, gave growers the necessary impetus when he founded a large winery at Rishon-le-Zion in the **Sefala Plain** south of Tel Aviv. This region, together with that of **Zikhron Ya'aqov** to the north of Tel Aviv, now accounts for at least three-quarters of Israel's wine. The Baron helped and financed many viticultural projects and persuaded wine-growers to start a Co-operative Society, which is still in existence today.

Other wine-growing areas quickly sprang up around **Binyamina** and **Zikhron Ya'aqov** in the north, and as far south of Tel Aviv as **Be'er Sheva.**

Modern wine-making techniques enable Israel to produce a wide variety of wines despite the hot dry climate. Most of the wines are light and medium dry, and growing exports are encouraging further experiments.

The Israelis drink about 80% of their own wine, but a large proportion of Israel's exports go to the USA; there is also a growing demand for Kosher wines.

More red than white wine is made, and the principal red wine grapes grown are the alicante-grenache, carignan, alicante-bouchet, sirah and cabernet, all of which were imported from France towards the

North Africa

The wine industry of North Africa has developed differently from that of other countries. For many years, North Africa was colonized by the French who supervised the planting of vineyards on a very large scale, particularly in the green, fertile valleys and hills of Algeria.

In the 1950s, Algeria and Morocco between them produced almost two-thirds of the world's wine, but because the Muslim religion forbids alcohol and the indigenous European population was – and still is – far too small to support the home industry, the wine was made for export. Vast quantities of wine were sent to France.

However, in 1962 the situation altered drastically. Morocco had won independence in the late 1950s, and now Algeria too declared independence. Lengthy and bitter argument with France, coupled with the latter's development of new techniques in wine-making, brought about the virtual cessation of the wine trade between the two countries. So new markets had to be found, and Germany and the USSR have replaced France as major buyers of North African wine.

The qualities that have given North African wine a prominent role in wine production are these: light acidity (making it ideal for blending with over-acid wines), high alcohol content (between 12–15%), and quick ageing. As a result of blending, enormous quantities of good *vins ordinaires* can be made.

Location of vineyards

Algeria
The Algerian vineyards are situated mainly in the provinces of Oran and Algiers. During the French administration, several wine regions were given VDQS status, and among the best known are the hills of Tlemcen, around Mascara and Mostagenem, in the Dahra region, and in the hills of Zaccar and Medea.

The vineyards are mostly planted with carignan, morrastel, grenache, alicante, clairette, faranah, and muscat grapes.

Morocco
Here the vineyards are comparatively new; many of them were not planted until after World War II. They are found to the east around the town of Oujda, to the south and east of the capital Rabat and stretching inland to the towns of Meknes and Fez, and also to the south of Casablanca.

The wine is mainly red and rosé, and is very light and pleasant to drink. The main red wine grapes used are carignan, cinsault, grenache and alicante-bouchet.

Tunisia
This country produces a few red wines, notably Thibar, Rhades and Kelibia, but her principal claim to wine fame is Muscat, a very sweet wine made from the grape of the same name.

Egypt
She has one of the longest histories of wine-making; but her modern wine industry did not begin until 1903 when the Gianaclis vineyards to the west of the Nile delta near Alexandria were planted. The Egyptian climate is very well suited to the vine. Most of the wine produced is white, the best known names including Cru des Ptolomées and Clos de Mariout; the best known of Egypt's red wines is Clos Matamix. Unfortunately there are very few regulations governing wine-making.

USA

The West Coast

California has always been considered one of the golden states of the Union and this is nowhere better demonstrated than in its wine production; the state makes 80% of all the wines in the USA. Although some excellent wines are produced in the valleys of the San Francisco Bay zone, about 60% of Californian wines are the less expensive, sweet dessert types. Fortunately, the consumer is becoming more discerning and there is a growing trend towards drinking the drier table wines whose more subtle nuances are not disguised by sugar.

There are approximately 420,000 acres under vine in California, planted in a wide variety of sites, for example, at 200 ft below sea level in the Coachella Valley, and through all the intermediate altitudes to 4,000 ft in the Owens Valley. Rainfall in the northern areas may reach 36 in, but in the southern semi-desert zones, it may only be four in a year.

The soils vary enormously from the

California, showing the major vineyard areas in this fertile state

granitic schists of the Napa Valley to the alluvial soils of the Central Valley and the arid sand areas of the south.

Indifferent wine has been made in California in the past because high yield, poor quality vines have been used such as alicante-bouchet and carignan for red wines and the sauvignon vert, colombard and thompson seedless for whites. Today, with the help of scientific research from the University of California at Davis, the vines are better matched to their local environment and, wherever possible, the more classic vines such as the cabernets, pinots, rieslings and sémillons, are used.

Location of vineyards

There are two major wine zones in California: the San Francisco Bay coastal region and the Central Valley; there is also a minor zone near Los Angeles. The valleys of Sonoma, Napa, Livermore, Santa Clara and San Benito run like fingers from the San Francisco Bay and benefit from its tempering influence; the vineyards here produce the finest wines.

In the warmer climate of the Central Valley zone – on the flat, rich soil of Sacramento, San Joaquin Valley, and the districts to the south – the sweet fortified wines, often a by-product of the table grape industry, are made.

California's wine labelling is some of the simplest to understand. It is also very informative, stating clearly the grape variety, the producer, the locality and, in exceptional cases, the vineyard.

California's wine history

The history of California's wines dates back to the Spanish Conquest of Mexico in the early part of the 16th century, but it was not until 1697 when the Jesuits first entered lower California that there were records of grapes being grown there at Mission San Xavier.

The early vines were of European origin, but there is only one positively identifiable type, the aptly named mission grape which is still grown in California today. For 130 years after the first missions were founded, the Church was responsible for introducing vineyards further and further north, to produce wines for their sacramental needs.

In 1832 the power and influence of the Church came to an end when the Mexican government secularized the missions; the cultivation of the vineyards and the production of wine came to a halt.

About this time, wine-making was taken up by pioneers such as Joseph Chapman and a Frenchman, Jean-Louis Vignes. The latter arrived from Bordeaux in the late 1820s and brought with him the knowledge and expertise to make high quality wines from his noble Bordeaux vines. In the following years many more men took to the culture of the vine, and their achievements appear all the more remarkable when one considers their non-viticultural backgrounds.

Until 1850 most of the grapes grown in California were of Spanish origin. It was not until the arrival in California of a versatile Hungarian aristocrat, Agoston Haraszthy, that the European *Vitis vinifera* varieties were imported in quantity.

Haraszthy was a man of vision; he quickly noted that climatic conditions were perfect for the vine in California and established his Buena Vista vineyard in Sonoma in 1857. Sponsored by Governor John G. Downey, he arranged an expedition to Europe to purchase vine plants in 1861. His tour took him to France, Italy, Spain and his native Hungary, and he selected root stocks from which today's Californian varieties have been propagated. On his return from Europe with 100,000 vines, he organized their distribution to growers in his state. He experimented with planting and pruning and passed on the results to his fellow vineyard owners.

During the early 1850s, the Gold Rush brought a great boost to Californian wine-makers because of the influx of European

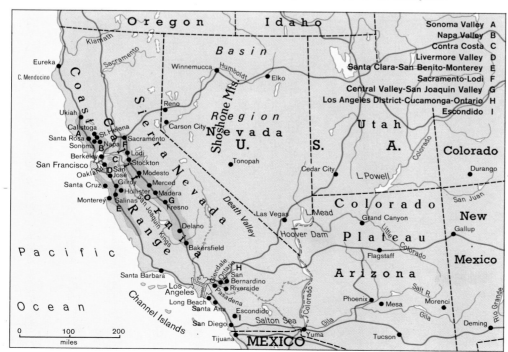

speculators. This boom lasted into the 1870s – a period when many of today's leading Californian wine names came into being.

However, prosperity and growth did not last; in 1873 there was a national economic crisis. Some vineyards were forced to close down and others had to sell wine for the production of vinegar. This crisis was followed by one more serious – an attack of the vine louse phylloxera.

The first signs of the phylloxera disease appeared in about 1870, but wine-growers took little notice since they believed that the rich Californian soils would sustain their plants. They were wrong; by 1890, the majority of Californian vineyards had been devastated and vineyard owners had to resort to the European remedy of grafting to American vines root stocks that had proved immune from the disease. These two disasters finally convinced wine-growers and wine-makers of the need to form a unified body to control the industry. In 1880, a State Board of Viticulturists was elected to advise and educate both the industry and the public.

The next crisis to hit the wine industry was Prohibition. In the first 15 years of this century, 6,000,000 immigrants arrived in the USA from Europe – and wine consumption increased accordingly, to the alarm of the rapidly growing temperance movement. Prohibitionists found their way to power through election in several states and in 1920 the National Prohibition Act was passed.

The output of wine was hit at an early stage; the production figures for 1912 were in the region of 50,000,000 gallons but by 1915 this had decreased to 12,000,000 gallons. Wine was still obtainable, although only officially for medicinal and sacramental purposes, and production was sustained until the Prohibition Act was repealed in 1933 when the industry had to re-establish its image. Aided by the State Board of Viticultural Commissioners, the University of California, the Department of Health and the Federal Government, new standards were laid down. Since that time Californian wines have continued to improve in quality; and today their high standard compares favourably with the wines from other parts of the world.

Above: vineyards on flat country outside Delano
Right: for the grape harvest in California much migrant labour is needed

The principal zones

San Francisco Bay

Some 45 miles north of San Francisco is the Sonoma Valley, a district noted for producing quality wines; it is separated from the neighbouring Napa Valley by the Mayacamas Mountains.

The wine history of this area can be traced back to the Franciscan missions, but their vineyards were taken over by the Mexican Mariano Vallejo in the 1830s. The most important man in Sonoma's early wine history was Agoston Haraszthy who founded his famous Buena Vista vineyard in 1857.

There are about 11,400 acres of vineyard covering the Sonoma Valley, Santa Rosa and the Russian river valley, including 28 wineries, five of which are in and around the town of Sonoma itself. The best known of these is Buena Vista, which

suffered mixed fortunes – the 1906 earthquake and conversion into a prison farm – before it was finally re-established in 1943 by Frank Bartholomew. The present owners make some good red wines from zinfandel grapes, still and sparkling whites, and some port- and sherry-types.

The other winery of note is Sebastiani, which is famous for its red wines, especially Barbera which is made from grapes of the same name, as well as some Cabernet and Pinot Noir wines.

A small but specialized vineyard and winery worthy of mention is the Hanzell property designed as a replica of the famed Clos de Vougeot in Burgundy. Its owner, the late James D. Zellerbach, wanted to make wines of the calibre of French Burgundies and therefore grew pinot and chardonnay grapes. It is difficult to make comparisons of wines from vineyard locations so far apart but one can say

that they are both fine and interesting. Other vineries in the district are Pagani Brothers, near Kenwood, and the Valley of the Moon winery situated on the east side of the Sonoma Creek.

In the Russian river basin area to the west of Santa Rosa there are 56 wineries, and the most important of these is Korbel, whose antecedents arrived here from Czechoslovakia in 1862. The company is known for its sparkling wines made by a somewhat automated version of the Champagne process, a Cabernet Sauvignon and a Pinot Noir red, some white wines from the grey riesling and the inevitable dessert wines.

To the north, the vineyard area stretches from Sonoma up into Mendocino county, following the Russian river valley and is concentrated around the town of Ukiah. The majority of the wines are reds of an average quality and may come

Left: a 'gondola' of wine grapes is dumped into a crusher
Above: the vintage in California is a thoroughly well run operation

from Italian Swiss Colony, Cambiaso, L. Foppiano, Parducci, Rege, Simi or Mendocino Vineyards.

The Napa Valley

The word *napa* in Indian means plenty — a very apt description for a valley so rich in vineyards and wines. Situated one hour's drive north of San Francisco, the valley stretches from Napa in the south, some 15 miles north through the elegant little town of St Helena, on to the small spa town of Calistoga. There are approximately 13,000 acres of vineyard, planted for the most part on the valley floor, but the quality of the small amount grown on the slopes of the valley suggests that some

good quality wines could be made there.

Climatically and geologically, this area is divided into two: the wide, lower half of the valley between Napa and Rutherford, which has a rich, almost heavy soil and a cooler climate than the upper half owing to the influence of San Francisco Bay; and the upper half of the valley, which has a gravelly soil well-suited to the vine, and a warmer climate afforded by the surrounding mountains.

Napa is the home of California's top quality red wines that are made from the cabernet sauvignon grape. They are full-bodied and take some years of maturing in bottle before they show their finest qualities. The pinot noir of Burgundy fame is also planted but does not give wines of the quality of the Cabernets, while the white chardonnay produces beautiful, subtle wines reminiscent of French Meursaults.

For wines of lesser quality, the useful zinfandel is grown; other European grape varieties do well in the valley but most growers prefer to concentrate on making increasingly fine wines from vines that have already proved well suited to the area and commercially successful.

There are many impressive wineries, mostly found in the upper half of the valley; they include Inglenook, Beaulieu, Louis M. Martini, Beringer Brothers, Christian Brothers (Champagne Cellars), Charles Krug and Hans Kornell.

On the east side of the valley is the beautiful new Chappellet winery and further north there are the cellars of Joseph Heitz and Souverain. On the west side there are the Schramsberg Champagne Cellars and the Sterling winery.

South of Rutherford in the lower half of the valley is the magnificent new Robert Mondavi winery and high up in

93

the Mayacamas the Christian Brothers have their vineyards around the Mount La Salle winery and Novitiate.

Apart from the wineries named, there is the continuing expansion of co-operative groups who play an increasing role in the development of the wine industry.

The Livermore Valley

In Alameda and Contra Costa counties, urbanization is encroaching on the prime sites of the early vineyards. Nevertheless the Livermore Valley survives as a distinct district, famed for its stylish white wines.

The term valley is used rather loosely here for the area is in fact a dried-up basin with a characteristic gravelly soil remarkably similar to that of the Médoc and Rhône Valley in France.

Charles Whetmore and Louis Mel first brought the sémillon and sauvignon vines from Bordeaux and planted them at Liver-

more in the 1880s, but today their Cresta Blanca property has lost its former renown. The most important wineries are the Concannon Vineyard and Wente Brothers.

The wines of this district were formerly the heavier-style whites but today controlled fermentations and early bottling combine to give a wide range of wines from a crisp, dry Mosel-type to the smooth, delicate Sauternes-type. Reds, ports and sparkling wines are also made in this district, an indication of the combined versatility of nature and man.

Five miles over the ridge from Livermore lies Pleasanton, known as much for its cheese as its wines. There are two wineries of note, Ruby Hill, which produces a wide range of wines from many different grape types, and Villa Armando, whose wines are mostly sold for distribution in the eastern USA.

In the south of Alameda county, near

San Francisco, is a dwindling wine district at Mission San José and Irvington. The firm of Weibel Champagne Vineyards is the most important in the district, making some interesting sparkling wines by the Charmat bulk process, some *solera*-blended sherries and a range of table wines from varietal vines. The other winery in south Alameda is Davis Bynum, but most of their wines are made from grapes processed at St Helena in the Napa Valley.

There are only two wineries in Martinez in Contra Costa; they are J. E. Digardi and Conrad Viano, who make the usual range of wines, port- and sherry-types from a number of grapes, including gamay, zinfandel, sauvignon, cabernet and

Below: grapes are pressed in modern automatic presses
Right: wine is matured in vast wooden tanks that look like traditional casks

barbera, grown in vineyards on the very fertile slopes of Mount Diablo.

Santa Clara and San Benito

South of San Francisco Bay lie the last wine-growing districts of the northern coastal region, Santa Clara and San Benito.

San José was the early centre for wine-growing in Santa Clara but increased population has reduced vineyard sites. There are still some of the original wineries in the south-eastern part of San José, but many are now buying their grapes from areas up to 100 miles away in the Pinnacles-Piacines region.

The towns of Los Gatos, Cupertino and Saratoga, which are situated to the west of San José, were particularly well chosen for wineries as they nestle in the foothills of the Santa Cruz mountains, and are not subject to fogs from the Pacific.

The major wineries in north Santa Clara are Almaden, Paul Masson, Martin Ray, David Bruce, Ridge, the Novitiate of Los Gatos, a Jesuit seminary where wines are made to support teaching activities, and Pichetti; between them they make up a vast spectrum of stylish wines.

Over to the south-east of San José, on the slopes of Mount Hamilton, is Mirassou, the sole survivor of the former Evergreen vineyard district. Like many of the wineries around San José, it too is moving its operations down to the Salinas Valley.

As you travel south from San José, the valley narrows at Hecker Pass. Here, around the town of Gilroy, the wine industry is dominated by Italian family-owned businesses such as Bertero, Conrotto, Guglielmo, Bonesio, Giretti, Pappani, Solis, Pedrizetti and others. As one might expect, the wines are mostly produced from Italian grapes such as barbera and grignolino, although many other varieties are used including zinfandel and cabernet for reds, and grey riesling, sauvignon and sémillon for whites. Apart from these table wines, much vermouth is made as well as the usual port- and sherry-types.

San Benito and Monterey counties are the developing districts for planting new vineyards to replace those around San José and other cities. Hollister is the main wine centre in San Benito, but to date the output is comparatively small.

When large companies were looking for new vineyard sites, they were attracted to the Salinas Valley, following research carried out by the University of California. It was discovered that valleys like Salinas provide cool air corridors running inland from the Pacific and give a cooler, more stable climate than even the Napa Valley. Wine-growing in the region is still in its infancy, but its potential is obviously great since such large businesses as Paul Masson, Almaden, Wente Brothers and Mirassou have already established wineries there. It is believed, but not fully proven, that by judicious selection of vines and sites, this valley may well produce the best wines in California.

South of Monterey county is San Luis Obispo. The county boasts only a small area of 400 acres around the town of Templeton and makes some average wines from zinfandel and a number of other grape varieties. The only wineries are Presenti, Rotta and York Mountain.

The Central Valley

The major lowland feature in California is the extensive inland Central Valley, the centre of the state's agriculture and also the largest bulk wine-producing region in the USA. In the hot summers, on rich alluvial soils, the vines give high grape yields that were formerly suited only to table use and for making sweet fortified wines. With the change in consumers' taste, there is now a demand for table wines so that many farmers have planted hybrid vines and the district is now making distinctive table wines.

In the northern half of the valley, drained by the Sacramento river, mass-produced dessert wines are made in Placer, Yolo, Butte and Amador counties, but the most important district is Sacramento-Lodi. Here, co-operative wineries dominate the scene, making a wide range of wines from grapes such as the cabernet and pedro ximenez.

South of Lodi, one finds an area which produces about 65% of the state's total output. Extensive vineyards are planted on the valley floor in San Joaquin, Stanislaus and Merced counties. The grapes are picked and transported to one of the 35 wineries located in the towns of Escalon, Manteca, Modesto, Salida and Livingston, and, although the table grape industry is important, wine production is also expanding. A large percentage of the wines are dessert types of average quality; for higher quality wines, some of the larger wineries buy entire crops from the Napa and Sonoma Valleys.

In viticultural terms, the climate is perfect for high grape yields: the rainfall is between 11–18 inches a year, hot summers average 18°C between June–October, there are rich, irrigated, alluvial soils, and vine diseases seldom occur. The most important wineries are Gallo, Cadlolo, Delicato Cellars, Franzia Brothers, Bella Napoli and Pirrone Wine.

Proceeding south down the San Joaquin Valley, one comes to Madera county and the wine town of the same name. There are two wineries in the district, Bisceglia Brothers and Ficklin, who produce California's best port.

Next to Madera is Fresno and at this point, where the valley is wide and flat, dessert wines predominate. The dry wines are disappointing because they lack acidity and leave a rather dull palate.

Wine companies in Fresno include Roma, United Vintners, Del Rey Co-operative, Farnesi, A. Nonini and Crestview. The vineyard districts extend southwards to Kings, Tulare and Kern counties at centres such as Hanford, Cutler, Tulare and a large acreage between Arvin and Delano in Kern county, but many wines are shipped elsewhere for processing and distribution.

Los Angeles district

Vineyards were first planted in and around Los Angeles in the 1830s, but as population increased, wine-growing districts disappeared.

The most important vineyards in southern California are one hour's drive east of Los Angeles at Cucamonga-Ontario in the Pomona Valley. The vineyards are planted in the scree at the foot of the San Gabriel mountains which form the northern boundary of the district, and the climate in these parts is warm and dry. Wines of all varieties are made but in general they do not keep well because they lack acidity. The trade, therefore, has a substantial 'take home' business and local distribution for many of the wines which may include so-called clarets, chiantis and burgundies. Zinfandel is used to make many of the reds, while some rosés are made from the grignolino grape, and some pleasant, but not outstanding, still and sparkling wines from varieties including emerald riesling. The mission grape and palomino were used for sherry-types. The other notable district in southern California is Escondido, producing Muscats.

Stainless steel tanks are now often used to ferment, store and age wine

The East Coast

Recent evidence suggests that North America was in fact discovered by the Vikings long before 1492 when Columbus sailed the Atlantic, and the name the Vikings gave to this land was Vinland. Such a name is appropriate because North America is the natural habitat of over 70% of the world's vine varieties. Unfortunately, few of these varieties make good table wine and it is the type of grape that divides the wine styles of the East Coast from those of the West.

The eastern states grow the native varieties of *Vitis labrusca, rotundifolia*, and *riparia* whereas California grows the European *Vitis vinifera*, the source of Europe's finest wines. This is a generalization but to the layman the difference becomes clear when a glass of wine from one variety is tasted against another; an East Coast wine has a 'foxy' or musty taste.

East Coast wine history

In the east, early settlers tried to make wine from native European vines that they brought with them but they could not withstand either the severe cold of the American winter or the humidity of summer – an ideal condition for diseases of the vine.

The first successful wines came from a North American-European cross by William Penn's gardener, John Alexander, after whom the grape was named.

Many experiments were carried out to find a vine that would produce good quality wines in the North American climate. They produced the varieties common today such as concord, duchess, delaware, catawba, ives, niagara and noah. (The wines take their names from the grape varieties.) Few of these grapes are of great importance in terms of wine production except perhaps the concord, which is used for Kosher wine. All the grapes are hybrids but the search continues for a hardy American-European cross. To overcome the characteristic 'foxy' flavour, many companies import Californian wines for blending.

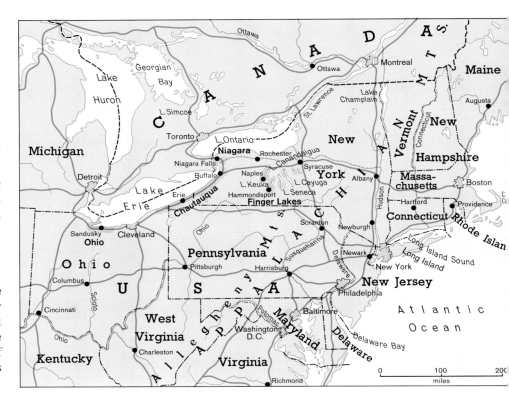

Above: East Coast wine districts are to be found in several states
Left: thompson seedless grapes, a New York varietal. Experiments continue today to find a grape variety that does not give a 'foxy'-tasting wine

Location of vineyards

New York

This region, which borders on the Finger Lakes some 200 miles north-west of New York, is the largest producer of American wine outside California. The vineyard were first planted in the 1830s and have expanded because public interest in wine has greatly increased.

The continental climate – very cold winters and hot summers – is not entirely suited to the vine, but the influence of humidity in the Finger Lakes district and nearby Lake Ontario provides a more temperate micro-climate than the surrounding countryside so that the vine can produce grapes and survive the winter. Even so, there are still the natural hazards of short periods of excessive winter cold, drought in summer and frost in the all-important ripening period in the autumn.

The Finger Lakes

The lakes are the result of glacial carving in the surface of the earth. The ridges along the lakesides, where most vineyards are to be found, rise to 1,600 ft and slope down to the water's edge, so providing good drainage.

Wine production is centred around two of the Finger Lakes. On Lake Keuka, at Hammondsport, Taylors-Mount Pleasant have their winery where, apart from their excellent Great Western sparkling wines, they produce red and white still wines from American varietals and hybrids, and process and bottle some Californian wines, particularly Muscatels.

To the north of Hammondsport on the western shore of Lake Keuka, Urbana have their Gold Seal vineyards and make their Charles Fournier sparkling wines. They also produce still wines and, like many other wine companies, are experimenting with the *Vitis vinifera* grape variety in the belief that the brightest prospects for the future lie in this variety or its hybrids.

At Naples, on Lake Canandaigua, the old-established firm of Widmers have their vineyard and winery and, unlike their counterparts at Hammondsport, they use only native American vine varieties. Their sparkling wines and sherries are, therefore, distinctive in their 'foxiness' but are none the less well made.

There are vineyards in the environs of Lakes Seneca and Cayuga but they do not have the importance of the former two.

The Hudson River Valley

There are two wine-growing districts in the valley, one at Highland and the other at Newburgh. The latter is about 70 miles north of New York City and is known more for its table grapes than for its wine; however, a fair percentage of the output of concord grapes is sold for use in Kosher wine.

Eighteen miles north of Newburgh is Highland, where the Bolognesi family, owners of the Hudson River Valley Company, make some good wines from native American varietals and hybrids.

View of recently built wine cellars at Naples, New York

Chatauqua

The tempering effect of Lake Erie gives the Chatauqua district a micro-climate suitable for wine-growing, similar to the Finger Lakes district. The district stretches from Buffalo, south-west down the south shore of Lake Erie, past Lake Chatauqua from which it takes its name, down to Ohio after passing through a small area of Pennsylvania. The most common grape in the district is the concord, the produce of which is almost exclusively used in Kosher wine.

Niagara

This is only a small district situated between Lakes Ontario and Erie. Here hybrid vines do well in alluvial soil, but the output is relatively small and the majority of suitable sites make up one of Canada's most important wine-growing areas over the border.

Ohio

The centre of Ohio's wine industry is located at Sandusky on the southern shore of Lake Erie. The district stretches from Port Clinton in the west to Vermilion in the east, and includes the Bass Islands off the lake shore.

The predominant grape is the catawba but the concord and some hybrids are also used. The largest company is Meiers, with centres at Sandusky and Silverton, near Cincinnati, who make a wide variety of wines ranging from still wines to vermouths, sparkling and dessert wines. Other companies worthy of note are Engels and Krudwig, and George Lonz.

Maryland

Although the state has good potential for wine-growing, for one reason or another it has never been exploited. There is, however, one vineyard of note at Ryderwood, near Baltimore, the Boordy vineyard, which is the property of J. and J. Wagner. The emphasis here is on the nursery side of viticulture, though the wines made are none the less excellent.

Michigan

Production is not as important in Michigan as in other states, and this is reflected in the quality of the wines which is only average. Delaware, concord and catawba vines are used to make still and sparkling wines from the vineyards in the south of the state at Paw Paw and Benton Harbour on the shores of Lake Michigan.

New Jersey

Former commercial interests in wine-making have waned in New Jersey in favour of the Finger Lakes district and California.

Virginia

Although vines are grown on some farms, wine production is not important here. The only vineyards of any note are in Albemarle and Clack counties.

Chile

Of all the countries of South America, Chile has the longest tradition of wine-making. According to the chronicles of Garcilaso de la Vega, the vine was introduced to Chile by a priest named Francisco de Carabantes who arrived from neighbouring Peru in 1535. At that time, missionaries were following up the expeditions of the *conquistadores* and planting vines to provide altar wine. By the first half of the 18th century, the reputation of Chilean wines was well established.

The development of the modern Chilean wine industry is due to a nobleman, Silvestre Ochgavia Echazaretta, who employed a French viticultural expert, a M. Bertrand, to organize the planting of vineyards. He discovered that Chile's soils were ideally suited to French vine stocks, and he introduced the first cuttings of the cabernets, pinots and other French vines grown today. The expansion of the wine industry from 1851 onwards was based on French principles of planting, pruning, fermentation and maturation.

In wine-growing terms, Chile is unique because she has never suffered the devastating pests and diseases affecting all the other wine-producing countries of the world. This fortunate situation is due to the geography of the country; in the north there is the inhospitable Atacama Desert; in the east the high Andes Mountains, and in the west the prevailing winds sweep in from the Pacific Ocean, creating conditions unlikely to foster diseases.

Indirectly, these conditions affect Chilean wines by making it unnecessary for the vines to be grafted onto American root stocks — a costly and laborious operation. However, it is believed that these stocks make a better wine than grafted vines.

The claret- and burgundy-type Chilean wines compare favourably with their European or Californian counterparts especially as they are comparatively inexpensive as labour is less costly in Chile. The elegant white wines are fruity, although sometimes they are left to mature too long, which makes them rather dark in colour so that they lack the refreshing acidity vital to a balanced wine. However, these are not necessarily faults but traditionally inherited methods of vinification and, perhaps, give Chilean wines their own distinction.

Today, Chile is the eleventh largest wine producer in the world, having some 281,000 acres of vineyard and making something in excess of 100,000,000 gallons per annum, of which only 1,500,000 gallons are exported. The government is conscious of this valuable export potential and is endeavouring to increase the overseas markets by continually improving wine technology and imposing strict quality control on all wines leaving the country.

Location of vineyards

Chile is about 2,800 miles long and 100 miles wide; it includes four different climatic zones ranging from the Atacama Desert in the north to the sub-Antarctic wastelands of the south at Tierra del Fuego, and the Andes Mountains are an impressive massif running down its eastern border with Argentina. There are three wine-growing zones: northern, central and southern.

The northern zone
This area stretches from the Atacama Desert in the north down to the Choapo river, where rainfall is negligible; irrigation in the vineyards is essential and is provided by diverting and channelling the melting snows of the Andes.

The luscious muscat is the grape most commonly planted and it produces sweet port- and sherry-type wines; it is also distilled to give one of Chile's popular spirits, Pisco.

The central zone
Chile's finest dry table wines are made in the central zone between the Aconcagua and Maule rivers. Climatically, it is perfectly suited to the vine.

Vineyard worker pruning vines in Chile's southern wine region; these vines have never been affected by phylloxera

Here the French and, in particular, the Bordeaux influences are noticeable. The best claret-type wines are made from the cabernet sauvignon and the cabernet franc vines; the merlot, malbec, pinot noir, petit verdot and trebbiano are used for full-bodied, robust and sometimes rather tannic red wines.

The Sauternes-style white wines are made from the sémillon and sauvignon grapes and the lighter, elegant dry white wines are made from the pinot blanc (chardonnay) grape of Chablis fame and, to a lesser extent, the riesling, which gives the finest white wines.

The indigenous país, a descendant of the criolla grape found elsewhere in the Americas, gives large quantities of grapes for ordinary wines.

The major centres of wine production are based on the rivers Aconcagua, Maipo and Cachapoal. Irrigation is used in many vineyards but Chileans do not believe it affects the quality of the wines.

The southern zone

This area stretches from the Maule river to the Bio Bio river and is less important than the regions to the north.

French vine varieties such as malbec, merlot, carignan and sémillon and the local país are often blended to make the *vinos corrientes* or everyday wines.

Chile and Argentina are South America's important wine-producing countries

Argentina

Argentina is the largest wine-producer in the Western Hemisphere, and lies fourth in the league of wine-producing countries of the world, making some 300,000,000 gallons annually from its 500,000 acres of vines. These facts come as a surprise for Argentinian wines are seldom available elsewhere. Home consumption is vast – the average amount drunk per head at the last analysis was 23 gallons (US) per annum.

The vine was first planted in Argentina in 1556 by a Jesuit priest Father Cedron. Today, the industry is run by the descendants of Italian immigrants who, in the 1880s, laboured to channel the melting snow of the Andes mountains into the semi-arid plateau around the town of Mendoza, and eventually succeeded in making it into a fertile vineyard area.

Argentina does not permit the use of hybrid vines in her vineyards. The familiar European varieties are grown; for red wines they are malbeck (as it is known locally), cabernet, pinot noir, gamay, barbera and sangiovese. The white wines are made from the criolla, pinot blanc, riesling, sémillon, palomino, pedro ximenez and various muscats.

Frequently different types of vine are mixed in the same vineyards and are even harvested and vinified together in the belief that one variety may provide what another may lack. In general, the wines are robust, alcoholic and often soft – a characteristic of wines from warmer climates, where the grapes develop a high sugar content and a corresponding loss of acidity, which tends to make the wines rather dull. The exception to this rule are the more elegant dry wines of the Rio Negro district, which have a crisp, balanced acidity.

Unlike her neighbour Chile, Argentina has suffered from most of the familiar vine diseases. Phylloxera frequently occurs even today and is combatted by flooding the vineyards; the fungoid diseases are treated by spraying.

The government controls all aspects of production through the Wine Institute in Mendoza. These controls include the plantation of different grape varieties, the market price of grapes, the alcoholic content of new wines and all new tech-

nical innovations, and they are especially stringent over labelling. The Argentinian wine industry is continually expanding and production now exceeds the demands of the home market. The government is, therefore, harnessing this potential and there is little doubt that these wines will begin to appear more and more frequently in overseas markets.

Location of vineyards

There are three major wine-growing districts: Mendoza, and the provinces of San Juan and Rio Negro.

Mendoza

This town is the centre of Argentina's wine industry and the wine-growing district which surrounds it is responsible for over 70% of the country's total output. All types of still and sparkling wines and large quantities of vermouth are made.

The red wines, made from the malbeck grape, are the most popular. The white wines, which are made from a number of varieties, particularly the criolla grape which is a cousin of the Chilean país and an alleged relative of the Californian mission grape, represent the larger part of the white wine production.

The wine industry in Mendoza and its environs is enormous; 10 companies dominate the scene, using the most modern mass production techniques of pressing, continuous fermentation and maturation in large tanks. Production on this scale, using grapes from irrigated vineyards and bulk processing, precludes quality wines of individual character. Wines in Argentina are an everyday drink and have no pretensions to grandeur; nevertheless, they compare very favourably with their commercial counterparts anywhere else in the world.

San Juan province

Immediately north of Mendoza lies the province of San Juan, the second largest wine-growing district in Argentina, which contributes 26% of the national total.

The vineyards stretch across verdant plains at the foot of the Andes and are nourished by the waters of the mountain streams. As they are further north than

Mendoza and therefore nearer the Equator, the warmer climate allows the mature grapes to become enriched with sugar and these are used to make the sweeter port- and sherry-type wines, and as table grapes.

Grapes that have just been picked are being loaded onto a truck in Mendoza

Rio Negro province

Argentina's best dry white wines and champagnes come from this province south of Mendoza, which contributes only 3% of the national total. The vineyards follow the banks of the Negro river, and irrigation is hardly required for the climate is very similar to that of the wine-growing regions of Northern Europe.

Some of the champagne houses are owned by well-known European champagne houses, and their labels bear a marked resemblance to the original. The wines gain their sparkle by one of three methods: the traditional *méthode champenoise* process of bottle fermentation, the less costly bulk Charmat process, and carbonization.

South Africa

As the Dutch opened up their colonies in the East Indies in the 17th century, an increasing number of ships took the route round the Cape of Good Hope, often making re-victualling calls at the little port which was eventually to become Cape Town. This was their first landfall after leaving Holland and it made a welcome break from the tedium of those long lengthy journeys was disease, particularly scurvy. Frequently as many as half the crew of a ship could perish during a voyage. By the time a ship reached Cape Town, it was common to find that most of the food on board was bad and the remaining water in the barrels undrinkable.

On consultation, Dutch physicians advised the use of brandy, a common antidote to disease in the French, Spanish and Portuguese navies. Holland was not a wine-growing country and was, therefore, unable to make brandy; her relations with the neighbouring wine-growing countries were uncertain so that she was obliged to look elsewhere for grapes for distillation.

Early mariners had noted that their port of call at the Cape had a very favourable climate for the propagation of the grape, similar to the wine regions of France. It was also ideally situated, half-way along the trade routes to the East.

In 1656, the Dutch East India Company sent out Jan van Riebeek to the Cape with the first vine cuttings, which were planted at Wynberg, later named Bosheuvel. On 2 February 1659, van Riebeek reported that he had produced the first wine from his newly planted vineyard. Nobody knows precisely what grape varieties he used but one was probably a muscadel.

Next to expand and influence vineyards

Pruning the vines in South Africa; each country has slightly differing methods

in and around the Cape was Simon van der Stel. He became governor of the Cape in 1679, and was responsible for the planting of the famous Constantia vineyard. His name was given to what is now one of the biggest wine-producing towns, Stellenbosch. Van der Stel already had experience of wine-growing, and passed on to less-experienced farmers the theories of selecting grape varieties, pressing, and general cleanliness of the cellar. In 1690, some 200 French Huguenots arrived, many of whom came from the wine-growing areas of France. They contributed a great deal to viticulture in the Cape, passing on their skills and traditions of wine-making, and settling at Franschhoek (French corner), Paarl, Drakenstein and Stellenbosch.

During the 18th century, Constantia wine achieved a considerable reputation and was much in demand in Europe.

In 1806 the British took possession of the Cape and with the aid of the so-called Imperial preference on import duties into England, wine exports boomed to 1,000,000 gallons in 1859. This heyday did not last, however, for in 1861 the English Prime Minister Gladstone repealed the tax system on foreign wines. The problems and cost of shipping from South Africa meant that the Cape wines could no longer compete on price.

At the tip of the continent of Africa, South African wine zones have a temperate climate

Following this setback, the vineyards were ravaged by phylloxera in 1885. However, the vines were substantially replanted at the turn of the century, only to meet yet another problem of over-production – the final blow to many growers who had not the finances to withstand such misfortunes. These circumstances heralded the formation of the co-operative movement in South Africa in the form of the KWV or Ko-operatieve Wijn-bouwers Vereniging, which controls the South African wine industry today.

Location of vineyards

The main South African vineyards lie in the south-west of the Cape. Here the climate is considered one of the most bountiful in the world for wine-growing. There are two main areas: the Cape or Coastal belt and the Little Karroo.

The Cape or coastal belt

This area stretches from the coast to the Drakenstein Mountains and includes the districts around the towns of Constantia, Stellenbosch, Paarl, Malmesbury, Ceres, Tulbagh and Wellington.

The vines are planted on slopes of sandstone, shale and granite, either as bushes or, for the higher quality wines, on trellises. The climate is consistent and rainfall averages about 25 in a year, most of which falls in the Cape winter of June–August. Summers in South Africa are in the months of December–February

and the harvest takes place in the autumn between February and March.

This steady climate is reflected in the wines; the quality is constantly good, unlike the European vineyard regions. The wines vary greatly in type from table to sparkling, Perlwine (semi-sparkling), and some sherry- and port-style wines. Both light- and full-bodied red wines are made from the hermitage, shiraz, cabernet and pinotage grapes, the latter being a cross between the hermitage and pinot, which has not grown successfully by itself in the Cape.

The main centres for red wines are Constantia, Paarl and Stellenbosch, while the *vins ordinaires* are made around Malmesbury and Wellington.

In general, the good red wines may be rather harsh when young, but soften after some bottle age, becoming very palatable indeed after three to five years. Most of the cheap wines are made from the hermitage grape which gives soft, pleasing, quick-maturing wines.

The white wines have improved considerably over recent years, aided by the technological advances made by the Stellenbosch-Elsenburg Wine Institute. Formerly, the warm climate produced wines which were fruity, more alcoholic than their European counterparts, but at the same time rather uninteresting on the palate. Today, owing to new techniques, these wines are light and delicate and surprise many wine-lovers overseas by their outstanding quality.

The principal vines for white wine are riesling, fransdruif (similar to palomino), steindruif, steen, sémillon, sauvignon and clairette blanche, the latter being used for Fonkelwyn (sparkling) and Perlwine.

The centres of white wine production are Tulbagh, Stellenbosch, Franschhoek, Durbanville and Paarl, the wine capital of South Africa.

Fortified wines

Since 1930, the South Africans have been making sherry, and when visiting Paarl, one is reminded that it lies on virtually the same latitude south of the Equator as Jerez de la Frontera, Spain, lies north of the Equator. Palomino, the classic vine used in Jerez, is also used here; the other vines are fransdruif and steen. Flor, a type of wine yeast forming on the surface of new sherry wine and an important prerequisite for light sherries, is used in the same way as in Spain, the only difference

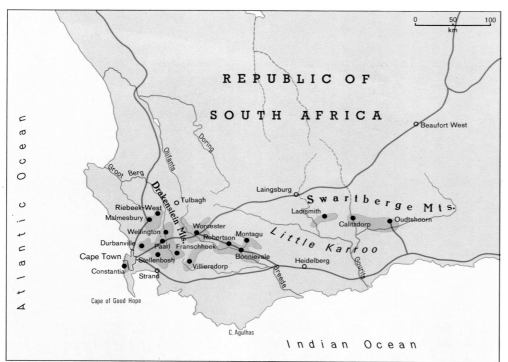

being that Stellenbosch University has now developed its own strains of flor yeast believing that this gives a more uniform quality to the wine.

The *solera* system has also been copied from Spain; this vital part of the sherry process is based on the fact that young wine when blended with old wine inherits the character of the old wine. South African sherries are now exported to many countries, and this is a reflection on the high quality of the wine.

The port-style wines are made from the hermitage and pontac grapes and combined with others of Portuguese origin. The technique of arresting the fermentation by the addition of natural grape brandy leaves some residual sugar in the wine exactly the same as the classic port wines. After this process, the wines are left to mature for a period of five to eight years before being blended prior to shipment. White, ruby, tawny and even vintage ports are made at Paarl, Riebeek-West, Stellenbosch and Strand in the Cape.

Little Karroo

The sweeter, heavier port-types are made in the Little Karroo. This district stretches from the Drakenstein to the Swartberg Mountains. Here the vines grow in rich alluvial soils, and the climate is hotter than in the coastal belt, with a lower rainfall of about 10 in, so irrigation is needed.

Worcester, Robertson, Montagu, Bonnievale, Ladismith, Calitzdorp and Oudtshoorn are the centres of production for these port-types, and other dessert wines, white *vins ordinaires* and some good quality brandies, many of which are consumed on the home market. The grape types used for these wines include the hermitage, pontac, shiraz, hanepoot and steendruif.

Today, the South African wine industry is under the supervision of the KWV whose job as a co-operative is to control minimum grape prices, the surplus for industrial use, storage facilities, particularly for fortified wines, the overall quality, especially of those wines intended for export, and the development and expansion of overseas markets. In these aims they are singularly successful for there is little doubt that the wines leaving South Africa now are extremely well made and popular.

Harvesting the grapes which takes place between February and March

Australia

The vine is not indigenous to Australia, but was planted by English settlers in the 1780s. Early settlers were encouraged by the British government who were keen to establish agriculture and primary industries and, recognizing the suitability of the climate, gave financial incentives to anyone who wished to plant vineyards.

To be able to import wine from Australia seemed the ideal solution to England's lack of vineyards; she would no longer have to secure supplies of wine from countries such as France and Spain with whom she was at war. In 1801, Napoleon Bonaparte sent emissaries to find out how the English were developing the new continent. They reported that vines were being planted and added that they believed that Australia was becoming England's vineyard. This was a generous estimate because it was not for another 60 years that wine was exported from Australia to England in large quantities.

Australia's wine history

The first man to be credited with planting vines was Captain Arthur Phillip, at that time governor of the new colony around Sydney. No-one is sure what vine varieties he planted and records vary as to their origins, some stating they came from the Cape, meaning South Africa, and others saying they were in his cargo when he left London. Whatever their source, the first vines were planted at Farm Cove, Sydney, in 1788. This site proved unsuitable owing to the humid conditions near the coast, and a better situation was found some 14 miles inland from Sydney at Parramatta, where three acres were planted in 1791.

The first commercial vineyard was planted by Captain J. Macarthur at Camden Park, using root stocks from the earlier plantings which were later augmented with vines which he bought during his visit to Europe in 1815–16.

He had two sons, James and William, both of whom continued in the family wine business and who helped their father to move his Camden Park vineyard to nearby Penrith in 1820.

Gregory Blaxland is reputed to be the first man to have exported wine from Australia and, although he did not export a large quantity, it was the forerunner of some of the Australian wines which later won awards at European wine fairs.

The most important figure in the history of Australian wine was James Busby, a Scotsman who arrived in Australia in 1824, when he was still in his early twenties. He was a schoolteacher by training but had spent some time touring the vineyard areas of Europe and, recognizing the potential of vine-growing in Australia, he made viticulture one of the subjects at the orphans' school in Sydney where he taught.

At that time, knowledge of wine and wine-making was very limited so Busby wrote and published the first textbook on the subject of viticulture in Australia. In the late 1820s he received a grant for 2,000 acres in the Hunter River Valley which he named Kirkton but, after planting part of this estate, he recognized that the wine he produced was limited by the lack of vine varieties and he therefore returned to Europe in 1830.

During this visit to Europe, Busby travelled through France and Spain, selecting vines he considered suitable for the Australian climate. On his return to Sydney he started a nursery and, although only about half his original 678 plants took root, he cultivated enough young root stocks to distribute to the major wine-growers of the time.

In these early days some vines were mislabelled which later led to confusion about the origins of some wines.

By the 1850s, exports were still small. In 1877 the arrival of the phylloxera louse caused extensive damage to vineyards in New South Wales and Victoria – a major setback to the Australian wine industry.

As soon as the remedy for phylloxera was found, vineyards were quickly replanted and, by the turn of the century, approximately 1,000,000 gallons of wine were being exported, mostly to England. These exports steadily increased until the outbreak of World War II and reached a peak of around 4,000,000 gallons in 1937.

The bulk of the wine exported was of the burgundy type, sold in flagons, and it was perhaps unfortunate that its popularity and reputation were based on low price and, in the case of some shippers, its 'tonic' properties (by which is meant its high iron content). This image proved a hindrance when the Australians tried to re-establish their wine exports after the war, and it was some years before they built up a new reputation as makers of a large range of high quality wines.

Today, wine and wine-growing in Australia fall into two categories: first,

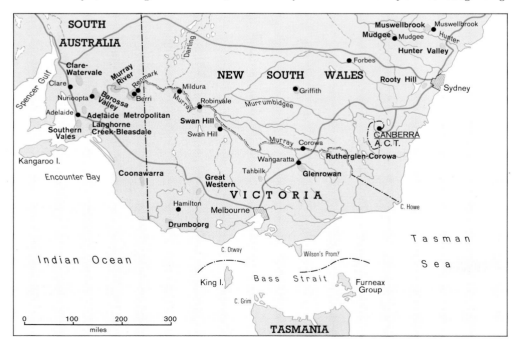

Left: major Australian wine zones are scattered throughout the country
Right: sparkling wine is made by the méthode champenoise *in Victoria*

high quality wines from low-yield vines planted on hillsides in upland country giving two to four tons of grapes per acre in a climate of long, hot summers, and an annual rainfall of about 20 in – as for example, in the Hunter River and Barossa Valleys. Second, the lower quality, fortified and dessert wines from high-yield vines from lowland, irrigated vineyards which may yield from 10–15 tons of grapes per acre, planted on rich alluvial soils, where there is an annual rainfall of about nine in – as for example, in the Murrumbidgee and Murray irrigation vineyard areas.

The Australian wine-maker such as Penfold's or Seppelt's is concerned with making a large variety of wines, unlike the Europeans who concentrate on making one wine in one area. The variety of wines produced in one winery may be the result of blending grapes either from several districts or from one small area.

Location of vineyards

New South Wales
This region became a state in 1824. At that time, it was the only state with any large vineyards. The modern centres of wine production are the Hunter River Valley, the Murrumbidgee irrigation area, Muswellbrook, Mudgee, Rooty Hill, Swan Hill, Corowa and Robinvale.

The Hunter River Valley
This is regarded by many as the home of Australia's best claret- and burgundy-type wines. The district is comparatively small, occupying some 2,500 acres of sandstone and loam soils of the valley which is 150 miles long and 70 miles wide.

Pokolbin is the main wine town and centre of production even though it is situated 17 miles south of the Hunter river.

The vines are all of the European *Vitis vinifera* species; the cabernets make the

deep, velvety, rich reds, and the sémillon the pale, flowery whites; for some reason, the last named grape is known locally as the riesling. The average wine production for the area is 140,000 gallons (US) but this figure will no doubt increase in future as more vineyards are planted.

Murrumbidgee irrigation area
This is the largest wine-growing district in New South Wales and consists of 5,000 acres of flat, rich alluvial soil around the town of Griffith, which itself lies about 20 miles north of the Murrumbidgee river.

The climate is hot and dry, but irrigation provides the necessary moisture for the vines so that the production of sweet sherry- and port-type wines is correspondingly large, averaging about 6,000,000 gallons annually. The red and white table wines of the district are not as successful as the dessert wines; they are big and soft, but lack the finesse of those from non-irrigated areas.

Corowa

Situated at the south of the state on its border with Victoria, this area is a noted producer of some of Australia's best dessert wines. Surprisingly its vineyards are not irrigated.

The remaining areas in the state are relatively small in terms of production; Penfold's winery at Rooty Hill makes the well-known Minchinbury champagne, while wineries at Mudgee and Forbes make table wines; those wineries at Swan Hill and Robinvale on the Murray river make sherry- and port-type wines.

Victoria

Vineyards were planted in the 1830s; the most important influence was Charles Joseph Latrobe whose Swiss background

Left: wine store in the Barossa Valley in South Australia
Below: grape harvest in the Barossa Valley, home of Australia's best wines

enabled him to persuade established Swiss wine-growers to emigrate and start up on their own. At the end of the last century, the state had more vineyards than the rest of Australia, but phylloxera struck in the 1880s, forcing many growers to turn to more profitable crops.

Today, the important districts are Mildura, Rutherglen, Glenrowan, Wangaratta, Tahbilk and Great Western.

Mildura

By far the largest of Victoria's wine districts is Mildura, an irrigated area on the Murray river which makes some good dessert wines and, more recently, interesting table wines.

Rutherglen, Glenrowan and Wangaratta

These scattered areas all produce robust, alcoholic red table wines and a few sherry-type and dessert wines. Wine-growers are experimenting with lighter wines.

Tahbilk

On the Goulburn river 76 miles north of Melbourne, is a property called Château Tahbilk, which makes some excellent firm claret wines from the shiraz and cabernet grapes, and uses marsanne, amongst others, for white wines. These wines are often austere in youth and need bottle age before they can be appreciated at their best.

Great Western

The vineyards of this district are planted in a volcanic and limestone soil on hills which form the Great Dividing Range about 100 miles west of Melbourne.

The district is renowned for sparkling wines which are sold under the Great Western label and are considered by many to be Australia's best. The red and white wines tend to be somewhat hard, needing a certain bottle age to develop their best qualities, and it is for this reason that many of the larger firms blend them with

wines from other districts which are deficient in acidity. The only companies making wine are Seppelt who have 650 acres, and Best who own a mere 20 acres.

South Australia

For many years South Australia lagged behind her neighbouring states in the number and area of vineyards planted, yet now she makes more wine than all the other states combined. The main reason for this is that the disease phylloxera, which destroyed many vineyards, left South Australia's unaffected – and so they remain today.

Many growers in other states, realizing the cost of re-planting and the difficulty of transporting and selling their wines at a profit, turned to more lucrative forms of agriculture.

Recent wine production figures top 30,000,000 gallons per annum and, although much of this is from the rich irrigated Murray River Valley, there is an emphasis on quality in other areas.

The main wine districts are: Adelaide Metropolitan, Southern Vales, Barossa Valley, Clare and Watervale, Langhorne Creek and Bleasdale, Coonawarra, Loxton, Renmark, Berri and Waikerie.

Adelaide Metropolitan

Adelaide is the state capital and was until recently a wine-growing district of some repute. The few vineyards that have survived urbanization are situated in the suburbs of Magill. Penfold operate their main winery there as well as Wynn, but they have also a good wine centre at Auldana. At Burnside, Martin have their Stonyfell property and Hamilton are at Glenelg.

Southern Vales

Thirteen miles south of Adelaide on the hills between the Mount Lofty Range and the sea is a district known as Southern Vales. Here, John Reynell planted his first vineyard in 1838; today, it is known as Reynella, the property of Walter Reynell and Sons who make some fine wines from the vineyards of the surrounding areas, including some fine quality red wines from shiraz and cabernet grapes.

South of Reynella in the rich ironstone soils of McLaren Vale, Edwards and Chaffey use rhine riesling to make their top-quality white wines from their Seaview property, and the firm of Thos. Hardy make some excellent dry red wines from their Tintara vineyard.

Barossa Valley, Clare and Watervale

The largest fine wine district, not only in South Australia but in the continent as a whole, is the Barossa Valley which lies some 30 miles north of Adelaide in the valley of the Para river, with the vineyard areas in and around the main towns of Tanunda, Nuriootpa and Angaston.

The district was opened up by a man of foresight, George Fyfe Angus, who in 1840 raised the money to bring out Lutheran dissenters; they later became the core of this essentially German community. The specialities of the valley are the fine wines made from the rhine riesling and the cabernet; they come from such renowned firms as Leo Buring's Château Leonay at Tanunda, Penfold and the South Australian Grape Growers Co-operative at Nuriootpa. The latter also make some fine sparkling wines under the Kaiser Stuhl label. Smith's Yalumba at Angaston and Gramp's Orlando at Rowland Flat are known for their fine late-picked rieslings, as Seppelt's are known for their cabernets grown in their impressive winery at Seppeltsfield.

Adjoining the Barossa Valley is the Eden Valley with several vineyards spread over its hilly countryside. The wines are made from the same grapes its neighbours use and are often purchased by companies in the Barossa Valley. The wineries of note are Henschke at Keyneton, and Hamilton at Springton.

In the Mount Lofty range 80 miles north of Adelaide is the district of Clare-Watervale. Like the Barossa Valley, this region was also settled by German immigrants, possibly because of its resemblance to the Rhine Valley in Germany. At Watervale the firm of Buring and Sobel make a fine Rhine Riesling, and at Clare one can find some distinctive, firm and well flavoured reds from such companies as the Clarevale Co-operative, Roland Birks and Stanley Wine.

Langhorne Creek and Bleasdale

Twenty-five miles east of Adelaide is the small district of Langhorne Creek and Bleasdale, situated on and irrigated by the Bremer river. On the rich alluvial soil the grape yields are high and the wines produced are a sweet dessert sherry-type and a big full-flavoured claret.

Coonawarra

Near South Australia's easterly border with Victoria and some 200 miles from Adelaide is Coonawarra, a district of about 10 square miles of red soil originally planted by John Riddock in 1890. Since that time, it has suffered from an onslaught of phylloxera and then a general lack of demand affecting Australian wines. However, Australia's new interest in table wines has meant that since 1950 wine companies have planted new vineyards.

As the district is so far south its climate is more temperate than most of Australia's other regions and the wines are consequently lighter and more acid. Many companies have successfully blended the wines with those from other districts, especially from the Hunter River Valley. As the emphasis is on quality, the grapes grown are the cabernet for the red wines, and the rhine riesling for the whites.

Loxton, Berri, Renmark and Waikerie

These are the centres for wine production in the South Australian section of the Murray River Valley irrigation areas. The district was developed as a resettlement scheme for war veterans in 1919, to produce grapes for the table and for distilling into fortifying spirit. Today, a high percentage of grapes grown is bought by the national companies and trucked to the Barossa Valley and elsewhere for making fortified wines.

Western Australia

The viticultural region of this state is situated near Perth on the sandy alluvial soils of the Swan and Canning rivers. Hot summers and an average annual rainfall of 35 in combine with the rich soil to give wines with high sugar levels.

Dry wines are difficult to make, but some soft, slightly sweet but palatable red wines are made from shiraz and malbec grapes. Some flowery and interesting whites are made from the rhine riesling and the sémillon but they lack the crispness these grapes show elsewhere.

The climate is suited to the production of sweet wines which are made from tokay, shiraz, grenache, frontignac, pedro ximenez and muscat grapes. Some develop an almost liqueur-like character similar to the sweet natural wines of France, much appreciated locally.

There are 60 wineries in the district and the best known are Sandalford and Houghton, and Valencia which are owned by the Emu Wine Company.

Profusion of grapes which will be blended to make firm, well-flavoured red wines

England

Although it is possible that a few small vineyards existed near some of the more permanent Roman settlements, there is no reliable documentary evidence to support the widely held assumption that the cultivation of the vine was first introduced to Britain by the Romans.

The first serious wine-growers in Britain were early Christian missionaries. When, towards the end of the 7th century, their supplies of imported wine were cut off they began planting their own vineyards.

After the Norman conquest in 1066, the number of vineyards, both ecclesiastical and secular, increased.

The sites of ancient vineyards may still be seen at Worcester, Gloucester, Tewkesbury, Hereford and Ledbury, and there is evidence that vineyards were planted in the village of Westminster, at Chenetone in Middlesex, at Ware in Hertfordshire, at Hanten in Worcestershire, and at Winchester in Hampshire. The Domesday survey also mentions vineyards in Essex and Berkshire.

By the middle of the 12th century, there were large areas of vines in the vale of Gloucester, and there is mention of vineyards at the Abbey of Ramsey in East Anglia, the Isle of Ely, and frequent references to royal vineyards at Windsor in Berkshire, Purley in Surrey, Stoke in Staffordshire, and in Hertfordshire and Huntingdonshire. There were also medieval vineyards at Lincoln, York and Bath.

The vine flourishes on chalky Hampshire soil

In 1152 Henry of Anjou married Eleanor of Aquitaine and came to the English throne two years later as Henry II. The great Bordeaux wine region thus came under English domination and the wine trade with England increased steadily. By the reign of King John, vast quantities of wine were entering Britain from Rouen and Bordeaux. There is evidence that at about this time a long-term change of climate affected British viticulture. By the reign of Henry III (1216 –72) the husbandmen of England were putting their land to more profitable use and the wine industry finally declined.

The first serious attempt in recent years to grow grapes for wine in Britain was made by the Marquis of Bute in 1875 at Castle Coch in Glamorganshire, and later at Swanbridge near Cardiff. These projects were not very successful, mainly due to the use of unsuitable grape varieties, and World War I put an end to them.

Some 30 years later, in 1951, Major-General Sir Guy Salisbury-Jones, inspired by the pioneer work of Edward Hyams, an author and broadcaster, and Ray Barrington-Brock, an enthusiastic scientist, who started a private viticultural research station at Oxted, Surrey, in the mid 1940s, planted 4,000 seyve-villard 5-276 vines, imported from France, on a chalky slope at Hambledon in Hampshire. Today, his vineyard, which has been extended to four acres, and now includes pinot chardonnay vines, is well known, and his clean, dry white wines are much sought after.

Other vineyards soon began to appear and in 1967 the English Vineyards

Major English wine-growing areas are in the south of the country

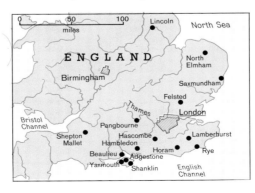

Association was formed, with the object of promoting the revival of viticulture in Britain. Today, the acreage of vines planted is thought to exceed 250, and over a dozen vineyards are now in full commercial production.

The most widely grown grape is the müller-thurgau, also known as riesling-sylvaner, but nearly all growers are experimenting with other varieties and crosses of promising European vines.

Most of the new plantings have been made on grafted stock to insure against phylloxera infestation. Some vines are, however, grown on their own roots; this is possible because the bug phylloxera is not endemic in Britain as it is on the entire mainland of Europe.

English wines, being derived from musts of comparatively low specific gravity, are light in style but pleasantly fragrant and with a remarkable intensity of flavour. Like the wines of the Mosel and the upper Loire Valley, their freshness and life form an important part of their appeal and they are usually best drunk young. Some are dry, while others are medium dry. Successful rosé wines exist, but as yet no grape has been found to produce good red wines.

The following are some of the leading wines and their growers: Adgestone (K. C. Barlow, Adgestone, Isle of Wight), Beaulieu (Mrs. M. Gore-Brown, Beaulieu, Hampshire), Bowden (W. L. Cardy, Pangbourne, Berkshire), Brede (R. D. Thorley, Rye, Sussex), Cranmore (W. N. Poulter & R. H. Gibbons, Yarmouth, Isle of Wight), Elmham (R. S. Don, Elmham, Dereham, Norfolk), Felstar (J. G. Barrett, Felsted, Essex), Hambledon (Maj.-Gen. Sir Guy Salisbury-Jones, Hambledon, Hampshire), Hascombe (Lt.-Com. P. Baillie-Grohman, Hascombe, Surrey), Kelsale (J. Edgerley, Saxmundham, Suffolk), King's Rew (Lady Montagu of Beaulieu, Hampshire), Lincoln Imperial (Maj. A. Rook, Stragglethorpe Hall, Lincoln), and Pilton Manor (N. de M. Godden, Pilton Manor, Shepton Mallet, Somerset).

In a world situation where quality wines are increasingly at a premium and supply is limited, the young English wine industry seems set for a successful future. Results have already proved that by the use of suitable grape varieties, modern methods of cultivation and the best of modern wine-making technology, high quality wines can be made in England as regularly as in other northern wine regions of Europe.

How to buy, store and serve wine

Knowing where and how to begin buying wine can be a daunting prospect for the beginner. With so many wines to choose from and so many different names to recognize, it is hard to shop wisely without being utterly confused by the ever-increasing numbers of wines carried by shops, supermarkets, independent wine merchants, brewery-owned and national chain-stores.

First decide what type of wine you want – white, rosé or red; sweet or dry – and then decide whether you want a branded wine, one bottled abroad or in the country of origin, or an estate-bottled wine.

Branded wines

These wines are the *vins ordinaires* and make up a large proportion of the popular wine market; they are attractive because they are cheap and well-made. Most groups or firms specialize in buying their wines from one region and the various labels they put on the bottles represent blends of wines from that region. You seldom find a branded wine with a distinctive single grape character although great care is taken to ensure that the wine is good and appeals to most palates. Labels usually bear popular but somewhat meaningless names rather than the district names associated with more expensive wines. Branded wines are often sold in litre bottles, carafes or half-gallon jars. Prices are in the cheaper range.

Wines bottled abroad are bought in cask in the country of origin and shipped to the country where the wine is to be bottled and labelled for distribution. The label states where the wine was bottled and also bears the name of the wine, its vintage if there is one and the place of origin. Wine bottled in the country of origin is a self-explanatory term. Prices vary considerably depending on quality and reputation.

Estate-bottled wines

Estate-bottled is a generic term for wine bottled on the property where it was actually grown and made; this term appears on the label (the terms *château*-bottled and *domaine*-bottled mean the same). Estate-bottled wines are normally top-quality; demand almost always exceeds supply because production of fine wines is carefully controlled and they are, therefore, expensive. Prices can vary enormously and are dependent on many factors: the kind of wine, its place of origin and reputation, vintage, supply and market trends. Some of these wines are priceless; most are costly and worth a special sacrifice.

Before you buy your wine shop around because considerable price-cutting occurs, even on branded wines, and offers are well worth taking up. If you buy a case or a dozen bottles at a time, you are entitled to a case discount and delivery is usually free.

Many wine merchants offer remnants or have end-of-bin sales and on the whole these are good value for money. Prices are low simply because the quantity of a particular wine stocked is no longer sufficient to warrant

holding it and the merchant wants to sell to make room for new stock. This is an excellent opportunity to experiment and try half-bottles.

Wine auctions are another means of buying wine, especially in quantity. Wines at auction are available for tasting beforehand and you should try to taste whenever possible. Note also where the wine is kept – if it is abroad or some distance away you will have to pay shipping and carriage costs – and how it has been kept – if by a merchant or in a known private cellar it should be in good condition; if from an unspecified source you are taking a chance.

The wines may be sold in minimum lots called parcels of a dozen or half-dozen bottles; sometimes parcels of mixed wines may be sold. In general, though, the parcels consist of three to four dozen bottles so you need to have somewhere to store that amount of wine. Unless you have cellar facilities and intend to lay down the wine, this could be a problem, and you may very well grow tired of it unless it is of outstanding quality.

You do not have to go and bid at an auction yourself. By consulting the person running the sale you can place with him a reserve price on the items that interest you and he will bid for you. Alternatively, a good wine merchant known by you personally will also make a bid on your behalf.

Wine clubs

Another way of buying wine is through a club. This system has several advantages, especially if you do not live near a good wine merchant. Orders can be made by post or telephone, advice is freely given on storage and laying down wines, tastings may be arranged several times a year, special offers may be available to members and introductions in foreign wine regions may even be arranged for members going abroad.

A wine club may save you money because it buys its wines direct from suppliers instead of going through a retailer; on the other hand, it may involve a large outlay because the wines have to be bought in bulk and club members may have to buy them by the dozen; this may in turn lead to problems of storage.

There are other points to bear in mind when buying wine through a club, such as the experience of the person in charge of buying the wine – a large scale buying operation needs someone who is well informed and understands the requirements of club members. No one can know everything about wine so a club run in conjunction with a reputable merchant or shipper should be able to guarantee not only regular supplies but also wines of reliable quality.

A wine club is a business and must therefore attract members; this may be done by offering bargains, particularly in spirits, for most people know what constitutes a fair price for gin or whisky. With cut-price wine, however, you run the risk of disappointment because an unfamiliar wine offered at a bargain price may not be worth either the price or the drinking.

A comparatively new and as yet largely unknown method of buying wine, especially in bulk, is through a wine broker. He acts just like any other broker. He usually offers an extensive but selective list, sometimes accompanied by detailed tasting notes. When a choice of wine has been made, he passes the order on to his sources of supply who will send the wine direct to the customer.

One final word on buying: if you want wine for laying down rather than for everyday drinking, buy it young. Any wine goes up in price as it grows older, even though its quality is not necessarily improving. Inflation is partly responsible for this but market trends are also influential, for if the supply of a top-quality wine is dwindling, anyone who possesses a few bottles of that wine can ask high prices.

Storing wine

People store wine for two reasons: to keep a stock for everyday drinking and to lay bottles down, particularly of very distinguished wines, which may need anything from two to 20 years to mature, such as claret, Burgundy and vintage port.

All wines benefit from a rest, especially after buying and bringing them home, and cellar space enables you to buy wine when it is least expensive so that, after a period of maturation, you can drink fine wines cheaply. Buying in bulk saves money as well because wine is usually cheaper by the case than by the bottle.

Even the smallest house or flat has some sort of storage space suitable for turning into a home cellar, for few of us today have houses with large underground cellars. Suitable places are cupboards, the space under the stairs, a bookcase, even a corner of the bedroom or garage, so long as the area chosen meets certain requirements essential for keeping wine in peak condition.

These requirements are absence of vibration, a constant temperature around 13°C, darkness and good ventilation. Vibration shakes up the wine so be careful how you position wine racks under the stairs; don't attach them to the underside of the stairs themselves. Lack of variation in temperature is more important than the actual temperature. The cooler the cellar the more slowly the wine matures, so choose storage space away from central heating or a fire. Dampness does not cause problems unless it is excessive. Strong light affects the colour and the natural development of wine so cover the bottles with a cloth if you cannot place them in the dark. Ventilation (but not draughts) is necessary to keep the air in the cellar smelling sweet.

Positioning the bottles

Bottles with corks should be laid horizontally so that the wine keeps the cork moist and expanded, which prevents loss of wine through evaporation and stops bacteria entering the wine through a dry cork; it also makes the cork easier to draw. Make sure, however, that the neck is not lower than the rest of the bottle because if there is any sediment it will collect on the cork, where it cannot easily

be removed. For the same reason sparkling wines with wired corks should also be laid flat.

Bottles with stopper corks should stand upright as the wines are not intended for laying down for a long period.

Many kinds of wine racks made of wood, metal and plastic are available and are ideal for home cellars with limited space, but they can be expensive. A handyman can make his own, or you can improvise and use the partitioned boxes in which wines are delivered or pieces of drainpipe or tubing stacked on top of each other. All that is needed is a system that ensures bottles do not roll about and can be easily removed without disturbing other bottles.

If you have a large stock of wines, keep a cellar book so that you can see at a glance how many bottles you have, what they are, how much you paid for them and when you should replenish stocks.

Tasting wine

Tasting wine is not difficult – basically it involves only your senses of sight, smell and taste. But interpreting these senses is a different matter and calls for experience and skill. Background knowledge such as wine names, types and regions can soon be learned by any keen wine drinker.

The obvious reason for tasting wine is to find out if you like it. However, a wine may have hidden qualities such as the degree of fruit, its balance, the amount of acidity and tannin, and its likely life span, which you will discover only by tasting. The ability to recognize and judge these qualities is part of the pleasure of drinking wine. It is acquired by experience, although some people appear to have a natural talent for it.

A well-known *négociant* and wine-taster of the Côte d'Or once said: 'In wine there is nothing absolute – it makes its own rules.' This is particularly true of wine-tasting; although types of wine have recognized and recognizable characteristics you frequently come across the exception to the rule.

To make tasting a worthwhile exercise, there are a few rules to follow.

1 Taste wines in the morning, before lunch if possible, when you still have a clean palate; it is best not to smoke as this can dull the taste buds.
2 With a range of wines, taste them in the most suitable order to give you a good basis for comparison: i.e. dry before sweet, young before old and cheap before expensive. Ideally, the wines, including the white wines, should be at room temperature. It is a matter of personal preference whether you drink red before white or vice versa.
3 Look at the wine carefully, smell it, then taste it – in that order. There is less risk of your opinion being influenced by the name on the label if you turn the bottle round and taste blind.
4 Try to get into the habit of writing short notes about each wine as soon as you taste it so that you build up a source of reference for future comparisons.

The order to follow when tasting is always appearance, smell and then taste.

Appearance

Colour tells you a great deal about a wine so examine it carefully. Basically the colours are red, white and rosé; the actual hue is important and this is best seen by tilting the glass over a plain white background such as a linen cloth. A candle flame may seem romantic but it is virtually useless except for assessing clarity. All wines should have a bright, lively colour which gives you pleasure to look at, but there are variations of colour dependent upon origin and age which tell more.

Red wines vary in hue from purple through various shades of red to red-brown and mahogany as they age. Purple indicates a very young wine, red indicates the transitional period between youth and the beginning of maturity and bottle-age; red-brown indicates good maturation occurring (for claret five or more years in bottle, for Burgundy three or more years depending on the quality of the vintage); mahogany indicates considerable maturity and mellowness (for claret 10–20 years in bottle, for Burgundy seven to 12 years in bottle); brown-amber *(madérisé)* indicates considerable age or oxidation in which case the wine may have started to deteriorate.

White wines vary in colour from a pale yellow-green to a deep amber and yellow. In general, white wines deepen in colour with age; dry wines usually have a straw-like colour and sweet luscious wines start off a rich golden yellow and become more golden and amber with age. Sherry is basically a pale straw-yellow; the deeper shades emerge after ageing and blending although the *olorosos* and brown sherries gain their colour mainly from specially prepared 'colour wines' which are added in controlled proportions.

A green tinge indicates a young white wine and is characteristic of Chablis and Mosel. Straw-yellow with a touch of green is a good colour for most dry wines; yellow-gold is a normal hue for any white wine which matures well; gold or amber indicates either a sweet wine or one with bottle age (a Burgundy develops a golden hue after about six years in bottle). Yellow-brown or old gold tinged with brown indicates a very old wine with considerable bottle age or oxidation; again, the wine may have started to deteriorate. Brown really applies only to sherry.

Smell

It is not easy to describe the various reactions on smelling a wine but in general a wine that does not smell good does not taste good. To release the nose or bouquet fill the glass about one-third full and hold it by the stem; gently swirl the wine up and around the glass and nose it. Very young wine has a raw smell, or no smell at all if its components have not yet had time to blend together. Mature wines have a more mellow bouquet and it is not unknown for old wines to give their best bouquet just as they are going over the hill on the palate.

Except in sparkling wines, beware of wines with a very sharp or prickly bouquet or with a strong smell of sulphur.

Countless terms can be used to describe the bouquet but unless they are readily understandable they are not much use. Basic terms used are acetic, austere, baked, clean, cooked, fragrant, grapy, green, little, musty, piquant, spicy, sulphury and sweet; definitions are given in the Glossary (see pages 12–16).

Taste

In general, the taste of the wine on the palate confirms the opinions formed by the nose. The most sensitive taste buds lie on the back and the front of the tongue which is why at wine-tastings people sometimes make extraordinary noises as they aerate the wine in the mouth. In anyone but a serious wine drinker, these taste buds tire after a few wines which is why it is a good idea to spit out rather than swallow every wine tasted. Do not be embarrassed about spitting out wine – it is infinitely preferable to suffering the ill-effects of swallowing many types of wine of different alcoholic strengths.

When tasting you should look for dryness or sweetness, flavour (i.e. body, fruit and balance), the proportion of tannin and acidity, and finesse or elegance, often called breeding.

There are countless terms that describe and denote the taste of wine; the basic ones you need to know are acid, balance, big, bite, bitter, body, coarse, delicate, dry, fat, finish, flinty, fruity, full-bodied, green, hard, heavy, light, luscious, meaty, medium dry and medium sweet, piquant, robust, silky, soft, supple, sweet, tannin and vigorous; definitions are given in the Glossary (see pages 12–16).

In red wines you should look for flavour and fruit, body and tannin; young wines can have an unpleasantly high tannin content but this decreases with bottle age. In white wines you should look for acidity although excess is not desirable.

Making tasting notes

Any system of notes is suitable so long as the notes can be quickly assimilated and give the following information: the date of the tasting; the name of the wine (i.e. district, vineyard and vintage); if in bottle, the name of the bottler; if estate-bottled, the name of the property; the price, appearance, bouquet and taste, as well as any general conclusions you may have. This may seem a laborious process but you, the wine drinker, are the one who will benefit.

Serving wine

Vital to the enjoyment of a white wine (and to some extent a rosé) is its refreshing quality; to a red wine it is the bouquet. It is, therefore, important to serve wine at a temperature best suited to retain and highlight these qualities.

White and sparkling wines benefit from a light chilling or cooling so that the refreshing quality and flavour are not dulled. Sweet white wines usually require a little more chilling than dry wines to counteract the initial impact of the dominant sweetness.

Rosé wine is a case for personal preference since chilling may in the case of a delicate wine, diminish the flavour and bouquet.

The best way to chill a wine is in a special bucket filled with ice chips. Place the bottle well down in the ice so that almost all of the neck is covered as well, with the cork facing upwards, and leave it for about 15–20 minutes before serving. Failing an ice bucket, use the refrigerator but never use the freezing compartment.

Red table wines should never be chilled with the exception of a good Beaujolais whose freshness and vitality are enhanced by a light chilling. A red wine should be brought to the temperature of the room in which it is to be served (this is the meaning of the French term *chambré*).

A wine that has lain a long time in a cool cellar should be brought up a day or so in advance and stood upright to allow any sediment in it to settle to the bottom.

Never raise the temperature of a bottle quickly by heating it in a low oven or standing it in front of an open fire because this can drastically alter the make-up and taste of a wine. If the bottle must be heated quickly stand it carefully in warm, not hot, water (about room temperature) for about 15 minutes.

Decanting

All fine red wines, but notably Burgundy, claret and vintage port, as well as some white wines throw a harmless but unsightly sediment. Decanting, or pouring the wine off into a new, clean container, separates it from this sediment. This needs a steady hand and a good eye.

To decant wine, hold the neck of the bottle against a strong light and gently pour the wine into the new container; as soon as any sediment appears stop pouring even if it means leaving behind a few inches of wine.

Decanting not only means the wine can be moved freely, since there is no longer any sediment to disturb, but also gives it a chance to breathe after its long stay in bottle, and to get rid of any slightly unpleasant smell or bottle stink that it may have acquired during that time. How long a wine should be left to breathe is open to argument – another case of wine making its own rules. It all depends on the character and degree of maturity of the wine. As a general rule, an hour and a half to two hours is enough for young, robust wines but 30 minutes to one hour suffices for mature wines. Very old, fine wines can be unpredictable so play safe and either draw the cork about 30 minutes before serving and pour straight from the bottle or decant just before serving.

Opening and pouring

Drawing the cork requires care, especially with old wine, rather than skill. There are many types of corkscrew available. The ideal corkscrew has a wide metal thread and is long enough to penetrate well into the cork.

A type popular with waiters is the one that has a small blade for cutting the capsule, a screw and a lever device all in one; it is compact and efficient. Pneumatic extractors are adequate and quick; the needle pierces the cork, air is pumped through it to force the cork out of the bottle. The sudden exit of the cork can cause spillage.

To open a bottle, first cut the metal capsule covering the cork; make sure it is removed below the lip of the bottle – if not it can impart a metallic flavour to the wine. Wipe the lip with a clean cloth to remove any mould or dust that has collected there. Insert the corkscrew through the centre of the cork, gradually turning it so that its tip emerges just below the cork. Grasp the neck of the bottle firmly with the cloth – the neck is the weakest part of a bottle and a cloth will protect you should the bottle split. Pull out the cork steadily, giving the corkscrew a quarter turn as you do so. Wipe inside the neck and outside with the cloth; the wine is then ready to pour.

Should the cork crumble or break off half way down, all is not lost. Either filter the wine through a clean, new piece of muslin or paper filter in a cone, or simply push the offending piece of cork down into the wine and use a clean knitting needle or skewer to prevent it from blocking the neck of the bottle as you pour the wine.

A bottle with sediment needs extra care when you open it. It is best to lay the bottle gently in a bottle basket without shaking up the wine and ease the corkscrew through the centre of the cork as before. Hold the bottle and basket firmly with one hand and gently pull out the cork with the other with the least possible movement. Pour the wine from the basket until the first signs of sediment show.

Sparkling wines need to be opened cautiously to preserve the precious bubbles of carbon dioxide. Chilling slows the action of the bubbles; to avoid agitating them handle the bottle gently. Remove the foil and the wire guard from the neck of the bottle, then ease out the cork. To do this, hold the bottle in one hand, take hold of the cork with the other hand and, using your thumb as a lever, slowly twist the cork and push it upwards. At the same time, turn the bottle in the opposite direction and pull it away from the cork which should just slip out. Popping corks may be a source of amusement but you are sure to lose some of the wine.

Choice of glasses

Wine is primarily for enjoyment, not show, so make your choice of glasses as simple as possible. It is not necessary to have different glasses for different wines; in fact there is a basic shape suitable for all table wines, including Champagne. The all-purpose wine glass is tulip-shaped, stemmed, at least 2 inches wide across the bowl and holds six to seven fl oz. Alternatively, a rounder, larger glass, known as a Paris goblet, holding about nine fl oz, may be used.

The glass should be plain and clear to show the true colour and clarity of the wine, so avoid fancy designs and, in particular, coloured glass.

The tulip shape and width of the bowl give you the fullest appreciation of the bouquet by allowing just the right surface area of the wine to be exposed to the air. Never fill a glass more than half full so that room is left for the bouquet to be concentrated in the upper half of the glass.

The stem is important and should be long enough to keep the heat of the hand away from the wine; this is particularly important for white wine. If you take the trouble to serve a wine at the temperature best suited to its qualities, don't spoil it by careless handling.

Many wine regions have, over the years, developed distinctive glasses whose shapes are intended to accentuate the virtues of their wines; such specialist glasses (see opposite) do not always fulfil these intentions nor are they necessarily practical. For example, the long-stemmed hock glass with its tiny bowl can be rather clumsy and the coloured glass sometimes used masks the colour and clarity of the wine. The popular and attractive saucer-shaped Champagne glass allows the effervescence of the wine to escape too quickly and does not concentrate the bouquet. However, the traditional, short-stemmed Champagne flute certainly shows off the sparkling qualities of this and similar wines and lets the bubbles travel gently upwards.

Glasses for fortified wines are generally smaller than those for table wines. The traditional sherry glass is the *copita* whose long, narrowing shape concentrates the bouquet very well; it can also be used for other fortified wines. Alternatively, a stemmed glass with a small round bowl (holding about three fl oz) which narrows towards the top can be used for sherry and Madeira. A larger version of the round sherry glass is ideal for port.

A balloon glass is generally used for Cognac but it should not be too big or else the bouquet will be lost through aeration. However, a large balloon glass is eminently suitable for drinking a really fine Burgundy.

Order of serving

It is customary for the host to taste each wine before serving it to his guests. Bottles of the same wine may be mixed in a single glass but if you are serving fine wines have a separate glass for each bottle because there can be great variations between them. Of course if you are serving several kinds of wine always use different glasses.

The order in which wines are served at a meal is usually as follows: a young wine before an older one, a dry wine before a sweet one and a delicate wine before either a robust or full-bodied one. In general, claret is served before Burgundy unless a young Burgundy is to be drunk with an older claret. A white or rosé wine usually precedes a red, except in the case of sweet wines which come at the end of a meal.

Partnering wine and food

What wine to serve with different food is really a question of common sense and consideration for others. A series of wines should be considered in relation to the dishes they will accompany; a very sweet dish will, for example, make any wine that follows it taste almost unpleasantly dry, and a medium dry wine drunk after a rich dish can taste thin and bitter. In general, wine should be chosen to complement or to contrast with the food. There are conventional partnerships of wine and food and the maxim 'white wine with fish, red with meat' will serve if you are really in doubt. However, you are not obliged to follow such recommendations nor do you have to serve wine with every course. Champagne is an excellent drink to serve throughout a meal but it is not to everyone's taste or pocket; as a rule serve fine wines only with fine food.

The following is a guide to partnering wine and food.

Hors d'oeuvres Dry or medium dry white (still or sparkling) wine or dry fortified wine such as sherry.

Soup A glass of dry or medium dry fortified wine such as sherry, Madeira or chilled tawny port.

Egg dishes; pasta Medium dry white, rosé or light red still wine.

Pâté Dry white sparkling wine, full-bodied dry white or red still wine.

Caviar; Smorgasbord Dry white sparkling wine or the traditional vodka or schnapps.

Shellfish Dry or medium dry white still wine.

Fish, general Any dry or medium dry white or rosé still or sparkling wine; red wine may be served but fish sometimes gives it a metallic flavour.

Fish, smoked Dry white still wine or dry or medium dry fortified wine such as sherry, Madeira or white port, or malt whisky.

Meat, white Any dry white or rosé still or sparkling wine, full-bodied white or light to medium red wine.

Meat, red Robust, full-bodied red still wine.

Salad None. Sharp flavourings like vinegar and lemon juice in dressings and mayonnaise give wine a bitter taste.

Cheese Any wine, but red is best of all, especially with strong cheeses.

Chinese food Medium dry white or rosé still or sparkling wine, or sweet white still wine.

Curry; highly seasoned dishes None. Strong flavourings spoil its taste; if a wine is chosen at all, make it an inexpensive, full-bodied red.

Dessert; fruit Medium dry, or sweet, white or rosé sparkling wine, or sweet white still or fortified wine.

Know your bottles

Many European wine regions use bottles with distinctive bottle shapes, which makes their wines easily recognizable. In recent years more and more wine countries have adopted these shapes for their own similarly styled wines. In the USA bottle shapes tend to follow those of the famous wine regions of France and Germany; for example Johannisberg Riesling comes in a bottle that looks like a Rhine wine bottle.

Bordeaux-style bottles are widely used throughout Europe and the New World; the straw-covered flask has come to be associated with Italian wine, particularly Chianti, and the German *bocksbeutel* has been adopted by Portugal for some rosé wines. The best-known traditional shapes are as follows.

Alsace
The Alsatian bottle is called a flute, is made of light-green glass and has a long, tapering neck.

Bordeaux
A narrow, square-shouldered bottle is used for all wines; dark green glass is used for red wine and clear glass for white wine. In addition to the standard 70-cl (approximately 24 fl oz) bottles Bordeaux wine comes in a half-bottle called a *fillette*, a magnum (equivalent to two bottles' capacity), Marie-Jeanne (three bottles), double magnum (four bottles), Jeroboam (six bottles) and Imperial (eight bottles).

Burgundy
A sloping-shouldered bottle with a short neck and a fairly full body is used for all wines; dark green glass is used for red wine and a lighter shade of green, almost yellow, is used for white. In addition to standard bottles holding 70 cl, Burgundy also comes in a half-bottle and magnum (two bottles).

The Beaujolais bottle sometimes varies from the basic Burgundy shape; it may be a bottle with a long neck that slopes out to an almost oval body and tapers in at the base. Le Piat de Beaujolais wine provides a good example of this bottle shape.

Champagne
The bottle slopes gently from the neck to a full body; it is dark green and made of very thick glass to withstand the pressure of the gas in the wine. The standard bottle holds 80 cl (approximately 28 fl oz). A magnum holds two bottles, Jeroboam (four bottles), Rehoboam (six bottles), Methuselah (eight bottles), Salmanazar (12 bottles), Balthazar (16 bottles) and Nebuchadnezzar (20 bottles).

Germany
The German bottle is similar to the flute of Alsace but with a shorter neck. Brown glass is usually used for wines from the Rhine districts and green glass for wines from the Mosel, Saar and Ruwer districts. The exception to the standard bottle is the squat flagon or *bocksbeutel* which is used only for wines from the Franconia wine district.

The Loire Valley
The bottle used is very similar to the Burgundy one, although it tapers from the neck to the body more gradually. Light-green glass is used for white wine, dark-green glass for red wine, and rosé wine usually comes in a clear glass bottle with a slightly longer neck.

The Rhône Valley
A bottle made of dark green glass, similar to the Burgundy shape but with a fuller body is used for all wines. A distinctive, squat, square-shouldered bottle is now in use.

Bottle capacities
The average European and British wine bottle holds 70 cl. The average American wine bottle holds approximately 75 cl (approximately 26½ fl oz), as does a bottle of fortified wine and a bottle of Cognac.

The average number of glasses you can expect to get from a bottle of wine is six from 70-cl bottles, eight from Champagne (or other sparkling wine) bottles if a small flute is used, 10 from a litre bottle or flask, eight to 12 from fortified wines and 10–14 from Cognac.

Bottle shapes below: 1 Rhine wine; 2 Mosel; 3 Beaujolais; 4 Italian Orvieto fiasco; 5 Hungarian Tokay; 6 white Burgundy; 7 red Burgundy; 8 Italian red – Barola, N. Italy; 9 Champagne; 10 Provence; 11 Italian fiasco – Chianti; 12 Franconian bocksbeutel – Portuguese wines; 13, 14 red, white Bordeaux; 15 Loire; 16 Port; 17 Alsace

1 2 3 4 5 6 7 8 9 10 11 12 13 14 15 16 17

Table of comparative vintages

Evaluations of wines are as accurate as possible at the time of publication. However, there are exceptions to the above because very good wines can be made when a vintage does not merit a high ranking, just as poor wines can be made in a very good vintage.

White wines that do not improve with age are not evaluated as far back as 1945.

Key to the symbols used in tables below:

Average year	🍾 (1 bottle)	Outstanding year	🍾🍾🍾🍾🍾 (5 bottles)
Good year	🍾🍾 (2 bottles)	Vintage year	outline bottle
Very good year	🍾🍾🍾 (3 bottles)	Not yet announced	glass symbol
Great year	🍾🍾🍾🍾 (4 bottles)		

In the table below, values are given as the number of filled bottles. (V) = vintage year (outline bottle); (NA) = not yet announced (glass symbol).

Year	Bordeaux red	Bordeaux white	Burgundy red	Burgundy white	Rhône	Loire	Rhine/Mosel	Champagne (vintage)	Port (vintage)
1945	5	4	3	3	4		4		(V)
1946	1	1	1		1		1		
1947	4	5	4	4	3	5	4	(V)	
1948	3	3	3	2	1	3	2		(V)
1949	4	4	4	3	4	3			
1950	3	3	1		3	3	2		(V)
1951									
1952	5	3	4		4	2	5	(V)	
1953	5	3	3	3	2	3	4	(V)	
1954	1	1		1	1		1		
1955	3	3	3	3	4	3	3	(V)	(V)
1956		1			1				
1957	4	3	3	3	3	3	3		
1958		3	1	1	3	2	2		(V)
1959	4	4	4	3	3	3	5	(V)	
1960	2		1		1	2	2		(V)
1961	6	4	4	3	4	4	4		
1962	3	2	3	3	3	3	3	2	
1963	1			2	2		2		(V)
1964	3	2	4	3	3	3	4		
1965					1				
1966	4	3	3	2	4	3	4		(V)
1967	3	3	3	3	3	3	3		(V)
1968				1	1				
1969	3	4	5	4	5	4	3		
1970	4	3	3	3	4	3	3		(V)
1971	3	2	3	3	2	3	5		
1972	2	2	1		3	2	2		(NA)
1973	2	3	3	3	3	3	3		
1974	2	2	2	2	3	3	1		
1975	3	3	1	2	1	2	3		(NA)

Classification of Bordeaux wines

Several official classifications of Bordeaux wines exist; the most notable are those of 1855 created for the Paris Exhibition of that year, covering the wines of the Médoc, Sauternes and Barsac. These rankings may not be rearranged and do not have AOC authority; today they are best used only as a guide.

In 1954 and 1959 the wines of St Emilion and Graves were given official rankings with the authority of AOC.

Reform of the 1855 classification would allow today's leading red wine estates (some 200) to be included. The elevation of Château Mouton-Rothschild in the summer of 1973 to the ranks of the Premiers Crus is seen by many to herald a potential reclassification of Médoc red wines.

The 1855 classification of the wines of Sauternes and Barsac

The white wines are classified in a similar way to the Médoc wines (see opposite page).

Twenty-two wines were selected and grouped into two classes of growth, except for one wine which is held to be in a class by itself.

Grand Premier Cru (Great First Growth)	Commune
Château d'Yquem	Sauternes

Premiers Crus (First Growths)

Château La Tour Blanche	Bommes
Château Lafaurie-Peyraguey	Bommes
Château Clos Haut-Peyraguey	Bommes
Château Rayne-Vigneau	Bommes
Château de Suduiraut	Preignac
Château Coutet	Barsac
Château Climens	Barsac
Château Guiraud	Sauternes
Château Rieussec	Fargues
Château Rabaud-Promis	Bommes
Château Rabaud-Sigalas	Bommes

Deuxièmes Crus (Second Growths)

Château de Myrat	Barsac
Château Doisy-Védrines	Barsac
Château Doisy-Daëne	Barsac
Château d'Arche (and d'Arche-Lafaurie)	Sauternes
Château Filhot	Sauternes
Château Broustet	Barsac
Château Nairac	Barsac
Château Caillou	Barsac
Château Suau	Barsac
Château de Malle	Preignac
Château Romer	Fargues
Château Lamothe	Sauternes

The 1954 classification of the wines of St Emilion

Premiers Grands Crus Classés (First Great Growths)

Château Ausone	Château Figeac
Château Cheval Blanc	Clos Fourtet
Château Beauséjour (Duffau)	Château La Gaffelière Naudes
Château Beauséjour (Fagouet)	Château Magdelaine
Château Belair	Château Pavie
Château Canon	Château Trottevielle

Grands Crus Classés (Great Growths)

Château l'Angélus	Château La Clusière
Château l'Arrosée	Château La Couspaude
Château Balestard-la-Tonnelle	Château La Dominique
Château Bellevue	Château Larcis-Ducasse
Château Bergat	Château Lamarzelle
Château Cadet-Bon	Château Larmande
Château Cadet-Piola	Château Laroze
Château Canon-la-Gaffelière	Château Lasserre
Château Cap-de-Mourlin	Château La Tour-du-Pin Figeac (Bélivier)
Château Chapelle-Madeleine	Château La Tour-du-Pin Figeac (Moueix)
Château Chauvin	Château La Tour-Figeac
Château Corbin (Giraud)	Château Le Couvent
Château Corbin-Michotte	Château Le Prieuré
Château Coutet	Château Mauvezin
Château Croque-Michotte	Château Moulin-du-Cadet
Château Curé-Bon	Château Pavie-Decesse
Château Fonplégade	Château Pavie-Macquin
Château Fonroque	Château Pavillon-Cadet
Château Franc-Mayne	Château Petit-Faurie-de-Souchard
Château Grand-Barrail-Lamarzelle-Figeac	Château Petit-Faurie-de-Soutard
Château Grand-Corbin-Despagne	Château Ripeau
Château Grand-Corbin-Pécresse	Château Sansonnet
Château Grand-Mayne	Château Saint-Georges-Côte-Pavie
Château Grand-Pontet	Château Soutard
Château Grandes-Murailles	Château Tertre-Daugay
Château Guadet-Saint-Julien	Château Trimoulet
Château Jean-Faure	Château Trois-Moulins
Château Le Châtelet	Château Troplong-Mondot
Château La Carte	Château Villemaurine
Château La Clotte	Château Yon Figeac
	Clos des Jacobins
	Clos Saint-Martin
	Clos la Madeleine

The 1959 classification of the wines of Graves

Red Wines	Commune
Château Haut-Brion	Pessac
Château La Mission-Haut-Brion	Pessac
Château Haut-Bailly	Léognan
Domaine de Chevalier	Léognan
Château Carbonnieux	Léognan
Château Malartic-La-Gravière	Léognan
Château Latour	Martillac
Château La Tour-Haut-Brion	Talence
Château Smith-Haut-Lafitte	Martillac
Château Olivier	Léognan
Château Bouscaut	Cadaujac
Château Pape Clément	Pessac
Château Fieuzal	Léognan

White Wines	Commune
Château Carbonnieux	Léognan
Château Chevalier	Léognan
Château Olivier	Léognan
Château Laville-Haut Brion	Talence
Château Bouscaut	Cadaujac
Château Couhins	Villenave-d'Ornon
Château La Tour Martillac	Martillac
Château Malartic-La-Gravière	Léognan

The 1855 classification of the wines of the Médoc

This general Médoc wine rating (fixed on a price basis) was accepted by the Bordeaux wine trade before 1855. Only 60 of the better vineyards were classified into 5 Crus, only 4 being accorded the highest rank of Premier Cru.

Premiers Crus (First Growths)	Commune
Château Lafite-Rothschild	Pauillac
Château Margaux	Margaux
Château Latour	Pauillac
Château Haut-Brion	Pessac (Graves)

Deuxièmes Crus (Second Growths)	
Château Mouton-Rothschild	Pauillac
Château Rausan-Ségla	Margaux
Château Rauzan-Gassies	Margaux
Château Léoville-Lascases	St Julien
Château Léoville-Poyferré	St Julien
Château Léoville-Barton	St Julien
Château Durfort-Vivens	Margaux
Château Gruaud-Larose	St Julien
Château Lascombes	Margaux
Château Brane-Cantenac	Cantenac
Château Pichon-Longueville-Baron	Pauillac
Château Pichon-Longueville-Comtesse-de-Lalande	Pauillac
Château Ducru-Beaucaillou	St Julien
Château Cos-d'Estournel	St Estèphe
Château Montrose	St Estèphe

Troisièmes Crus (Third Growths)	
Château Kirwan	Cantenac
Château d'Issan	Cantenac
Château Lagrange	St Julien
Château Langoa Barton	St Julien
Château Giscours	Labarde
Château Malescot-Saint-Exupéry	Margaux

Troisièmes Crus *continued*	Commune
Château Cantenac-Brown	Cantenac
Château Boyd-Cantenac	Cantenac
Château Palmer	Cantenac
Château La Lagune	Ludon
Château Desmirail	Margaux
Château Calon-Ségur	St Estèphe
Château Ferrière	Margaux
Château Marquis d'Alesme-Becker	Margaux

Quatrièmes Crus (Fourth Growths)	
Château Saint-Pierre	St Julien
Château Talbot	St Julien
Château Branaire-Ducru	St Julien
Château Duhart-Milon	Pauillac
Château Pouget	Cantenac
Château La Tour-Carnet	St Laurent
Château Rochet	St Estèphe
Château Beychevelle	St Julien
Château Le Prieuré	Cantenac
Château Marquis-de-Terme	Margaux

Cinquièmes Crus (Fifth Growths)	
Château Pontet-Canet	Pauillac
Château Batailley	Pauillac
Château Grand-Puy-Lacoste	Pauillac
Château Grand-Puy-Ducasse	Pauillac
Château Lynch-Bages	Pauillac
Château Lynch-Moussas	Pauillac
Château Dauzac	Labarde
Château Mouton Baron Philippe (called Mouton-d'Armailhacq until 1956)	Pauillac
Château du Tertre	Arsac
Château Haut-Bages-Libéral	Pauillac
Château Pedesclaux	Pauillac
Château Belgrave	St Laurent
Château Camensac	St Laurent
Château Cos-Labory	St Estèphe
Château Clerc-Milon-Mondon	Pauillac
Château Croizet-Bages	Pauillac
Château Cantemerle	Macau

Wine brotherhoods

Wine societies and social groups stemming from the historic vintners' guilds have been in existence in France for centuries, but the idea of using them to promote the sale of wines, particularly abroad, is comparatively recent. Every French wine region has a wine brotherhood devoted to the business of growing, shipping and drinking the local wines, but only a few of them have branched out internationally. Regular meetings are held and on ceremonial occasions senior members of the brotherhoods are resplendent in colourful robes.

Tastevin activities

The largest and most famous brotherhood is the Confrérie des Chevaliers du Tastevin (Brotherhood of the Knights of the Winetaster's Cup) of Burgundy whose following is now world-wide. The Confrérie was first launched in November 1934 by Georges Faiveley, a wine merchant, and Camille Rodier, both members of the local Chamber of Commerce. Two annual local events were chosen as a springboard: the auction of wines from the famous Hospices de Beaune vineyards and a vintners' feast, known as the Paulée, held in Meursault, a village renowned for its fine white wines.

Rodier reasoned that by publicizing the high prices commanded at the auction by the select Hospices wines whose vineyards were among the very best in the Côte de Beaune, the low-priced wines made elsewhere in the region would be overlooked. At Meursault local growers congregated for the annual holiday, bringing with them bottles of their very finest wines for all to taste. To inject a little class into what was really a country fête Rodier, with the help of a retired French journalist called Georges Rozet, instituted a literary prize to be given annually for the work that had done most to promote Burgundy. Today that prize consists of 100 bottles of the finest Meursault; current high prices make it a prize indeed.

Other ceremonies were devised which, together with the auction and the Paulée, have become part of the general activities of the Chevaliers. Since 1934 regular dinners and initiation ceremonies, with up to 600 guests at a time, have taken place. They used to be held at Caveau Nuiton, the cellar headquarters of the Chevaliers at Nuits-St-Georges, and the Hôtel-Dieu in Beaune. In recent years the Chevaliers have held meetings called Chapitres practically every Saturday during the year except in July and August in their new, luxurious headquarters of the Château du Clos de Vougeot.

Franco-American ties were formed that same year; the American Ambassador to Paris, William C. Bullitt, set a precedent that has been followed ever since when he accepted an invitation as guest of honour at a spring ceremony of the Chevaliers. Shortly afterwards Jules Bohy became the first Tastevin representative in the USA and organized the first American dinner and initiation at the Hotel St Regis, New York, in March 1940.

The advent of World War II temporarily suspended the activities of the Chevaliers du Tastevin, although in 1944 the Confrérie was given the Château du Clos de Vougeot by vineyard proprietors whose interests then were in the potentially priceless plots of land surrounding it rather than in the 600-year-old *château*, badly in need of repair and renovation.

Rodier once again came up with an idea; he suggested founding the Societé des Amis du Château du Clos de Vougeot, a tax-exempt, non-profit-making body separate from the Chevaliers du Tastevin, which would conserve and restore the *château* as an eventual headquarters for the world-wide promotion of Burgundy wines. Gifts of money were soon forthcoming, especially from America, and in 1948 the French government declared the *château* a building of historical interest.

Expansion in the USA

Meanwhile, the American branch of the Chevaliers du Tastevin was growing and local groups called Sous-commanderies were meeting several times a year. The Confrérie now numbers over 1,200, has 18 Sous-commanderies and its distinguished members include generals, judges, diplomats, writers and businessmen as well as people in the wine trade.

As in Burgundy, membership is for those who truly love wine and camaraderie and are willing to spend their money for both. The Confrérie prides itself on creating the best possible menus for its dinners and on its most lavish presentation of Burgundy wine, white and red; for the members are sworn to 'defend the interests of French wine in general and of the wines of Burgundy in particular' and at Tastevin festivities the only other wine allowed is French Champagne with the hors d'oeuvres and dessert.

The emblem of the Chevaliers du Tastevin, since adopted by many other wine brotherhoods, is the little silver cup used for tasting wines drawn from the cask. *Tastevin* literally means 'taste wine' and should be pronounced *'tâte-vin'* (tuttvin), not *'tasse-de-vin'*; the word is now a registered trade mark of the brotherhood. The Confrérie's own Tastevinage label may be used on wines which have been approved by a special committee.

New wine societies

Since 1958 the Chevaliers du Tastevin have not been alone in their efforts to promote French wines. Bordeaux also has a number of local brotherhoods whose American interests are represented by the Grand Conseil de Bordeaux founded by a group of *château*-owners and *négociants* including Edouard Kressman, a member of an old family of Bordeaux shippers, and Henri Martin, President of the Interprofessional Council of Bordeaux Wines. The latter Council ruled that the Bordeaux wine societies – the Jurade de St Emilion, the Connétablie de Guyenne and the Commanderie du Bontemps du Médoc et de Graves – were to be represented by the Commanderie de Bordeaux; an American, H. Gregory Thomas, who was already Grand Sénéchal of the Chevaliers du Tastevin, was chosen as Grand Master.

Thomas called the dinners of the Commanderie de Bordeaux Parlements and the first one was held at the

Brussels Restaurant, New York, in October 1958 when 20 Commandeurs were inducted in all. In contrast to the large gatherings of the Chevaliers du Tastevin, the Parlements are more intimate affairs with rarely more than 40 people present.

Other wine-growers have successfully publicized their wines, particularly those of Champagne whose cellars in Reims and Epernay never fail to attract visitors. But they have no brotherhoods abroad like the Chevaliers du Tastevin and the Commanderie de Bordeaux to further their interests.

There are British branches of many French wine brotherhoods whose activities are, however, on a smaller scale than those of their American and French counter-parts. Their induction ceremonies for new members are usually held once a year and several ceremonies have been held in London by leading wine orders, among them the Compagnons du Beaujolais and the Commanderie de Grande Bretagne des Chevaliers du Sacavin.

In view of rapid increase in wine consumption in the western world the international success of the prestigious brotherhoods of Burgundy and Bordeaux should encourage wine-growers in Europe and America to follow in their footsteps. Modern wineries may solve economic problems for the cheaper end of the market but it is plain to see that there are still many people willing to pay for the enjoyment of drinking and talking about wines that have been made with loving care in time-honoured ways.

Selected reading list

Allen, H. W. *A History of Wine*, Faber & Faber, London 1961; Horizon Press, New York 1962.

Amerine, M. A. and Singleton, V. L. *Wine: an Introduction for Americans*, University of California Press, Berkeley 1965.

Balzer, R. L. *The Pleasures of Wine*, Bobbs-Merrill, Indianapolis 1964.

Brejoux, P. *Vins de Loire*, Société Française d'Editions Vinicoles, Paris.

Broadbent, J. M. *Wine Tasting*, Wine and Spirit Publications, London 1968.

Cocks and Feret *Bordeaux et ses Vins*, Feret et Fils, Bordeaux 1969.

Cox, H. *The Wines of Australia*. Hodder & Stoughton, London 1967.

Croft-Cooke, R. *Sherry*, Putnam, New York 1955.

Port, Putnam, New York 1957.

Madeira, Putnam, New York 1961.

Fisher, M. F. and Yavno, M. *The Story of Wine in California*, University of California Press, Berkeley 1962.

Forbes, P. *Champagne: the Wine, the Land and the People*, Gollancz, London 1967; Reynal, New Jersey 1968.

Grossman, H. J. *Grossman's Guide to Wines, Spirits and Beers*, Scribner, New York 1940, (revised) 1964; Muller, London 1966.

Gunyon, R. E. H. *The Wines of Central and South-Eastern Europe*, Duckworth, London 1971; Hippocrene Books, New York 1972.

Halasz, Z. *Hungarian Wine Through the Ages*, Collet's, London 1962; Arthur Vanous, New York 1962.

Hallgarten, S. F. *Rhineland – Wineland*, Elek Books, London 1951; Arlington Books, London 1965.

Alsace and its Wine Gardens, André Deutsch, London 1957.

Jacquelin, L. and Poulain, R. *The Wines and Vineyards of France*, Hamlyn, London 1962; Putnam, New York 1962.

Jeffs, J. *Sherry*, Faber & Faber, London 1961, (revised) 1971; British Book Centre, New York 1971.

Johnson, H. *Wine*, Nelson, London 1966; Sphere Books, London 1968.

The World Atlas of Wine, Mitchell Beazley, London 1971.

Lake, M. *Classic Wines of Australia*, Jacaranda Press, Queensland 1966.

Langenbach, A. *German Wines and Vines*, Vista Books, London 1962.

Larmat, L. *Atlas de la France Vinicole*, Societé Française d'Editions Vinicoles, Paris.

Leedom, W. S. *Vintage Wine Book*, Vintage Books, New York 1963.

Lichine, A. *Encyclopaedia of Wines and Spirits*, Cassell, London 1967; Knopf, New York 1967.

Wines of France, Cassell, London 1952, 1969; Knopf, New York 1969.

Opperman, D. J. *Spirit of the Vine*, Human and Rousseau, Cape Town 1968.

Penning-Rowsell, E. *The Wines of Bordeaux*, International Wine and Food Society, London 1969; Stein & Day, New York 1970.

Poupon, P. and Forgeot, P. *A Book of Burgundy*, Lund Humphries, London 1958; Hastings House, New York 1959.

Rainbird, G. M. *Sherry and the Wines of Spain*, Michael Joseph, London 1966; McGraw-Hill, New York 1966.

Ray, C. *The Wines of Italy*, McGraw-Hill, Maidenhead, Berkshire 1966; Penguin, London 1971; Penguin, Baltimore 1972.

Roger, J. R. *The Wines of Bordeaux*, André Deutsch, London 1960; Dutton, New York 1960.

Schoonmaker, F. *Dictionary of Wines*, Hastings House, New York 1951.

The Wines of Germany, Hastings House, New York 1956, 1966.

Encyclopedia of Wine, Hastings House, New York 1964, 1969; Nelson, London 1967.

Sichel, A. *The Penguin Book of Wines*, Penguin, London and Baltimore 1965, (revised) 1971.

Simon, A. L. *A Dictionary of Wines, Spirits and Liqueurs*, Barrie & Jenkins, London 1958; Citadel Press, New York 1963.

Wines and Spirits, the Connoisseur's Textbook, Skilton, London 1961; Transatlantic, New York 1961.

Wines of the World, McGraw-Hill, New York and Maidenhead, Berks 1967.

Wines, Vineyards and Vignerons of Australia, Hamlyn, London 1967.

Acknowledgments

Sources of photographs on the following pages:

Mary Evans Picture Library: 5, 6, 7.
Karquel: 17, 21 right.
Roberts, Jeremy: 18, 54.
Phédon-Salou: 19, 23, 24 bottom, 27 top, 28, 50 top.
Comité Interprofessionnel du Vin de Champagne: 20.
Bottin, J: 21 left, 49.
Mariorossi, C: 22, 59, 62, 63 left, 64, 65, 66, 67, 68, 69, 71, 72 left, 73, 81, 82, 88 bottom, 89.
Galliphot: 24 top left, 26 top left and bottom.
Atlas-Photo: 25.
Rapho: 26 top right.

Grégoire, A: 27 bottom, 29, 34 top, 38, 44 right, 46 top and bottom.
Wine and Spirit Education Trust: 30, 40 top, 78, 112.
Perceval, Alain: 31, 35, 45, 48.
L'Institut Technique du Vin: 32, 33, 34 bottom, 43.
Magnum/Riboud: 36, 37, 41.
Top-Réalités: 39 left, 40 bottom, 51 top and bottom.
Trémallat, L: 39 right, 42, 44 left.
Ribière, J: 47 left, 50 centre and bottom.
Images et Textes: 47 right.
Deinhard & Co.: 52, 53, 56.
Spectrum: 55, 75, 77.
Austrian Tourist Office: 57.
Swissair: 58.
Quaglino, A: 61.

Archivio P2: 63 right.
Italian Trade Centre: 70.
Prato, M: 72 right.
Thuillier, R: 76.
Hennell, P: 80.
Teltscher Brothers Ltd./Nicholas Barrington photograph: 85.
Picturepoint: 86, 87, 91 top, 98, 100, 102.
Israel Wine Institute: 88 top.
Wine Institute of California: 91 bottom, 92, 93, 94, 95, 97.
Reckitt & Coleman Ltd.: 99.
South African Wine Farmers Association Ltd.: 103, 105.
Seppelt, B. & Sons Ltd., Adelaide: 107, 108.
Dickens, Douglas: 109.
Australian News and Information Bureau, London: 111.

Index

Page references to photographs are printed in **heavy** type. See also Glossary, pages 12–16